Wartime Style

M000238704

Also by Lora Ann Sigler

Clothes Make the Character: The Role of Wardrobe in Early Motion Pictures (McFarland, 2021)

Medieval Art and the Look of Silent Film: The Influence on Costume and Set Design (McFarland, 2019)

Wartime Style

Fashion and American Culture During 20th Century Conflicts

Lora Ann Sigler

McFarland & Company, Inc., Publishers
Jefferson, North Carolina

This book has undergone peer review.

ISBN (print) 978-1-4766-8718-6
ISBN (ebook) 978-1-4766-4840-8

LIBRARY OF CONGRESS AND BRITISH LIBRARY
CATALOGUING DATA ARE AVAILABLE

Library of Congress Control Number 2022043412

© 2022 Lora Ann Sigler. All rights reserved

No part of this book may be reproduced or transmitted in any form or by any means, electronic or mechanical, including photocopying or recording, or by any information storage and retrieval system, without permission in writing from the publisher.

Front cover images: unidentified woman modeling marching costume for Chicago suffrage parade, June 6, 1916 (Library of Congress); J. Howard Miller's inspiration for Rosie the Riveter (National Archives); Female worker on the Baltimore and Ohio Railroad, Glenwood, Pennsylvania (National Archives)

Printed in the United States of America

McFarland & Company, Inc., Publishers
Box 611, Jefferson, North Carolina 28640
www.mcfarlandpub.com

Table of Contents

Acknowledgments

My thanks go first to my husband, who has been of invaluable assistance throughout this entire publication process—my in-house IT tech, proofreader, secretary, and critic. Without his help, this volume would have taken twice as long and caused twice as much forehead slapping.

Secondly, but just as importantly, to the folks at McFarland for their kindness, patience, and, above all, their enthusiasm for my projects.

Just to mention a few of those: my primary editor, Layla Milholen, who has seen me through three books now, and who has never been anything but the kindest of friends and ready to help in any way; Charlie Perdue, who not only assisted me with great patience, but familiarized me with grist mills and grits; Virginia Tomlinson, Operations; Lori Tedder, Administration Specialist; Kristal Hamby in Marketing; Susan Kilby, Development; all cheerful, warm and helpful. And not in the least, the least—all those unsung folks who make my book a book: the formatters, the illustration scrutinizers, the people who gave their permissions to use their images, those at the presses, and those I may have forgotten.

Lastly, but again, most importantly, my family—large, noisy, and opinionated, but ever in support of Mom. Your love keeps me afloat.

Preface

The inspiration for this volume grew out of research done for an earlier project, which concentrated on the beginnings of moving pictures and their influence on society—in particular, within the areas of costume and set design. While that earlier work explored some of the societal *Zeitgeist* prompting general fashion trends, I grew more and more interested, not only in the choices made by costume, fashion, and set designers during the time period of my focus, but in further pursuing the reasons for those choices in time periods which ranged further afield. It was already obvious that trends in *clothing* fashion run, more or less, in step with prevailing social conditions. Moreover, those fashion trends in wardrobe revealed a reciprocal relationship with film trends throughout the changing decades; nevertheless, certain historical moments stood out. A compelling number of those trends, I felt, could be collectively grouped under the heading *War*. Primarily, the "Great" World Wars I and II, which along with Vietnam, will be the central focus of this volume. Nevertheless, the discussion will also touch briefly on three other devastating, and certainly world-involving, conflicts of the last 200 years: the Crimean debacle, the American Civil War, and the Korean "Police Action." Those conflicts, which were not gifted with a "Great" sobriquet, have nevertheless left their own enduring influences on later culture. The overall question to be asked is: Does war demonstrate a particular effect on fashion that can be traced throughout the war periods? In other words, is there a common response, no matter what the styles of the period dictate, or does each conflict require a separate fashion response peculiar to that era? Moreover, does the *Zeitgeist* of that particular moment place tacit restrictions on what the response may be? In speaking of fashion, I use the word in its broadest meaning—it also encompasses film and cultural trends.

Publications on wartime wardrobes and their influence have generally focused on just one war. For example: Lucy Adlington's *Great War Fashion*, Nina Edwards' *Dressed for War,* both British publications, which concentrate entirely on World War I, as well as Geraldine Howell's *Wartime Fashion,* also a British publication, which discusses World War II. All three are excellent sources but with a narrower focus. More recently, there have been more articles appearing on World War II, as well as the Cold War. Surprisingly, almost nothing could be found on Vietnam in this regard. A comparative study of the differences or similarities in fashion over the course of several wars, and the possible impetus behind them, has been rather overlooked. However, an interesting master's thesis by Lauren Topor does look at several wars, although focusing on the military jacket.

This study will try to rectify that omission by focusing on fashion trends which appeared during the three most devastating wars of the 20th century, including a brief excursion into the 19th century. I will discuss what effect wartime conditions had on streetwear, costume design for the movies, and societal attitudes. Again, I stress that reciprocal relationship. Like conjoined twins, none can exist without the others. Along with fashion trends, I will provide some background on the wars themselves. For all of us, World War I has faded into the background of ancient history; furthermore, there are fewer and fewer who recall World War II. For those under forty, Vietnam is just as remote as the two World Wars. Therefore, there is a need for brief excursions into a broader field of view, although these discussions will be brief because this book is not a history of wars.

By looking at both costume for films and everyday wear for the populace, we may see a pattern emerge. If it does not, why not? Can the reasons be discerned? Differences or similarities which may be seen among conflicts are simultaneously societal/attitudinal, psychological, and/or practical. Matters of dress fall under the umbrellas of all three and may lead us to a greater understanding of ourselves and our seeming need for conflict. While this may appear to be a frivolous assertion, dress is one of our most important avenues to take the temperature of either a nation or the global village as a whole. As we know, wars are never over when the treaty is signed—the psychological and societal ramifications continue well afterwards, and continue to build, resulting in pervasive societal changes. Fashion, I would argue, holds up the mirror to those changes.

Whichever war a nation's people must live through, conflict is assuredly on everyone's mind continually and with dread. On occasion, however, there have been some, let's say, *peculiar* attempts made to put a good face on the dreadful situations that confronted them. I was particularly intrigued by one inexplicably chirpy fashion blurb from World War I which referred to "war's brighter side!"[1] Rather than a total indifference to the ravages of war, this bespeaks a very human need to make the best, and most hopeful, of circumstances. As demonstrated by the defiance of wartime restrictions, such as the appearance of the "war crinoline" of 1916, we will see in all wars that, in spite of the constant reminders, the human spirit can contain only so much pain before it rebels. We will examine both the compliance and the rebellion.

World War II seems to have demanded a return to conservative values, much more so than the 1914 to 1918 struggle which led to the Jazz Age, and further to pre–Code Hollywood. In contrast to either of the previous conflicts, Vietnam seems to have led to a state of perpetual confusion which is still reverberating after nearly half a century.

Although an in-depth psychological examination is outside the scope of this volume, a few observations will be made in an attempt to determine the *why* of the aftermath years following each conflict.

Introduction

With war come restrictions, whether you are directly involved or only on the periphery. Foodstuffs are less available, hired help is less available, transportation is difficult if not altogether impossible, and contact with loved ones dries up to a trickle. What is less frequently examined is the effect these restrictions have on fashion. What are the psychological implications of semi-privations, and how are these manifested in what we put on our backs to face every day? To answer that question, men will not be ignored—neither their courage in the face of unspeakable conditions, nor their service on the home front when unable to join the military forces. Nevertheless, the emphasis will be more on the female perspective. We will be concentrating more on the arc of their fashion, both in real life and the "reel" life of films. Furthermore, we will look at their personal involvement in war, both on the home front and the actual fighting front.

Chapter One looks back briefly to the 19th century, before war became the mechanized juggernaut it was in the 20th. The horror of those earlier conflicts arose not from death falling from the sky, or from great mechanized beasts that rolled over the countryside dispensing it, or from cannon that reached for frightening miles. That particular "hell" came from septicemia, when a minor wound meant agonizing death; from disease for which there was no amelioration; and from close-up combat where one looked his possible death literally in the eyes. Nevertheless, that century also marks the establishment of what would later become practice—professional nursing, the primitive groundwork for antisepsis, and some concern for finding the actual causes of disease through research.

World War I—the "war to end wars"—is discussed in the next four chapters. Chapter Two describes not only some of the fashion changes wrought by the war, but also fashion innovations which were in place at the start of the war. Those "shocking" designs were already shaking up society before 1914. With the advent of a new vocabulary of war however, of which mechanization was the leading word, for the first time, women were pressed into *acknowledged* roles of active service. Thus, for their expanded roles, an entirely new vocabulary of clothing had to be devised to accommodate those activities. Chapter Three investigates the influence of motion pictures and the new Hollywood in presenting the changes in fashion trends put before the eyes of the public. It also discusses the influence of the first actors to be considered "stars," both as fashion leaders and as influential voices for the war effort. This chapter will also emphasize women in the work force as a newly recognized phenomenon by filmmakers. What was the probable resultant effect on costume design? What was the reciprocal response of filmmakers during the war, as well as after? Chapter Four then investigates the part the newly established movie fan magazines played in further expanding the influence of the movies, on fashion in general, and the new styles created for women's new roles. Chapter Five looks at the worldwide depictions of men and women in propaganda posters, which were produced to raise awareness of the war effort and stimulate patriotism. Where the attention is focused on women, were the portrayals true-to-life, or simply idealized and sentimentalized versions of women's actual roles? Did the images correspond with the way women were *received* in their active roles? Did they influence what the populace as a whole wore? This chapter explores those questions, as well as the utility of those propaganda efforts. Chapter Six then discusses the aftermath of the war and some of its lasting societal consequences on both fashion and society.

The next four chapters, Seven, Eight, Nine and Ten, shift the focus to World War II. These chapters, although employing a treatment similar to that used for World War I, slightly alter the former order. Chapter Seven begins this section with the analysis and comparison of wartime movies with regard to their subliminal influence on the fashion world. The chapter examines both those whose scenarios stemmed directly from the war and those which either gloss over the war or ignore it completely—whether it be romance, mystery, comedy, or history. The chapter includes some of the most well-known movies of the '40s. It will also touch on less well-known films which were wardrobed by well-known names in the costume design field. These latter movies held their own with regard to their influence on the fashion world. Chapter Eight discusses the audience's efforts on the home front and the concomitant tie-in with fashion, and then Chapter Nine takes another look at wartime propaganda posters. The chapter's focus is not only on the productive results of their patriotic exhortations, but also their essentially unintended effects where fashion and society are concerned. Chapter Ten summarizes the overall effect on fashions for the woman and man on the street. Then, Chapter Eleven again turns to the societal repercussions of World War II's aftermath and the long-lasting effects on the coming decades.

Chapter Twelve will examine the chaos of Vietnam and its essentially anti-fashion fashion. It begins with a short summary of the facts surrounding the war—the lead-up to it, the involvement of the United States, and the political quicksand which drew the United States in further and further. After that, the chapter focuses on the kaleidoscope of '60s and '70s fashion with an eye to both exploration and explanation—if that is possible. As the most controversial conflict of modern times, Vietnam prompts these questions: How is the Vietnam controversy reflected in fashion, societal behavior, or politics? Is there a lesson to be learned for the present? Has the upheaval of the period become normalized? In the popular phrase at the time of this writing, is this the "new normal"? This chapter provides some discussion of the attitudes and opinions expressed by the opposing sides, both for and against the war. The complexities of the conflict were such that a final conclusion can only be attempted, even from that nearly fifty-year distance. Chapter Thirteen looks again at propaganda posters from the Vietnam War, demonstrating the startling difference in attitude which prevailed during those contentious years. Chapter Fourteen presents some of the movies about Vietnam, but which came after that debacle. These can scarcely be called unbiased, as the war's lasting shadow still hung heavy over the filmmakers, some of whom were actual veterans. Chapter Fifteen repeats the issues of the war's aftermath in a similar manner to the previous chapters on the subject.

The epilogue attempts a summing up of the backward looks the book has taken, discussing those similarities and/or differences first mentioned in the preface. The attitudinal complexion of the different periods—the *Zeitgeist*—is examined a little more closely and some conclusions drawn; however, a thorough discussion is outside the scope of this volume.

Fashion is mainly our focus, but some readers may be inspired to follow the subject matter in further research. Appendices A, B, C, and D discuss some topics of interest only touched upon in the text and give a fuller exposition of the subjects.

One

Saluting the Past

"War is Hell."
—William Tecumseh Sherman
address, 1879/80

Whether he just flatly said, "War is Hell," "It is all Hell," "War is cruelty," or any of the many other variations of the quote attributed to him, the much-criticized General Sherman knew exactly what he was saying even if his precise words are lost to time.[1] A veteran, during the American Civil War, of the first Battle of Bull Run, Battle of Shiloh, Siege of Corinth and the Vicksburg Campaign, just to name a few, he was well acquainted with that hell. A short examination of that blot on American history's escutcheon will provide ample proof that he knew whereof he spoke.

Although the American Civil War is arguably one of history's most discussed, interpreted, and disputed conflicts, most scholars agree that it centered on the role of slavery. Many have suggested a variety of reasons: economic hardship (of course, if you have to pay people for their work); states' rights to self-governance; and abuse of federal authority, among others. In the end, it boils down to the right of one human to own another human. This volume will not attempt to add to that dispute; it will concentrate, instead, on the "hell" Sherman addresses, its societal ramifications, and effect on common practices.

First of all, more *Americans*—our troops on both sides—lost their lives in the Civil War than in *nearly all* the next *ten* wars combined. At least 620,000, although this number is considered by many to be too *low,* some estimates run as high as 750,000.[2] Even the staggering 405,000 of World War II could not compete. The most sobering aspect of this statistic is that twice as many died of disease as of wounds in battle. Sanitation was non-existent, floors were covered with blood and waste, men were simply left lying in their dirty, bloody clothes, and the germ theory was in its infancy. Typhoid, smallpox, and measles were rampant, although attempts at isolating the sufferers were made. The worst affliction was "hospital gangrene" which spread quickly from one wound to another and from one patient to another. A flesh wound could rapidly become life-threatening, and the only recourse was drastic amputation. William A. Hammond, who had been raised to the rank of general and appointed Surgeon General by President Lincoln, was one of the earliest to consider the necessity of sanitary practices but they were hit-or-miss, at best.

During his tenure, Hammond introduced a number of reforms: he raised admission requirements for the Army Medical Corps; increased the number of hospitals; and ordered an increase in ventilation. Along with those put in place, he also proposed a permanent military medical corps; a permanent military hospital; and centralization of medications issuance. In addition, he banned the use of calomel, a mercury compound, believing it dangerous. This caused an uproar among many of his colleagues, who accused him of trampling on their rights of free practice. The fact that he was absolutely correct about the lasting ill effects mattered little against their combined complaints, nor did his arrogant personality stand in his favor. His biggest mistake was to fall out with Secretary of War Stanton, causing the loss of an ally, which ultimately led to his court-martial on purportedly trumped-up charges, and his subsequent removal from office. Thereafter, he devoted himself to neurology, becoming professor of nervous and mental diseases at Bellevue, then again at New York University, and served on the faculty of the University of Vermont, Burlington. He, and the few others who believed in the necessity of sanitary conditions, e.g., Joseph Lister and Louis Pasteur, as well as Florence Nightingale and Clara Barton, were fighting an uphill battle in the 19th century. Sadly, personality too often factored in the opposition.[3]

Enter the Ladies!

Before the Crimean War, all "nurses" had been male—orderlies, with little or no formal training—however, the pendulum was beginning its feminine swing. First on the female-nursing war scene was the English Florence Nightingale, the acknowledged founder of modern nursing practices. Born in 1820 in Florence, Italy, and named for her birthplace, she was a precocious child and formidable scholar, able to read and write French, German, Italian, Greek and Latin. Also well-versed in mathematics, history and philosophy, she was never content being *just* a woman but enjoyed serious discussions of politics, philosophy and other "unwomanly" subjects.

Three-quarter portrait photograph of Florence Nightingale. Demure pose, elegant satin dress and lady-like lace cap, negated by the steely look in the eyes (Library of Congress).

Always religious, she felt nursing was a call from God to serve, and over the objections of her family, she was able to secure a spot at the Institution of Protestant Deaconesses in Kaiserswerth, Germany. Receiving only two weeks of training in 1850 and another three months in 1851, she embarked on her chosen career, first as Superintendent of the Institution for Sick Gentlewomen in Distressed Circumstances, an establishment which was not prospering until under her supervision. She changed the name to the Hospital for Gentlewomen during Illness, instituted a number of reforms, and also admitted wives and daughters of the clergy, as well as those of military and naval personnel. At the outbreak of hostilities, she departed for the Crimea as the leader of a group of nurses who were assigned to Scutari.[4] She and her group were greeted with hostility, filth, short supplies, inadequate and uncooperative staff, and seriously wounded men crowded together with little or no consideration for their comfort.[5] Very shortly after her arrival the horrendous Battle of Balaklava and Battle of Inkerman occurred, overwhelming the already desperate conditions (Nightingale referred to it as the "Kingdom of Hell") and forcing the resistant doctors to put the female group to work. Nightingale herself bought much needed equipment with the aid of funds from the *London Times* and got soldiers' wives to help with the laundry. She insisted on cleaning up the wards and laid down her standards for care—baths, clean clothing, clean dressings, and enough food. Her habit of wandering the wards at night to check on the patients earned her sobriquet of "Lady with the Lamp." Her success in lowering the mortality to around 2 percent (at least in the press reports, it was actually higher and kept under wraps) also earned her acclaim. Her efforts were not without a price however; she fell ill with brucellosis and felt the lingering effects of the disease for the rest of her life.[6] This was a constant danger for the women, who worked at least twelve-hour shifts and were continually exposed to a veritable encyclopedia of diseases.

Along with the establishment of nursing standards, and at least a basic concept of hygiene, the war in Crimea employed some of what would become modern warfare practices: the use of railroads; use of the electric telegraph; the first trenches; the first professional war correspondents; and the first employment of blind artillery fire (firing at an enemy which could not be seen). In spite of this, owing to the failures of those in charge, the war became "an iconic symbol of logistical, medical and tactical failures and mismanagement."[7] The most successful and lasting reform, for medical practices at least, was brought about by Nightingale. Unfortunately, the mismanagement of those in charge has not been ameliorated through subsequent generations, as we will see in the discussion of the conflicts which follow.

After returning from the front lines, Nightingale, despite her lingering ill health, chose to devote herself to a continuing effort at reforming medical practices. A fund for the training of nurses was established in her name (the Nightingale Fund) and was generously endowed. In 1859, she wrote a well-received book—*Notes on Nursing*—detailing her ideas. The publication served for generations as part of the curriculum for not only the Nightingale School but others and is still considered a classic. By 1882, her nurses were uniformed, had professional training and were frequently employed as matrons at leading hospitals. Although approaching blindness and declining health slowed down her productivity, she nevertheless retained an interest in what went on in her field until her death at ninety, still leaving a large body of work to be published. In perpetuity, her groundwork legacy lives on with the professional care, now taken for granted, in our hospitals.

Undoubtedly due to the success of Florence Nightingale during the Crimean War, as well as Nightingale's recognition by the United States government, the political activist and social reformer Dorothea Lynde Dix entered the Civil War fray. Always a tireless advocate for the mentally ill, and well-aware there was a need for reform, she offered her services and managed to become the Union's Superintendent of Army Nurses in 1861. Her efforts were met with resistance both from the male nurses *and* the doctors, who felt their authority undermined, and also by the attitudes of a Victorian society which looked with disdain on a "working" woman. Southern women in particular, who provided care for both sides, would feel this censure most strongly.

Ignoring these difficulties, Dix persevered and raised a small army of women volunteers who were expected to conform to the strict guidelines she set up. Ages ranged between thirty-five and fifty, and, because she feared that younger women were in danger from both the soldiers and the doctors, she decreed no jewelry or makeup, and black or brown dresses with no hoops. Although actual nursing uniforms were still well in the future, Dix wisely realized that the drab colors and unfashionable styles, reminiscent of ordinary soldier's uniforms, provided some measure of protection for her ladies, demonstrated professionalism, and set them apart.[8] Somewhere close to three thousand women eventually served under Dix's tutelage and followed Dix's guidelines.[9]

Dix's efforts were duplicated in New England by Clarissa (Clara) Harlowe Barton,[10] who performed a like service for the wounded in Massachusetts. Northern women were assigned nursing posts without the need of Dix's endorsement, so she was somewhat eclipsed by Barton's efforts.

Born in Massachusetts in 1821, Barton was the daughter of a militia captain who had served with General "Mad" Anthony Wayne in his battle with the Northwest Indians. A natural-born scholar, she started school at age three, excelling easily. Extremely shy as a child, her only friend seems to have been a girl with the amusing name of Nancy Drew. Equally a natural-born caregiver, she nursed her older brother David after a severe head injury, long after the doctors had given him up.[11] When her parents relocated to a farm, in a surprise reversal of her previous practice of avoiding friendship, she socialized with her male cousins and evidently kept up with them easily at horseback riding, climbing, and other so-called boyish pursuits. A female cousin assisted Barton's mother in schooling her in feminine social skills and reining in her more tomboyish behavior.

After becoming a schoolteacher at seventeen, she taught for twelve years, and made her first steps into social activism. Along the way, she entered into a "romantic friendship" with her principal, when she studied at the Clinton Liberal Institute in New York—the relationship lasted for several years. In 1861, she moved to Washington, D.C., working as a clerk in the U.S. Patent Office, and became the first woman to receive a clerkship in the federal government and the first to be paid a salary equal to that of the men. This unseemly show of equality resulted in continual harassment from the male clerks. Owing to this opposition, her position was reduced to copyist and she was finally fired on the grounds of her politics.

When the war broke out, she first took supplies directly to some of the wounded soldiers, then organized a group of women to gather and provide not only food and clothing, but also medical supplies. In 1862, she got permission to work at the front lines, helping both Union and Confederate soldiers, providing the same services, along with reading to them, trying to keep their spirits up, and consoling them at death.

Photographic records of nurses are few but poignant.[12] In one of the most iconic images to come out of the Civil War, nurse Annie Bell was posed with two unidentified soldiers looking as though she is just about to serve one of them a cup of something. We would know almost nothing about this historically important photograph if it weren't for Annie's letter home to her mother. This revelation of the importance of a nurse's presence was included in a cache of random ephemera found by a collector of Civil War memorabilia, Chris Foard.

Foard, a registered nurse who specializes in items related to nursing, has amassed a collection amounting to around 3,200 items, including rare books, images, newspapers and medical instruments. His important images include, besides the Annie Bell photo, several rare photographs of particular interest to me, because they provide graphic proof of Dix's proscriptive rules of dress while actively serving. One of these is of Maria Hall, taken by Matthew Brady soon after the Battle of Antietam, picturing a seated Hall holding what seems to be a letter. She is clad in a dark-colored, hoop-less dress with a hooded cape flung loosely over her right shoulder. The only relief from the subdued impression is a touch of white around the collar and cuffs.[13]

A more telling image is a carefully arranged photograph of an Armory Square Hospital ward in Washington, D.C. There is no sign of the seriously wounded and dying—the men are all dressed in their uniforms, shaved, and sitting at attention. Unobtrusively placed in the background are the nurses in their drab dresses, minus hoops, and modestly posed. The very fact of their subdued appearances demonstrates Dix's proscriptions in action.

Susie King Taylor in her uniform of an American Army nurse with the Union forces (Wikimedia Commons).

White women were not alone in their service to the war. Considered the first African American Army nurse, Susie King Taylor, who had been born a slave, gained her freedom at fourteen and served on Morris Island with the Union 1st South Carolina Volunteers. In one photographic image, Taylor is shown in the uniform she wore while serving—a military-style jacket in a dark, sober color with a hoop-less skirt and a long veil attached to a semi-bonnet. The photo introduces us to a woman of strength, determination, and professionalism.

Culturally speaking, owing to the nature of their roles throughout most of history, women were more suited to nursing than men. It's not that the men did not care, but owing to the nature of *their* historical roles, they were less able to express feelings, less able to hold hands, comfort like a mother, or take a dying young man in their arms—and really, let us be honest, less concerned with cleanliness. Young men, away from home for perhaps the first time, often felt the need for surrogate mothers and welcomed a kindly face and hand.

Nursing was hard, backbreaking, and

heartbreaking work, conditions were deplorable, and appreciation scant more often than not. What inspired these devoted women on both continents to persevere in the face of almost insurmountable obstacles? Perhaps it's true, that women just can't help it—their nurturing instinct is so strong they just must sacrifice themselves when an opportunity is presented. I offer this notion without a firm basis of evidence. More probably, is it that women feel the same call of duty that men do, and for centuries this was their only way to serve?

Wearing their drab clothing proudly, the women of the Crimea, the American Civil War, and countless other conflicts, found that way.

Two

The "War to End Wars"

World War I (1914–1918)

"...there is no doubt that the course and character of the feared 'European war' ... will become the first world war in the full sense of the word."[1]

—Ernst Haeckel

The events leading up to the outbreak of hostilities in 1914 have been discussed at length and further analysis is outside the intent of this volume.[2] Nevertheless, the uneasiness and social upheaval of the coming chaos were not only already touching day-to-day lives, but already reaching the world of fashion and need further examination.

Virtually everyone has heard an account of the assassination in Sarajevo, by the young Serbian Gavrilo Princip, of the Archduke Franz Ferdinand of Austria and his morganatic wife Sophie,[3] which led to a declaration of war. This was, in the first instance, Austria-Hungary against Serbia, however that was just the trigger. The response of the general public—the "shock and awe" to quote the recent past—occasioned a series of events that led to the allies of both participants declaring all-out war—and has also been delineated in detail.

Nevertheless, less of a comparative nature has been discussed with regard to the effect on clothing trends and the responses of the fashion houses after the actual declaration was made. The tendency has been to concentrate on separate wars. However, there is a carryover from war to war.

As I have asserted, trends in fashion are neither a trivial nor a frivolous subject, fashion reflects the *Zeitgeist* of the populace as a whole vis-à-vis their situations; clothing is a vital part of ourselves and our well-being. To a significant extent, an individual's psychological state can be determined by their wardrobe choices. This doesn't necessarily hold true across the board, but if you see a friend gradually becoming more and more careless of appearance, it's time to worry. On a broader scale, a similar assertion is true of an entire society. The coming societal upheaval was made particularly evident in dress, with the events of 1914–1918, but was, as the few examples already provided demonstrate, discernable even before that.

By 1912, gowns had already drawn close to the body and suits with a masculine air were popular. Just a touch of the pouter pigeon look, from the late 19th century, was still evident in day dresses, although coats had taken on a more columnar silhouette. Collars were still frequently high around the throat, but a more relaxed appearance was evident on many of the popular "Waists" as blouses were called. Skirts were assuming a slender silhouette; however, waistbands were still at the waist and had not yet begun their downward plunge. One eyebrow-raising addition to female wardrobes, and precursor of the future, was the harem-pant look popularized by Paul Poiret and seized upon by the more adventurous.

We could have seen Dutch actress Sophie de Vries-de Boer outfitted in an ensemble consisting of the notorious harem pants under a tailored apron-like skirt which buttons up both sides, with a white collared and cuffed dark bodice. Self-consciously posed to seem casual, she reads as though unaware of the photographer.

Much mocked in cartoons, along with the "jupe-culotte," the harem style was the beginning of the end for men's "wearing the pants in the family." The jupe-culotte still continues in contemporary fashion, transmogrified as the cropped, wide-legged, skirt/pants combo of today.[4]

Poiret disingenuously boasted that he had liberated women from the slavery of their corsets. However, he failed to foresee the serious consequences resulting from his introduction of the hobble skirt. Rather than freedom, he had imprisoned them just as securely and was quoted as proudly saying: "[I] freed the bust [but] shackled the legs."[5] Skirts, as I mentioned, were already narrowing, but the diameter of hobble hems became ridiculous—some as narrow as fifteen inches in circumference—and proved dangerous. Several women were seriously injured while wearing them. An unfortunate few were actually killed due to their inability to use their legs to save themselves from a disastrous accident. Even those who survived without incident found their activities seriously restricted. Getting on a streetcar was nearly impossible as lifting the knees was not in the cards without either splitting the seams or lifting the skirt to thigh length (not even considered).

According to streetcar history, in 1912 New York began running special cars with no step, and Los Angeles followed suit in 1913. To circumvent the difficulties, designers featured clever innovations such as concealed pleats or slit/wrap skirts.

As to the origin of the hobble concept, a probably apocryphal anecdote is told about Mrs. Hart O. Berg, the first American woman to fly in an airplane in 1908. While aloft for two minutes and seven seconds, Mrs. Berg tied a rope to her skirt to keep it from blowing in the wind. In a most fortuitous coincidence, a French fashion designer was in the crowd at the exhibition and saw her leaving the plane. *Et voila!* The hobble skirt was born.[6] Whatever, and whoever, the truth, Poiret took credit. Fortunately for women's survival, the hobble fashion mainly faded with the advent of the war.[7]

With the outbreak of open warfare, the permanent residence of some form of trousers in milady's closet was assured after 1914. As outlined in the Introduction, a whole new vocabulary of fashion was necessary when women assumed the more varied and active roles of the absent men, such as the above-mentioned "harem pants"; "resort wear"; "outdoor sporting"; and so on.[8] This new vocabulary was hardly greeted with approbation. In fact, the response was more often negative than otherwise, among those who were watching from the sidelines. Since much of the new mode of dress took on a seriously masculine bent—not just trousers but entire ensembles—some older women, but most especially men, tended to react with both disdain and condemnation. Nina Edwards, in her excellent book on British World War I fashion, *Dressed for War,* writes of one young British soldier who wrote to his beloved that he hoped she was not wearing pants, because he found them "disgusting."[9] The implication being, of course, that he would find her the same. Women shouldered that burden of social ostracization just as they did the burdens of farm and factory work, entering the war effort with zeal. As

Hobble skirt by Paul Poiret. Note panniers as well. Everything you wouldn't want in one tidy package (illustration by George Barbier, Wikimedia Commons).

we see, women who entered the workforce in the First World War were forced to walk a tightrope (forgive the pun): their work was essential, yet their presence was resented—even by other women. Mocked, branded unfeminine, yet increasingly necessary and their contributions increasingly vital.

Women's duties on both sides of the "pond" were as diverse as those of the men's had been. Not only were they in safer positions such as clerk or ambulance driver, but also in heavy industry and munitions. There are many photographs which attest to the reality of their employment on what could be called the "home front lines." One dramatic image is of the interior of a vast factory in the United Kingdom, where masked women in coveralls, hair securely tucked out of sight, are wielding sledgehammers pounding the caps on bombs, elbow to elbow with their male counterparts.

The "ladies" took to the outdoors, as well. An endearing photo of an all-female survey crew, from the 1918 Minidoka Dam Project in Idaho, USA, shows a smiling group of four kitted out in puttees and boots, posed with theodolites and other surveying instruments. The resemblance to male surveyors is not just in their clothing, their demeanor is androgynous as well—with the possible exception of the cheerful smiles. They could be just "some of the guys," which is undoubtedly the impression they wished, and needed, to present. No flirtatious airs, no girlish poses, just a serious professional work crew, wearing serious professional work garb. Rough work shirts, baggy pants, boots, and loose masculine jackets that say "we can do it." Furthermore, there is an unspoken joy that pervades this photograph. These are not say-cheese-for-the-camera smiles—these surveyors are pleased with themselves and pleased with their jobs.

Unidentified female surveyors with the Minidoka Dam Project in Idaho, c. 1918, looking very pleased (U.S. Bureau of Reclamation).

Another candid shot, now part of the National Archives and Records collection, is of a woman at work in Glenwood, Pennsylvania, on the Baltimore and Ohio railroad. I quote the caption in full:

> Attired in overalls, more than 30 women are doing men's work in the shops of the Baltimore & Ohio Railroad, at Glenwood, Pa. Although only a beginning, this encroachment by the fairer sex, on a field peculiarly adapted to men, will soon become more general, and as more and more of our boys take their places on the firing lines in France, fresh additions to our armies of women workers will come in the natural course of events, until, in a few years, if the war lasts that long, the male worker will be a curiosity. The photo shows one of the workers, and proves the belief that women are not physically fitted for arduous labor is a fallacy.[10]

Once again, women are wearing the most practical garments they could obtain, which certainly meant trousers rather than skirts. Men who disparaged pants-clad women surely must have known how much more dangerous and impractical skirts would be, but failed to feel that to be a consideration. The ladies frequently paired their pants with men's rough work shirts and bandanas around their necks. If you're working on the railroad, it's best to look as rough and ready as possible.

The combination of humorous dismissal and faint praise in the above quote is representative of the schizophrenic attitudes which surrounded the subject of women stepping competently into the places of the men, as more and more disappeared into the trenches. In the interest of fairness, the United States had attempted to hold on to its neutral status until it became obvious that position was untenable. This late entry into the fray may have given the American society a shorter time to get used to the whole idea of war in the first place, and women doing men's jobs in the second. They conveniently forgot that worldwide, women (and children) had already comprised a significant percentage of factory workers from the dawn of the Industrial Age. Before that era, women worked as domestics, farm hands, cloth manufacturers, vendors, and brewers, standing shoulder to shoulder with the men but somehow invisible. One interesting twist, coming from women's employment in more traditional masculine jobs, is that domestic service, long the purview of females who needed to work, plummeted, as women found better paying positions in industry. Good, while it lasted.[11]

Better paying, but still far from the salary rates of men. Owing to the fact that women were willing to accept the lower salaries and work just as hard, this caused a worry that returning servicemen would not be able to regain their positions after the war. Two things occurred: women were fired precipitously; or if they were able to keep their jobs alongside the men where it was needed, they were still paid much less.

In 1918, the female transportation workers in London went on strike to demand equal wages. The strike spread to the towns and adversely impacted the London Underground, resulting in the establishment of a committee by the War Cabinet to review the matter. The committee hemmed and hawed over the problem in their report. Yes, they believed in equal pay for equal work, but you know how it is with women—"lesser strength and *special health problems*" (emphasis mine)—therefore the inevitable weaseling. Where, when, and if they conceded that women should be paid the same as men, this was to revert immediately on the cessation of hostilities to the lesser salary. Otherwise, less money was all that was warranted.[12]

As an interesting, and rather infuriating, revelation of just how overlooked women's contributions had been, Barton Hacker, retired Senior Curator of Armed Forces

Unidentified female worker on the Baltimore and Ohio Railroad, Glenwood, Pennsylvania. She probably wears a man's small pants and shirt with the sleeves and cuffs rolled up (photograph by War Industries Board, Wikimedia Commons).

History at the National Museum of American History, expressed astonishment on seeing a collection of women's uniforms at the museum saying, "I never realized how many thousands of American women had volunteered in World War I." The real surprise for him was the fact that many of the uniforms were not from the military, such as the United States Women Executives, but belonged to civilians who were as organized as any army and dressed the part to boot.[13] Photographs of an amazing array of over sixty different uniforms, for as many diverse service occupations, make the extent of women's contribution forcefully evident. And yet, these represent only a part of the jobs taken on by women for the duration of the war. Still missing, as the museum states on their website, are such occupations as factory workers, munitions workers, or women police and mail carriers.

Some of the spiffiest, as well as one of the most militarily styled, was the uniform of a general of the Salvation Army. Others, such as the ensemble of the First Vice President of National War Work, as well as the Overseas and United States representatives of the YWCA, with their elegant hats, capes and business-like jackets and skirts, were equally impressive.

Evangeline Booth, the founder of the Salvation Army, wears her self-designed uniform here as she shakes hands with a regular Army officer. As a working model for the uniform, she borrowed freely from the British Women's Army (WAAC) with its

Founder of the Salvation Army, Evangeline Booth, shaking hands with a regular Army officer, c. 1915. She wears her official Salvation Army uniform, which was modeled closely on those of the women serving in the British WAAC (Library of Congress).

high collar, rows of buttons, and little epaulets on the shoulders. An attractive woman with a slender figure, she is amusingly posed in a fake office with desk and chair on what appears to be dirt, and a drawn-in backdrop which doesn't quite cover the foliage at the left.

A fair number of the ensembles sported Sam Browne belts and/or epaulets, and the Winter Field outfit of a female member of the United States Marine Corps demonstrated that she protected herself with a heavy double-breasted trench coat. The trench coat was a new style at the time but now a fashion staple. The Woman's Land Army is represented at the museum by two models in boots or gaiters and trousers, and one in a motor corps driver's uniform.[14]

What is of interest is that many of the women made their own uniforms at home to a common standard. Joining an organization did not necessarily mean an automatic gift of a made-to-order outfit. As a matter of fact, many women complained in the beginning that they were often given men's uniforms with trousers sized to fit a small man. As Nina Edwards emphasizes, this was true in both Great Britain and the United States, where attitudes were equally equivocal. She states "...authorities were slow to allow women's uniforms to be designed with female body shape in mind, and the resulting resentment was matched by the ingenuity some spent in adjusting the fit...."[15] As her quote demonstrates, women were desperately needed but should not, at the same time, show that they could actually do just as good a job—which well-fitted work garments would tacitly imply. Women, nonetheless, threw themselves into the challenge with enthusiasm and a repudiation of corsets.[16]

Organized first in Britain, the Women's Army Auxiliary Corps (WAAC, then later just WAC), which had its counterpart in the U.S., were billeted in many places along the Front. In this image, we see an unidentified example of very official looking ladies in their khaki uniforms, which, in spite of the skirts, look much like the men's. This particular group are shown on parade in Rouen, France at the Western Front. There is no mistaking the determination and purpose radiating from their squared shoulders and firmly set jaws. If there is fear, it is well tucked away in the oversized pockets attached to their waists.

The women were held to high standards very similar to those of Dorothea Dix in the 1860s. Wearing all khaki brimmed hats or caps; jackets or overcoats; and skirts (which had to be no more than twelve inches above the ground); they were also expected to be physically fit and did specified exercises every day.

The appearances of the lady warriors are deceiving: while they look official, they were faced with the same prejudice women faced in every area of endeavor. For one, there were no officers in the WAAC, it was taken as a given that only men could receive a commission. Therefore, females in charge were called Controllers (or Officials), Forewomen, Assistant Forewomen, and just plain workers (who corresponded to Army privates), in lieu of an appellation which would make them sound like officers. Another, and more important facet of the difficulties, was the issue of their salary. Even though the rule was that for every woman given the job *of a man,* a man was to be released for duty, and even though women were occupying that same position, women were consistently paid less for taking the identical job. The thankless duty of Mrs. Chalmers Watson, a medical practitioner who had been given the job of overseeing the WAACs, was to have an almost daily fight over this contentious issue. By February 1918, nine months before the end of the war, Chalmers Watson finally gave up in exhaustion and resigned

U.S. Women's Army Auxiliary Corps members assembled in Rouen, France, at the Western Front, c. 1918. These ladies look unassailable, and as stalwart as any Yank or Brit (Zackerson21, Wikimedia Commons).

from the post of Chief Controller. She was replaced by a Mrs. Burleigh Leach, who presumably experienced the same difficulties, but was saved from complete collapse by the cessation of hostilities.[17]

Scurrilous rumors dogged the women from the start, no matter their country of origin. British newspapers began accusing the women of being too friendly with the troops at the front and having to be sent home pregnant. An official investigation revealed that of six thousand British WAACs in France between March 1917 and February 1918 only twenty-one had become pregnant. The senior investigator, Miss Tennyson Jesse, dryly opined that was a lower rate than in most British villages.[18]

That fact did not stop the criticism of those dedicated females. The mere idea of women serving either in combat, or near it, was simply deplored. An anonymous pamphlet written by "A Little Mother" essentially stated that women were created to procreate and, in a most peculiar argument, men were created to take it on the chin. Even would-be feminists argued that women's job was to bear armies rather than arms.[19] Nonetheless, in the November 1917 issue of *Photoplay,* Gladys Brockwell asks, "Speaking of Man Power in this War—What About Woman Power?" Ms. Brockwell illustrates her own question by appearing in full soldier kit with rifle at the ready, believing that "woman must now prepare herself to go right on the firing line as a soldier if the occasion demands it," owing to the fact that "if the struggle continues long enough at the terrible rate already set, there will be eventually more able-bodied women than there will be men fit for the service." It did not quite come to *that,* however Ms. Brockwell certainly made a cogent point. She continues, "If there ever was a time when lines of prejudices should be erased, that time is now.... If woman wants man's prerogatives—to vote and all—she should be willing to share man's ... work if there is any necessity for it."[20]

Just as the WAACs, nurses at the Front were set apart by their identical attire, which as Dorothea Dix had instinctively known, psychologically protected them to a certain extent. Prominently displaying red crosses on their apron bibs, and crowned by their crisp, white caps—some with longish veils—they served without rank or commission, just grit, selflessness, and professionalism. (On the Western Front alone, ten thousand Americans, and a probable fifteen thousand British—the count is uncertain due to the hostility they faced—were deployed. Many British women, unable to find acceptance within their own countrymen, were obliged to serve with the French and Belgians, although Queen Alexandra's Imperial Military nurses were tolerated, probably due to their snob appeal.[21])

The work was hellish and appreciation for their work was seldom forthcoming from either the doctors, or officers, with whom they were thrown together. As in the American Civil War, however, the wounded men were more grateful for a kind face, a kind hand, and a semblance of caring.

Vera Brittain's gritty memoir, *Testament of Youth,* as well as her poignant poetry, underscore the difficulty and thanklessness of their labor. Her resentment pours forth in her:

Lament of the Demobilised

"Four years," some say consolingly. "Oh well,
What's that? You're young. And then it must have been
A very fine experience for you!"
And they forget
How others stayed behind and just got on –
Got on the better since we were away.
And we came home and found
They had achieved, and men revered their names,
But never mentioned ours;
And no-one talked heroics now, and we
Must just go back and start again once more.
"You threw four years into the melting-pot –
Did you indeed!" these others cry. "Oh well,
The more fool you!"
And we're beginning to agree with them.[22]

Brittain had experienced the horrors firsthand. Losing both her brother and her fiancé, along with becoming seriously ill due to fatigue and overwork in the wards, she well knew the price of war. Her resentment of her parents, whom she considered complacent bourgeois even before the war, only became more profound on her return and echoes continually in her memoir.

Again, as in earlier wars, dress played an important part in bolstering the image of the nursing profession. All white uniforms, with crisp white aprons, were the most frequently pictured in photographs; however, there was a darker alternative. Referred to as an "overall," it was of deep blue "nurses' cloth," yet still sported the crisp white apron, white collar and cuffs, and white cap. There was also a military-style uniform in the same blue, with high collar, and overseas cap. Handsome deep blue capes completed the ensembles with prominent red crosses decorating all versions.

The utter impracticality of white amidst the filth, mud, and blood of the Front goes without saying. Nevertheless, photographic images of those dedicated women show them starched, spotless and as virginally white as brides before the ceremony. Certainly symbolic, the white spoke of innocence, untouchability, and cleansing. For young men, thrust into the hellholes of the trenches with their never-ending cold and damp, unable to bathe, unable to change, unable to get warm, a group of all-white uniformed, ministering women would have seemed a vision of angels. Which is certainly why they were photographed that way. At least, that is, what was undoubtedly intended. If any nurse actually did wear all white, it's barely possible that her day might have started out that way, but by the end, the ideal would have vanished under the coat of bodily fluids the uniform had been baptized with. Laundry, no matter what the uniform color, was an everyday ritual before a nurse could seek her bed, exhausted.

American nurses were represented by about 8,000 personnel belonging to the American Red Cross, in combination with the smaller American Army Nurse Corps of only 403 on active duty and 170 in the reserve. Civilian nurse volunteers usually worked with the American Ambulance Service in Paris or at a French Army field hospital in Belgium.[23] In some cases, they were supplemented by the VAD (Volunteer Aid Detachment) who got even less respect, even from their fellow nurses, for not being "real."

The VAD were mainly voluntary British women with a wish to serve. They were regarded with suspicion because they lacked the training and discipline of professional nurses, and sometimes had the audacity to criticize. In spite of their dedication, and in spite of their growth in ability and performance, when the war ended leaders in the profession agreed that they should not be allowed on the register of nurses. A poor return for the hours of equal labor, deprivation, and dedication shown by these devoted women, who did not have to be there. Some VAD nurses went on to become prominent

Queensland nurses stationed at Biggenden, c. 1918, and dressed all in white, at least for the photograph. Note the little fellow in Aussie uniform in front (State Library of Queensland).

names in other fields, Agatha Christie, Enid Bagnold (the author of *National Velvet*), and the aforementioned Vera Brittain among them.

In Britain, women served in the newly created Royal Air Force, called simply enough the Women's Royal Air Force (WRAF), a service which only existed from 1918 to 1920. Information on them is scant, but images abound, thankfully. Their uniforms were, in the main, the ubiquitous military-styled jacket over a full, gathered skirt. There are, however, photographs of them inspecting planes, and/or actually servicing them, wearing a mid-calf length white coverall. Their caps were distinctive: a stiff bill; a banded, pleated bonnet with a central insignia; and short flaps which presumedly folded down on the sides. One dashing image is of a woman in a brass buttoned and belted jacket with two large envelope pockets, over laced-up jodhpurs and nearly knee-high buttoned-up boots. Her cap is embellished with what look like faux flying goggles and the patch on her shoulder bears the legend Royal Flying Corps. The women rode dispatch motorcycles—although they were not allowed to ride at night—serviced planes, or were clerical workers, however I could find no verification that any of them actually flew or received flight training.[24]

Not just female dispatch riders passed along information during the war. Trained female signallers operated in much the same way as the men. Here are three uniformed, but unidentified, female members of the British Territorial Corps performing maneuvers with the signal flags. One sends a message with the flags, a second sights through her telescope to presumably see the return signal, and a third takes notes. They do *look* official.

Three unidentified female signallers of the British Territorial Corps. One performs semaphore maneuvers with the signal flags, while the second sights through the telescope and a third takes notes (Library of Congress).

Loving Hands at Home

Even more important, in its way, than the need for factory replacement workers was the Women's Land Army in both the United States and the United Kingdom. Food production was essential for those at the Front, as well as those supporting them at home. A propaganda recruitment poster for the American Women's Land Army depicts two women carrying an overflowing bushel basket and wearing the latest in farmerette chic: gaiters, below-the-knee-length bloomers, worn with voluminous tunics and straw hats. Behind them, a woman astride wears a khaki version of the same attire, however her khaki color suggests a regulation Army uniform and adds an official aura to the depiction. She rides a plow horse, which she guides just with her left hand, while balancing a *very* large rippling American flag in the other. The advertisement touts the University of Virginia Training School's two-week course for the Army. The tuition is free but there is a $5.00 a week charge for board.

When not growing the food for the Army, Home Front Moms were hard at their knitting needles. Heeding the rallying cry "Knit for Sammie!" (Uncle Sam's boys, i.e., Doughboys), Americans young and old were urged to turn out wool sweaters, socks, and headgear for the troops. The fanzines were quick to take up the cry with articles such as "Quick Watson, the Needles!" which pictures several "film queens" hard at work over their needles and "by and by some gallant soldier boy in the front-line trenches will be handed a package...." We see Louise Fazenda, Beverly Bayne, Pauline Frederick, Anna Little and others, all popular names at the time, doing their bit.

American Women's Land Army poster, c. 1918. Blousy tunics over bloomers tucked into gaiters. Woman astride wears khaki uniform in similar style (poster by Herbert Paus, Library of Congress).

Even before the winter of 1917, the American Red Cross was already asking for one and a half million wristlets, mufflers, sweaters, and socks. Socks were the most important—the trenches were permanently wet and cold, and the "Trench Boots" the soldiers wore were deplorable. Purportedly water-repellent, in truth they fell to pieces rapidly under the damp conditions, and the iron heel and iron hobnails conducted the freezing cold directly into the feet of the troops. In 1918, a *slightly* better design (the "Pershing" boot) was distributed which provided the improvement of an extra sole. This was accompanied by the drawback of rigidity, making it impossible for the soldier to bend his foot. Completely lacking in insulation as well, they might as well have been two ice cube trays. The men took to wearing two pairs of socks under boots two sizes larger than their normal. An endless supply of socks was desperately needed.

Knitters went to work with a will. Not all possessed the same degree of skills; nevertheless, even a somewhat askew product kept a soldier warm somewhere. Some of the somewhat askew were tactfully reworked by the better-practiced before they were sent abroad. As might be expected, Tyro knitters learned quickly as they sat—everywhere—with their work in their laps. Restaurants, theaters, church, social groups, anywhere they went, garments in all stages of development went with them.

The Seattle Times (Washington state) added its voice to the appeals by encouraging those who could not knit to buy yarn for those who did, saying: "...there were many dear little old ladies who were anxious to knit for the Red Cross, but who could not afford the 75 cents to pay for the initial allotment of the yarn." The *Times* explained that a fund had been established by the Seattle Red Cross to provide for those "dear little old ladies," and asking for donations.[25]

Pattern books trotted out dozens of ideas for balaclavas, scarves, socks, gloves, and caps to wear under helmets. The latter items were indispensable. The saddest and most telling pattern however, which came from a pattern book entitled *Service Woolies,* was for knitted items called "Amputation Covers." The horror evoked by this simple name was unspeakable. Gladys Brockwell, of the military bent (see above), insensitively suggests that women should spend more time "devoting ... to actual military training than to knitting."

Home sewers also made their contribution diligently, but not always well. One popular British patter ditty of the day was called "Sister Susie's Sewing Shirts for Soldiers," the lyrics of which went in part: "Some soldiers send epistles, say they rather sleep in thistles, than the saucy, soft, short shirts for soldiers sister Susie sews."[26] Nevertheless, women applied themselves with the same energy as they did to knitting.

Women were also encouraged to make their own clothes. When America entered the war in 1917, materials for home sewers grew tight everywhere, because the United States had been exporting a fair percentage of their textile production to Europe to ease shortages there.

An article in the December 1917 issue of *Photoplay* by Elizabeth June Christie touts the benefits of the home-sewing skill. Of course, that was a cleverly disguised advertisement for the "Women's Institute of Domestic Arts and Sciences, Inc.," a profit-making organization. The Inc. rather gives it away. Elizabeth June purportedly runs into a friend who is wearing a dress that inspires admiration. When she is told it is "homemade" and where her friend learned to produce such a marvel, Ms. Christie just has to attend the same Institute. After extolling the incomparable assistance of the Institute, Ms. Christie kindly appends a coupon directing unwary but aspiring home dressmakers to obtain the proper information.[27] While I have been satirical here, the governmental encouragement to sew at home was genuine. The department stores, with their ready-to-wear, inexpensive garments, were wooing women by the scores away from homemade clothing when store-bought could be procured so easily. The war sent these shopping enthusiasts backward a step or two.

This was rather a catch-22. For their own wardrobes, British women were already facing shortages of material for clothing, as were their sisters in the United States as soon as America entered the war. Although there was no official program for rationing among any of the Allies, manufacturers were encouraged to conserve the bulk of their output for the war effort. This caused even more shortages in the United Kingdom because, as I said, a large percentage of the textiles used for clothing came from the United States. As a result, magazines carried many articles offering sprightly suggestions about how to make over older clothing to look refreshed and newer, with the addition of some little trifle such as a flounce, collar, or scarf. This trend led to mocking articles and cartoons claiming that old was now the rage and that women were trying to outdo each other in looking as worn out and shabby as possible. Even to the point of buying new garments that had been "aged." Does this sound anything like the ripped jeans and tee shirts of today?

Les femmes in France faced similar shortages, so understandably, French fashion plates for 1915 start out with a similar close-to-the-body silhouette for both the United Kingdom and the Continent as dictated by rationing. These conservative styles are unaccountably overtaken at the end of the year by the "war crinoline," which almost overnight turned wartime fashion on its head. A possible reaction to Paul Poiret's "hobble skirt," or just war fatigue in general, the war crinoline consumed yards of gathered fabric. Previously competent women suddenly blossomed into millions of American Southern Belles. Juxtaposed with tailored jackets for walking suits, the contrast was almost comical. In an interesting attraction-of-opposites' way, nevertheless, the slightly more masculine and tailored look of the jacket combined with the pouf of the skirt, was actually attractive and more flattering to female figures. Wearing a fitted blazer over a wider skirt somewhat mitigated the antebellum resemblance.

The first to feature this perplexing development (in view of the circumstances) may have been the French *Gazette du bon ton* magazine, which went on hiatus from 1917 to 1920, but was around long enough to set a style before its interruption. Considering that France was deep in the business of war, it makes the foray into parachute imitations all the more inexplicable. Rather unfortunate as well, because the fashion all too often combined the worst aspects of Louis XIV (hip panniers) and Southern Belle (fussily gathered skirts). Froth was definitely in for 1916 and 1917.

Of course, there is froth and then there is *froth*. In the May 1916 *Photoplay,* there is a decidedly enticing example, probably designed by Lucile. As insubstantial as cotton candy, actress Margaret Greene wears a fluff of sheer tulle in a "flesh" color (pale pink) with handkerchief hem and embroidered bands, girdled with silver and punctuated by silver roses on the satin belt and down the skirt. A lace camisole shields the bodice from over-enticement but plunges far enough to still be flirtatious. Ms. (well, Miss) Greene, never quite a star, had a short but relatively major film career from 1915 to 1919. Beside her eight screen credits, there is little information beyond her husband's name and her birth and death dates.

Then there is the "other" froth. The stage and screen actress Jane Grey, in the same *Photoplay* issue, is clad in a gown by Lucille which she wears in the 1916 film, *The Test.* Again, of flesh pink tulle with a silver satin under-gown, it has all the features one doesn't want—droopy, cap-sleeved bodice with deep vee neckline filled in for modesty with the satin, hip flounces on the tulle overdress, which are not quite panniers, and an overall fussy and unfinished look. This is surprising for Madame Lucille, whose elegant and extravagant gowns were usually the height of taste. The silver satin under-gown would have been lovely on its own but is overdone with the tulle. A heavy-featured and mature-for-her-age appearing actress, Ms. Grey (née Mamie Larock, 1882/3) is particularly at a disadvantage in girlish frou-frou.

Lucille French's (no relation to designer Lucile) flowery, but also most intriguing, article in the July 1916 issue of *Photoplay*, "War-Time Fashions: Always the Same," takes window dressers and designers to task for the trend, albeit somewhat obliquely. However, she brings up an interesting point, and a possible answer to the article's title, which affords food for thought. She discusses an interview with Virginia Pearson, whom she describes as a "daughter of the stage," but "now of the screen," posing a question about what she describes as a "coincidence." This is the interesting observation that, throughout history, women in wartime seem to blossom out in tight-waisted ensembles over voluminous skirts. Ms. French and Ms. Pearson agree that this is a prevailing trend. They look back at the French Revolution and the American Civil War as examples which support their (non)answer, which they believe is that "coincidence," with fashion just turning in a circle back to the starting point; or possibly an attempt to counter the awfulness of reality with some fantasy. *This* author considered the "coincidence" in light of the wars discussed in this volume but saw none, with the exception of the not-mentioned Korean War when circle (poodle) skirts with frilly petticoats were all the rage.

Ms. Pearson models the trend with several frocks of the fun, frothy variety. In particular, a silver and salmon-pink evening gown accessorized with marabou fan. The charmeuse bodice is squared, ending in a tiny lace ruffle below the waist, with a full-circle lace skirt over an opaque under-skirt of the same material as the bodice. This ethereal bon-bon is worn with white curve-heeled, high-buttoned shoes.[28]

By contrast, Lucille French's article in the following issue for August, displays "Outing Fashions" (outing refers to outdoor activities, i.e., sporting) which are "All Our Own." While still war crinoline to the max, these are considerably toned down and tailored for daytime activities. Tennis fashion, for example, is a sash-belted, striped blazer with contrasting collar, pockets and cuffs, over a white skirt. I partially quote the caption: "The striped blazer is universal this season—the newest thing in sports coats ... the Milanese silk which tubs [sic] with all the expediency for the tourist...." Nevertheless, it is guaranteed to slow the wearer down to a crawl on the courts. Also shown is a Tyrolean-styled hiking suit (the caption refers to a Norfolk jacket) with knee-length breeches above gaiters, a jaunty hat with feather, shirt and tie, and a pair of really stylish two-toned, low-heeled oxfords (I have an identical pair). Made of khaki drill cloth, the ensemble looks stifling for the August wearer, and the shoes are ridiculous for hiking, however adorable.[29]

In the United States, the *B. Altman Fall and Winter* catalogue for 1915 shows the same long tunic and narrow skirt we see in European styles at the beginning of the year. These elegant walking suit ensembles often echo men's belted jackets with a slim skirt or feature more feminine models with gracefully curving jacket hems over a single- or double-flounced skirt. This trio of up-scale fashionistas portray all of these examples. On the left, our model's jacket swoops low in the back over her double-flounced skirt with button detail. The central figure wears a swing-back jacket, also with a curving hem, over her double-layered tailored skirt, and the third model is clad in a jacket

B. *Altman Fall and Winter* catalogue, 1915. Long tunics over slim skirts. Jackets sometimes with curved hems, skirts sometimes with double-flounce look. Masculine influence with feminine execution (Wikimedia Commons).

borrowed from the boys with straight lines and a below-the-waist self-belt. Envelope pockets complete the masculine influence.

By late 1915 or early 1916, ladies everywhere had caught up to the continent. The flounced skirt was still very much in evidence, however it had now taken on the dimensions of a bumbershoot, as these charming ladies strolling in the rain attest. A slight hint of military style adorns the left-hand figure of the facing trio, and just possibly was the intention for the sprightly young lady on the right. Our umbrella carrier wears a wide, dark belt with hanging pendant, looking rather like the chatelaine of the castle. The figure who glances over her shoulder, with her back turned to us, is wrapped in a voluminous overcoat with fur collar and contrasting banded hem. The

Gazette du Bon Ton. **French ahead of U.S. with skirts that could be used to parachute the ladies into the war zone. Military look on the young lady farthest on the left (Wikimedia Commons).**

foreground trio have come out in their gaiters; however, our overcoated young woman is tippy-toeing along in the most impractical of heels.

A *Vogue* cover, which decorated the August 1916, United States issue, displayed the war crinoline, but gave an ethereal touch to the concept, rather like Virginia Pearson's salmon-pink and silver creation. That illustration proved that the Americans might be a little tardy but still on top of the French styles. A lovely fantasy figure, of an earth-bound angel skipping across the sands, the imagined design takes the flounce and pleat as far as they will go. With sleeves resembling downy wings and adorned with pleats of the same feathery texture composing the swan-like skirt, the figure suggests Odette in transition. Alas, it's only fantasy, the reality was not necessarily so sublime. The artist was George Wolfe Plank, an American rival to George Barbier and Erté. Associated for many years with *Vogue* magazine, Plank has been compared a bit unfairly with the Art Deco style of his fellow illustrator at *Vogue,* Helen Dryden, although he was already well-known before she became both a rival and colleague.

Dryden, who was a little younger than Plank, was also a highly successful illustrator and industrial designer. She was contracted to *Vogue* from 1909 to 1922 where her work resembled Barbier's in its light touch.

During that time, she was also employed as a costume designer, and in the '20s, an industrial designer. In the '30s, she worked for Studebaker Automobiles and was rumored to make $100,000 a year. Ironically, in her later years, Dryden was reduced to welfare, living in a ten-dollar-a-week apartment paid for by the city, sadly forgotten. Basically self-taught, her work is romantic, innovative, and yet reminiscent of both George Barbier and Erté[30] in its Art Deco stylization. These two French designers were the primary influences on both Plank and Dryden.

These were the Art Deco years—roughly 1909–1940. The coining of the term itself came later and was attributed to the English art historian Bevis Hillier in 1968. It was a contraction of the French *Arts Décoritifs* style, first displayed at the Paris *Exposition Internationale des Arts Décoratifs et Industriels Modernes* in 1925. Growing out of the *Art Nouveau* movement, it used similar motifs but imposing geometrical angles on the sweeping curves of the earlier style. Art Deco also drew from the influence of the Fauvists, Cubists, and the *Ballets Russe,* mingling them all with abandon in color and shape.

Upper class magazines such as *Vogue* or *Harper's Bazar* (changed to *Bazaar* in 1930), featured Art Deco covers and patronized such famous names as Erté to decorate their interiors with his illustrations. Seeming to rise above war, privation and restriction, Art Deco appeared to aim its bow directly at the psyche, creating a world apart from the reality forced upon everyone. This was especially true in the case of Erté.

Erté's exotic designs, with their swooping sleeves and over-the-top execution were not for the shy violet or the modest purse. However, if you had the confidence of Catherine the Great, and the resources of the Bank of England, you could make every head spin. Two examples for the March 1917 issue of *Vogue* demonstrate that clearly. For one, "La Robe de Cendrillon" (Cinderella's gown). I quote the caption in full—they say it so well: "...is a gown for the modern ball sufficiently alluring to captivate the most exacting of princes. Erté has combined black and white chiffon most elaborately and embroidered the interesting sleeves and every edge with crystals and jet."[31]

The designer's obsession was with sleeves—every garment paid close attention to the way sleeves flowed, draped, trailed, or bloused airily. On this robe for a modern Cinderella, the sleeves are a wheel of sheer fabric with the crystal and jet embroidery

A Helen Dryden cover for *Vogue*, June 1913. In her light, delicate touch we can easily see the influence of George Barbier (Wikimedia Commons).

fanning out in spoke-like application. At the sleeve bottom hem are two jet and crystal tassels. Milady's upper arm is encircled like the wheel's hub. The attaching seam is just on the shoulder, giving the impression of a just-about-to-be-bared limb. The neckline is a vee which is trimmed with embroidery and continues down the front of the gown to below the hem. In this, even the plainest of serving girls would draw every eye.

A second figure on the same page wears "La Richesse," the bodice of which consists of ropes of dangling jet beads, the tasseled "sleeves" blending into what can only be called the "façade" of the bodice. As architectural in its construction as the girders of a bridge, and yet as ethereal as a mist, the neckline plunges to a high-waisted skirt which melds with the bust and cascades floorward in rivulets of silver brocade lined with black chiffon velvet.

For Erté, the war was something to ignore as one would a buzzing fly. Other than a slight hint of militarism in the high collars on his heavy overcoats, which nearly conceal the face of the wearers, and the beaked or tilted caps which accessorize them, all is elegance and mystery. Never conceding a thing to restrictions, his designs were as expansive (and expensive) as imagination would allow.[32]

A George Barbier illustration of a *femme fatale* in a misleadingly demure pose. Her necklace looks like a noose; nevertheless, a hint of the battle of the sexes (Wikimedia Commons).

Much more superficially restrained and seemingly demure, George Barbier's illustrations have less substance than Erté's but are their equal in imagination. Strangely, he could be much more erotic—frequently raunchy, in fact. I would say earthy, to be polite, but that term falls short of description. He combines his unabashed voluptuousness with a light touch that suggests the figures would dissolve if regarded too closely.

In one example, a young lady stands between two Ionic columns attired in a Grecian-inspired gown which narrows to hobble dimension at the hem. Ostensibly innocent, she fiddles suggestively with a double string of pearls. One strand reaches to below her waist, the other, longer strand she holds out like an imprisoning chain which she seems about to toss over the head of any unwary male. Behind her a tame panther lies at her feet in Sphinx-like pose. So simply executed, so menacing subliminally.

In another, a hint of forbidden love shows up in the image of two women—or, more properly, one woman and what appears to be an adolescent. The older female is completely nude and the younger clutches a sheer fabric which is slipping to the floor. Holding the youngster's head in her grasp, with their mouths only inches apart, the older figure plucks an apple from a bough which intrudes into the room. The whole is executed with the lightest of strokes.

In yet another, Vaslav Nijinsky, the great dancer of the early 20th century, creeps lasciviously up on a prone Ida Rubenstein in an illustration of the 1910 Paris ballet, *Schéhérazade*. He reaches for her bared breast with a lecherous grin as she clutches an oversize rose and throws her other arm over her head in compliance.

Other designers, who worked in the same Art Deco vein, were Louise Chéruit and Jacques Doucet. Chéruit, one of the first women at the head of a major French fashion house, operated her salon from 1906 to 1935. Her work has the same ethereal nature of Barbier's, whose influence is obvious, given to similar flowing lines, frequently with the look of a frothy meringue. Not only is Barbier's influence manifest, but she is also working within the stylistic influence of Art Nouveau with its softer curves. Although many fashion houses shut down during the war, her salon remained open, however she was touched by scandal and accused of being a German spy. She retained some control

The famous Nijinsky with a compliant Ida Rubenstein in *Schéhérazade*, c. 1910. He leers rapaciously, while she appears unresistant (George Barbier, Wikimedia Commons).

over her enterprise from seclusion, but after the war was seen as old fashioned and overdone—she retired in 1923.

Doucet was a little more substantial, but with a similar flowing line approach and a penchant for flounces. In the '20s, under the continuing influence of the Art Deco trend, his designs took on a more geometric feel. A walking suit from 1915 displays both aspects. The two-piece suit consists of a bolero-length jacket which dips lower in the back, where there is a pleated panel from the waist to the hem with a slight swing to it, and deep cuffs on the sleeves. The skirt, pleated all around, sports two levels of bell-shaped flounces. The whole is done in a crisp black-and-white check.

Paris fashion, in its peacetime glory, all but disappears during the war years, to be resumed immediately after. Many fashion houses were forced to adapt to the restrictions of war in order to remain active. Nevertheless, for many designers, the reality of war was a faraway thing, barely considered with relation to the average woman in the street. In spite of this, less affluent women sought for at least a semblance of *haute couture,* even in the face of privation—making do with "refreshed" garments or more economical copies in order to resemble the *haute monde*. For the well-to-do, who were not touched in quite the same way, designer wardrobes were an escape from that reality, because, like their less well-off sisters, they were not immune to death.

THREE

The (Reel) Time Wars

The Allies

The moving pictures had already, by the onset of the war, captured the world in their sway. By 1916, when the United States entered the fight, Hollywood had become *Hollywood.* From a literal cattle town—there were regulations about how many cows could be driven down the streets—it was now the center of movie production: under Carl Laemmle, Universal Studio had opened in the San Fernando Valley in 1915; Famous Players, which had just merged with the Jesse L. Lasky Company, had become Paramount; Thomas H. Ince, the "Father of the Western" had built his first studio, known as Triangle Studios—later it would become M.G.M.; and William S. Hart, the famous cowboy star, had his own studio.

Unlike the earliest years, stars had become *stars* by this time and were featured in fan magazines such as *Photoplay* and *Moving Picture World.* In gushing articles with titles like "Boys! Here's the Way to Win," lovelies like Enid Markey, Helen Holmes, Theda Bara, and the sweet-faced, prolific but short-careered Ormi Hawley, paraded their charms to entice the male readers to become moviegoers.[1] These same stars endorsing the latest fashions implied that their distaff readers could attain the same heights. Knowing their audience well, the magazines tended toward women and fashion for much of their content, along with blurbs discussing the latest releases. Each issue was devoted to several pages of full-size portraits of the stars, male and female, with short bios adulating each one.

The newspaper world was equally aware of the pervasive influence of the movies; many editorials and articles expressing both concern and favor were written regarding this issue, without—it must be added—coming to any conclusion. It didn't matter. Aye or nay, films were here to stay, and audiences flocked in weekly droves to be influenced.

Amidst the chaotic social upheaval caused by war, one must ask the question: How did Hollywood react to the fact of worldwide conflict?

Oddly, the most affecting films about World War I came *after* the war was over. *The Four Horsemen of the Apocalypse* starring Rudolph Valentino came out in 1921, *Wings* was released in 1927, and the powerful *All Quiet on the Western Front* in 1930. During the war, nonetheless, there were a handful of movies addressing some of the personal quandaries resulting from divided loyalties, such as *The Little American* (1917), directed by Cecil B. DeMille, where an American girl finds herself in love with a German soldier and not very attracted to his French counterpart. It starred the very popular Mary Pickford as the "Little American."

The plot is rife with improbable coincidences. For example, the "German soldier" is trapped into serving in the German Army by his French rival for Pickford's (as Angela Moore) affections, even though he is living in the United States and has no sympathies for the German cause. The Frenchman (Raymond Hatton) arranges it for Karl (Jack Holt, Jr.) to be sent to Hamburg where he is immediately obliged to join his regiment.

Blithely going on an overseas trip, Pickford's ship is torpedoed but she manages to make it to France (on a raft!). She then tries to visit her French aunt only to find that the woman has died and she is now the heiress of the chateau. Inconveniently, her aunt's chateau is also filled with wounded soldiers. She stays to selflessly nurse the wounded, only to have a contingent of Germans enter the chateau where she is ministering, get drunk and plan to rape her. In trying to flee she is discovered by a German soldier who *just happens* to be Karl. The commander is going to shoot Pickford, but Karl interferes to save her and receives the same sentence. The French bomb the chateau, the pair manage to escape, only to be found by the French who are then going to shoot Karl. Pickford convinces them Karl is actually a hero rather than an enemy; nevertheless, it is because of *her* services that they are allowed to fly to America where Karl will be a prisoner of war for the duration.

Pickford is her usual adorable self, although her signature long curls are fastened up through much of the movie—the curls flow when she is before the Huns. Over the course of the movie, she wears a succession of "cute" outfits: a quasi-uniform with cap; a sweet ankle-length ballgown which is drenched when the ship goes down, clinging to her in a revealing manner; a black, or possibly dark green, satin dress (with a demure lace collar) when she is brought before the Germans; and in a publicity poster, a man's military overcoat and wooden shoes. Still, a more mature wardrobe than her usual Pollyanna style, with the possible exception of the ballgown which is frothy and frilly. The costume designer is uncredited; however, later analysis has attributed the designs to Lucile (Lady Duff-Gordon).

When the film was released, the United States had not yet entered the war, although they had already declared war on Germany. Despite that fact, the Chicago Film Board banned it from exhibition, on the grounds that it was anti–German and that it might start a riot. On appeal, and two jury trials, the film was approved for showing in Chicago.

Hearts of the World (1918), starring the Gish sisters, Lillian and Dorothy, and directed by D.W. Griffith, was another of Griffith's heartbreakers. Also featuring Robert "Bobby" Harron and Ben Alexander, of much later *Dragnet* fame, as his little brother (Erich von Stroheim is an uncredited Hun), the story follows two families who are neighbors, one with a boy and one with a girl (Lillian Gish). Obviously, they are going to fall for each other. The boy (Robert Harron as Douglas Gordon Hamilton) is American but feels an obligation to do his part in the French Army, because war breaks out just as they are going to marry. Griffith manages to get in a little intertitle self-serving propaganda, in the guise of anti-war sentiment, by referring to the Civil War as no solution to the "black-white problem" and dramatically telling of the many *Southern* lives lost.

Lillian (as the girl, Marie Stephenson) does a lot of hoeing and looking slatternly; her look doesn't improve even when the intertitles tell us of her growing interest in fashion. Dorothy (the Little Disturber, a rival for the boy) doesn't do any hoeing but dresses only slightly better. Her outfit is mainly working-class "French" (beret, you know). She does wear one outfit with a lace-collared jacket that is actually semi-attractive. There is no wardrobe credit, but this is, generally speaking, still early for professional costume designers on many films. In which case, Lillian may be wearing a good bit of her own wardrobe, which is simply altered slightly to look French peasant.

Unadulterated melodrama, the movie is oddly not up to some of D.W. Griffith's early shorts and certainly not in the same league as his *Broken Blossoms* (1919), also starring Lillian Gish. The acting by both Gish girls is mostly atrocious, with Lillian the winner of the mugging award. Griffith was a pacifist and perhaps was going against the grain when making *Hearts of the World,* which may have led to his overdoing the direction of the Gish girls.

By the time *Hearts* was made, anti-German sentiment had reached its zenith, so the "Hun" could be shown as bestial without fear of banning. Unfortunately, the anti-fashion sentiment was just as obvious, not to mention the unconcern with even a slight touch of accuracy in costuming. Surprisingly, Lillian Gish, who was known for expecting perfection, apparently offered no objection to a simply thrown-together wardrobe.

As can be seen from the Chicago ban on *The Little American,* as well as the examples of the war posters, American attitudes toward the war were far different from those of the Europeans, including the British. Since a great many settlers in the eastern and midwestern United States were either German-born or German extraction and sensitive about their heritage, they were vocal in their responses to "brutal Huns" depictions. A *Photoplay* article by Karl Kitchen, from May 1916 (see Appendix B for the entire text), serves to prove this rather important point. Kitchen is in Berlin at the height of the hostilities, and yet writes as though he were taking tea at the Plaza. He speaks of the only place the average Berliner can go, to forget "their grief" resulting from the war, is to the movies, and of the fact that Vienna and Budapest have not been so "poignantly tainted" so they can laugh at the comedians while the Berliners only smile. "Even in Brussels," he states, they can enjoy this uplifting pastime, although he does add "forget[s] ... the grief that came with the grey-clad hordes from the East."[2]

This strikes one as unbelievably strange: first of all, that you can be an American out-and-about socially in Berlin after a declaration of war; secondly, that Kitchen can be so dismissive of Belgium's devastation; thirdly, that he obviously does not regard the Germans as "enemies"; and lastly, that he has no fear for himself. He goes into considerable detail about spending his first night in Berlin at the movies, sitting in a loge with three German officers. Of male fashion interest, they sported full-dress uniforms consisting of hip-length jackets, striped trousers, accessorized with swords, epaulettes, and medals, and monocles on all three. Kitchen—judging by the accompanying cartoons—is resplendent in white tie and tails! Completed, naturally, with white gloves and what look like spats.

He provides no synopsis of the film except to say it was a pretty good detective film, but he does give us its title and the names of its stars: Mia May and Max Landa in *Sein Schweirigster Fall* (*His Hardest Case, 1915*).[3] He tells us that he has seen no films made outside of Germany or Sweden, and, to him, "surprisingly" few American movies (he saw only one). French and British product had been banned and even though Germany is not officially at war with Italy, he has seen no Italian films.

He complains that moviegoing is more expensive in Germany than in the U.S., and doesn't run continuously. Nevertheless, he seems to spend an inordinate amount of time there and discusses a number of his experiences in detail. As an example, Kitchen describes the antics of Max Pallenberg, whom he calls the "Teutonic Charlie Chaplin," in *Der Rasende Roland* (literally *The Frenzied Roland,* or more probably Roland the Maniac) and how funny he was. Although, as did the entire audience, he takes the second feature on the double bill, *A Ghetto Tragedy,* very seriously. All present give it a rousing round of applause. He finishes up his opinion of the evening's entertainment by praising the excellent newsreel of the Kaiser reviewing his troops. He is more surprised that there is also a newsreel of the English King George reviewing *his* troops. He goes on to relate a reel that deals with the presentation of medals to a group of servicemen which included both English and French soldiers. The French officer kissed the recipients on both cheeks, including a Black soldier who may have been from Senegal, and the audience burst into laughter at "Der Schwartzer."[4]

Kitchen's tone is jarringly insouciant. How can he be unaware that the 1916 Chantilly Conference had estimated Allied casualties to be 485,000, and German deaths at some 630,000, *just at the Somme* (emphasis mine)? Did he go to France? Ypres was in ruins. The Battle of Verdun was in full swing—the engagement lasted ten months—French casualties alone amounted to 450,000; the Germans an estimated 350,000. His attitude is sadly rather representative of the many unaware Americans as well as a few Europeans.

Allied propaganda emphasized that the Germans of both wars were rapacious enemies; it comes as a shock to find they were not looked at in the same way by every "patriotic" American. When you look at the horrific statistics from both sides, you see that neither Kitchen's view nor our own are entirely correct. War really is "hell" for millions of ordinary young men, who just happen to be on one side or the other, and who never get a chance to live.

That having been said, rape was indeed later determined to be ubiquitous, so the picture of brutal Huns and rapacious enemies is not so far from the mark. The Belgians, whom Kitchen dismisses so cavalierly, could attest to that—the civilian population was severely mistreated. At least 6,000 were killed outright on flimsy and/or capricious grounds, and 17,000 more died as a result of expulsion, deportation, imprisonment or court-ordered death sentence. In the main, the atrocity reports were true, in particular the incidences of rape, but recent scholars have discovered that some stories may have been fabricated or exaggerated to stir up patriotic enthusiasm for the war. What remains absolutely true is that the Germans ravaged Belgium to the point that it never regained its pre-war economy.

Much propaganda was devoted to the "rape" of Belgium in order to stir up contributions to the war effort. A poignant poster is a case in point—against a backdrop of a burning town, a bestial figure in a German helmet drags away a young girl for obviously nefarious purposes. Rape is always the consequence of war. Invading armies tend to behave in an identical manner—shoot the men and rape the women—a sign of their complete control.

What else did the Allied newspapers have to say? Well, in spite of their cartoons, the *New York Tribune* discussed the "Ten Allies" Ball which raised $50,000 for war charities, along with a feature piece on Miss Ruth Law, an intrepid lady flyer who broke the record for a Chicago to New York flight, and "swept across the night sky in a whirl of magnesium flames." Awareness seemed to be confined to social events. Headlines about the war were confined to optimistic—and skewed—blurbs such as "Allies Raid German Trenches." At first, reporting was fairly accurate and gave a clear picture; then, government censorship stepped in and laid a firm hand over "adventurous" articles and the correspondents were constrained to downplay the real slaughter and promote the idea of victory. Although some hold the view that correspondents deliberately withheld bad news, some recent voices, however, have called for an alternative view—that the correspondents did what they could but the officers, such as the British Field Marshall Haig, complained, causing a reversal of truth to myth.[5] Therefore it's only too possible that Kitchen was as ignorant as a child of the true devastation surrounding him but not directly in his field of view. It is presumed, nevertheless, that the American correspondents, who were still technically neutral, wrote with a more objective eye. The United Press representative, William G. Shepherd, successfully reported on the first German use of poison gas on the Western Front in April 1915 and the first Zeppelin raid on London in September of the same year. There was no problem getting the air raid past the censors because the propaganda benefit was enormous. But by 1916 so many correspondents had been ejected that it moved former president Theodore Roosevelt to write to the British Foreign Secretary, Sir Edward Grey, that "the consequence of ejecting correspondents was that the only authentic war news … was coming from the German side."[6]

In the meantime, on January 24, 1916, the Military Service Bill calling for conscription of men for service was passed in the British House of Commons and shortly thereafter their draft began. At home, toward the end of February, Germany and Austria-Hungary notified the United States they would sink any armed merchant ships from the first of March onward. The United States' answer seemed to be to invade Cuba for the third time, which they did almost immediately.[7] However, a few days later they finally got around to rejecting the German declaration and demanding reparations for the sinking of the Lusitania. There was consciousness of the war danger among some but, on the face of it, there appeared to be little more response from the government than from the general public.

What little information leaked out to the public came from the Committee on (not for) Public Information, created by President Woodrow Wilson only eight days after declaring war—April 14, 1917. In charge of the committee was the journalist and activist, George Creel. His commission and mission were essentially to sell the war.

Creel was the perfect choice. He had previously written the script for *Saved by the Juvenile Court,* and a number of other propagandistic stories which were made into films. Owing to his familiarity with the movie industry, he preferred using film to market his propaganda product. He rapidly turned out several newsreels, mostly short films and some feature-length, such as *Pershing's Crusaders* (1918), *Women's Part in the War* (1917), *America's Answer* (1918), and *Our Colored Fighters* (1918). The last title was a documentary produced by the Downing Film Company, which featured the 15th New York Regiment colloquially known as the "Harlem Hellfighters."

Meant to rally African American support for the war, the publicity posters depicted a smiling Black infantryman marching in front of an all-Black unit, or standing before the flag, surrounded by vignettes of courageous action. The 15th were to be deployed at the French Front and the film had the full cooperation of the Army. A more compelling lithograph by the artist E.G. Renesch of Chicago, "*Our Colored Heroes*" pays tribute to the bravery of Pvt. Henry Johnson and Pvt. Robert Needham, who fought the Germans raiding their encampment steadfastly in spite of being wounded, outnumbered, and in the face of grenades.

At the outbreak of hostilities there were four standing all-Black regiments—the 9th and 10th Cavalry and the 24th and 25th Infantry. Eager to serve, in just one week

Pvts. Henry Johnson and Robert Needham of the 15th New York Regiment, fighting the Germans singlehandedly, in spite of wounds, superior numbers, and grenades (Lithograph, E.G. Renesch, National Portrait Gallery, Smithsonian Institution).

after the declaration of war, the acceptance of Black enlistees had to be curtailed by the War Department because the quotas had been filled. In an inexplicable reversal, draft boards were doing all they could to induct African Americans, *especially in Georgia* (emphasis mine), who in the end, made up 13 percent of inductees.[8] Overall, the United States Army was less discriminatory than other branches of the services, and Blacks did fairly well in khaki uniforms during the war. After the war, discrimination was worse than ever with the heavy implementation of the already in place "Jim Crow" laws, which had been named after a minstrel show character. This character had been created around 1830 by Thomas "Daddy" Rice, who was possibly to first to blacken his face with burnt cork. "Daddy" danced a jig while singing the song "Jump Jim Crow." Rice was supposedly "inspired" by seeing a Black stableman named Jim Crow who was physically impaired.[9]

The marginally better treatment of Blacks in the Army may have inspired some with hope for a better future. With that hope in mind, in January 1920, the African American director Oscar Micheaux released the lovely and moving film *Within Our Gates*. Written and produced by the director, *Gates* starred Evelyn Preer as Sylvia Landry, a young schoolteacher from the South who travels North to raise money for poor Black children. While there, she is subject to the advances of the stepbrother of the cousin she is visiting.

She rebuffs him and he later proves his degenerate character by murdering a gambler. The cousin proves just as treacherous because she arranges for Sylvia to be "discovered" in a compromising circumstance by her fiancé, whom her cousin also loves. Rather than believing her, he tries to strangle her but is stopped by the cousin, who is not willing to go that far. Sylvia goes home, a failure on both counts—no money, no engagement.

She agrees to go back to the North at the urging of the Reverend Jacobs, who runs the Piney Woods School, which will close without more funds. Immediately on arriving in Boston, her purse is stolen, but it is recovered by one Dr. Vivian (Charles D. Lucas). Unfortunately, Sylvia is hit by a car driven by the wealthy Elena Warwick (only billed as Mrs. Evelyn), who, in recompense, generously gives her $5,000 for the school, but increases it to $50,000 when a Southern "friend" tries to dissuade her.

Dr. Vivian, in the meantime, is trying to find Sylvia, and runs into the cousin by chance. Alma tells Sylvia's life story—the audience sees it in flashback. It seems Sylvia was adopted by her family, the Landrys. Although short on cash, they manage, somehow, to provide her with an education. Her adopted father, Mr. Landry, had been falsely accused of the murder of a wealthy white man, Gridlestone. A mob attacks the family, lynching them and one of Gridlestone's servants. Gridlestone's brother chases Sylvia and tries to rape her, but in tearing at her clothing he notices a scar. He recognizes the scar and realizes that she is actually his daughter by a local Black woman, and that she is the one whose education he has paid for. The attempted rape is stagy and unconvincing, however the lynching is portrayed with the nearly newsreel matter-of-factness I mention, which makes it all the more wrenching.

After hearing all of her story, Dr. Vivian meets with Sylvia to tell her of his love. He also urges her to love America and be proud of African American contributions. He is full of hope for the future with a new start for the "New Negro." The movie is melodramatic, beautiful, matter of fact and tragic all at the same time. We know, with a century of hindsight, that those hopes did not materialize. And, at the time of this writing, are still a struggle, although improved.

Throughout, Preer as Sylvia is fashionably, but always modestly, well-dressed. Her wardrobe is frequently white or light-colored. I would venture to suggest that this is a deliberate device on the part of Micheaux. Her scheming false friend, played by Floy Clements, is nearly always in dark clothing. This device is particularly effective, symbolically, in the rape scene as the rapist pulls a dark coat off Sylvia revealing the virginally white dress beneath.

As Public Information Head, we see that Creel avoided controversy at all costs. Of a certainty, *Within Our Gates,* with its unabashed racial message, would introduce more controversy than he could handle. Movies with depictions of strikes, labor riots, poverty, or slums were also rejected for export because of the "bad testimonial to the value of democracy," which would be obvious in spite of the *Within Our Gates* hopeful ending.[10] Bravery, sacrifice, not to mention moral necessity, were drummed like a John Phillip Sousa march and seemed a successful tactic to change the minds of a most unwilling audience.

A firm believer that the image of class harmony would enhance the war effort and a booster of the films which ostensibly promoted this harmony, Creel rejected many other "problem" films such as *The Eternal Grind* (1916) which dealt with "a phase of American industrial life which is a blot on American institutions."[11] The "blot" which *Grind* dealt with were sweatshops.

Grind starred Mary Pickford, in a tear-jerking scenario, as Louise, a sewing machine worker in a New York City sweatshop. Louise acts as keeper of her two younger sisters, Amy (Loretta Blake) and the sickly Jane (Dorothy West) and also as an activist in the shop. The sons of the sweatshop owner, Owen Wharton (John Bowers) and Ernest Wharton (Robert Cain) become interested in the factory girls. Owen, an upright settlement worker, falls honestly in love with Mary, but Ernest, a Casanova type, persuades Amy to be his mistress. The last sister, Jane, is growing increasingly ill with consumption, and Mary asks the owner, James, for some money to procure treatment, which he refuses. Ernest, hearing of the dilemma, offers money if Mary will become his mistress as well. Outraged, she goes after him with a gun and forces him into a literal shotgun marriage to Amy. Disaster strikes when Owen is melodramatically knocked unconscious in a serious accident. When he hears Owen call out for Mary, James begs her to see him. She agrees to go, only on the stipulation that James will improve sweatshop conditions (that's love for you). After Owen is on the mend, he and Mary plan to get married. Meanwhile, marriage, improbably, has turned Ernest into the model husband. He and Amy are now in bliss, the sweatshop is an ideal workplace, and everyone is thoroughly satisfied. Everyone except Creel, that is, who thinks this resolution smacks more of class disharmony.

Also on the rejection list was *A Little Sister of Everybody* (1918) starring the young, and very petite, Bessie Love. Featuring immigrants and dealing with labor woes, it was just too much for Creel in the class harmony department.

Little Sister features Bessie Love as Celeste Janvier (Miss Heavenly January in ironic translation), who lives with her immigrant grandfather in a tenement on the Eastside. Grandfather is a kindly, humanitarian, socialist (horrors). Celeste takes after him and has been nicknamed "the little sister of everybody" for her friendliness and kindness. She has turned down several unworthy suitors, when the young son of the factory owner (George Fisher as Hugh Travers, Jr.) where she works has to take over due to his father's sudden death. Hearing that the workers want to strike, and needing to know why, he poses as one of them to discern the nature of the problems. Meeting Celeste, he immediately falls in love and promotes her to a better position (she doesn't know who is the source of the promotion). Overhearing that an anarchist is planning to kill the owner, she runs to find and warn him, only to learn that it is the man she loves and has believed is a poor fellow worker. Travers then agrees to better conditions at the factory, earning the respect of the anarchist, Marask (Hector V. Sarno). Travers and Celeste then become a permanent couple.

This obviously seditious combination of not only striking workers, but socialists who are immigrants on top of it, anarchists who want to better workers' deplorable conditions, and uppity female kin of immigrants (who save the day), was more than Creel could endure. The advertising posters, in complete opposition, refer to Bessie as the "Glad Girl," akin to Pollyanna, and go on to affirm: "Your audiences—every audience everywhere—are calling for sunshiny plays with stories that induce cheerfulness...." Such a story is "*A Little Sister of Everybody.*"

The film is presumed lost with only one or two stills to tell us what Celeste's wardrobe may have included. However, it seems to have been fashionable in a demure, not particularly affluent, way. In one full-length still Celeste (Bessie) is posed in a full-skirted day-dress with horizontal stripes circling the gathered skirt, and vertical stripes of the same material on the bodice. The sleeves are plain with a ruffle at the wrist,

Pathé

The Glad Girl

BESSIE LOVE

Is Announced in the Happy Play

"A LITTLE SISTER OF EVERY-BODY"

Your audiences—every audience everywhere—are calling for sunshiny plays with stories that induce cheerfulness, with stars that are masters at making the heart glad. Such a story is "A Little Sister of Everybody." Such a star is Bessie Love!

Produced by Anderson-Brunton Co.
Story by Wm. Addison Lathrop.
Directed by Robert Thornby.

You are wasting your opportunities if YOU ignore advertising.

The adorable Bessie Love as the "Little Sister," printed in a magazine in April–June 1918. Her dress makes her look even tinier than she was but is still flattering and doesn't overwhelm (*Motion Picture News*, Wikimedia Commons).

and what looks to be a wide Pilgrim collar at the neckline; a huge pocket descends from the waist. Maidenly, but up-to-the-minute, the hem length is about four inches above the ankle, giving us a glimpse of dark hose and kitten-heeled shoes. As Bessie was curvy, but very tiny, the dress is surprisingly flattering; one would expect that much material to overwhelm her. Instead, it makes her look like a porcelain doll.

Certainly, another film which must have given Creel fits of indecision was *Fit to Fight* (1917). This little gem was produced when it was discovered that an unusually significant percentage of the servicemen were suffering from sexually transmitted diseases of one sort or another. The problem had been largely ignored in both Britain and the United States; however, by the time the United States had entered the war, it had grown to such a proportion that a blind eye could no longer be turned. A "major crusade" was launched under the auspices of attorney Raymond B. Fosdick with the government stamp and the propaganda movie was considered part of the solution. *Fit to Fight* tells the story of five young men, all but one of whom consort with streetwalkers. One of the seduced, Kid McCarthy, uses prophylactic precautions and escapes without a problem, but the other three wind up with unpleasant consequences. McCarthy calls Billy Hale, the young man who avoids temptation, a mollycoddle and Hale licks him a fight, thus proving otherwise. McCarthy decides to mend his ways. The three who have had the unpleasant consequences are shown in the hospital and referred to as "useless slackers." Kevin Brownlow, commenting on the film, suggests dryly, "Many in the audience may have ruminated on the fact that unpleasant though the disease might have been, a stretch in the hospital was preferable to an unspecified period of trench warfare."[12]

The 1919 version of the movie, now titled *Fit to Win,* was broadened in scope after the war and the script was altered to show the troops returning. Kid McCarthy has died bravely at the Front and Billy Hale has been promoted to captain and medaled. Because the movie was shown only to carefully segregated audiences, that may have solved Creel's dilemma.

Needless to say, the films of Lois Weber were not those that would make the cut. A writer/director who challenged D.W. Griffith for the unofficial title of most important filmmaker of the 1910s, Weber ignored war in favor of "problems" closer to home. Birth control, abortion, poverty, and religion, or sometimes a mix of all of the above, were her *métier.*

Nevertheless, not all her movies were concerned directly with contemporary problems. Some of her extant film product is of great lyrical beauty and addresses social criticism obliquely. *Hypocrites* (1915, also known as *The Naked Truth*) comes to mind. The film was banned in Ohio, and caused riots even in New York City, based on Margaret Edwards' full-frontal nudity, which made the title right to the point. Although overwrought to the point of hysteria, the film is so exquisitely lovely that one can forgive it much. The story is of Gabriel, an early Christian monk and a contemporary minister (both played by Courtney Foote). The monk is murdered by a mob when he reveals a statue of "Truth," which is a sculpture of a naked woman. The contemporary Gabriel's congregation is wealthy and upscale, but are revealed in several vignettes, where Margaret flits around in a double exposure (pun intended), to be greedy, avaricious, and sex mad. Controversially shocking in its day and very slow for present day audiences, it is, nevertheless, a work of art. Although some of the film was unrestorable, enough of the movie remains to be worth seeing for lovers of silent film.

Margaret's wardrobe as "Truth" undoubtedly demanded little in the way of budget over-runs. She wears an attractive ensemble only in the beginning. Gabriel wears either a voluminously white monk's habit or minister's garb.

The greedy hypocrites are dressed to the nines in the latest fashion and *quell horreur!* dance the latest dances. The symbolism is heavy but compelling as some sinners

Margaret Edwards (nude) and Courtney Foote (monk's costume) in *Hypocrites* (1915) that raised a few eyebrows, which confirmed the aptness of its alternative title, *The Naked Truth* (Paramount Pictures, Wikimedia Commons).

attempt to climb with Gabriel to a mountaintop. These are mainly women or children, a number of whom crawl painfully upward—some falling backward in despair.

In a fascinating reversal of that prior stance on confronting social problems, only two years after *Hypocrites* Ms. Weber, in an interview article in the October 1917 issue of *Photoplay,* claims she is not going to make any more propaganda pictures. Because, according to Elizabeth Peltret, author of the article, "The world, according to this greatest of all woman directors, is like a man with a jumping toothache. What a man with a jumping toothache wants more than anything else is to forget his tooth." This proclamation, while there is no clear explanation, may owe to the United States entering into the war. A time, one might think, that would be just the time for propaganda films.[13]

No conflict, no disharmony, and virtually no war—these were Creel's goals to lull the populace into contribution and acceptance without a hint of knowledge. Nevertheless, as discussed in Chapter Two, the fan magazines were taking serious looks at the war, although the emphasis was more on how it affected the film industry and only peripherally with what the effect was on the moviegoing public. As that chapter pointed out, this was mainly in service of increased ticket sales disguised as concern for lifting morale. In the service of "It's an ill wind that blows no one good," one good thing that was blown toward the movie industry was that American-made films were now foremost in the world and the organization we know by the collective name of "Hollywood" slowly formed into the formidable force it has become. Allied film production had ground nearly to a halt and as Kitchen's article demonstrates, little of note was being produced even in Germany.

The House I Live In

Wardrobes of the audience were not the only personal items influenced by the movies and movie magazines. Homes and their furnishings also fell into step with the slowly burgeoning presence of "Hollywood."

An influx of Easterners relocating to the West, seduced by what they read and saw, created a need for suitable places to put them. From 1910 to 1917 a host of modest bungalows sprang up in such balmy neighborhoods as Pasadena, Orange, and San Diego, all in California. To celebrate the opening of the Panama Canal, the Panama-California Exposition (not to confused with the Panama Pacific International Exposition in San Francisco) opened on January 1, 1915, in San Diego, California, sparking an interest in the revival of Spanish Baroque style. Even before that, the Pueblo Revival style, which originated in the Southwestern states of New Mexico and Arizona, as well as the Craftsman bungalow were already in place. However, the Spanish Revival style was a true California native.

Fanzines, such as *Shadowland Magazine,* not only featured clothing, makeup hints,

A house in San Jose, California, in the Spanish style, probably c. 1919. The arched windows, tile roof, and little kiosk-like entry porch are all characteristic of Spanish Revival (photo by David Sawyer, Wikimedia Commons. www.flickr.com/photos/18702768@N04/2816282981/).

and tips on demeanor mingled with their articles on the stars, but frequently expanded their discussion to include home décor. Displaying tasteful interiors and exteriors, they bore titles like "The House and Home Doctor (George B. Case)," who, using Thomas Ince's California house as an example, offered suggestions on how to achieve the same blend of art and luxe in your modest bungalow. Another article shone the spotlight on "Where Doug Lives," giving readers an intimate glimpse into the lifestyle of Douglas Fairbanks, Sr. Because the photos were black and white, readers had to see, with their minds' eyes, the "predominant colors" of "buff and blue." The captioned photographs set readers salivating for something like that as their own and drew them by the hundreds of thousands to that sunny spot where the stars lived close to the ground.[14]

Rule Britannia

Animation played a significant part in British propaganda filmmaking. One exceptional example is *The Bully Boy* (1914/15). Drawn by a wonderful artist by the equally wonderful name of Lancelot Speed, it chronicled the destruction of the Rheims Cathedral by the Germans—considered an act of egregious barbarism at the time. Speed first draws an image of an ordinary-looking man and quickly transforms him into the Kaiser. After that he limns a marvelous image of the cathedral captioned "The World's Greatest Gothic Work." Speed (who lives up to his name) then draws a howitzer similar to Big Bertha, calling it "The Work of the World's Greatest Goth," continuing with the shelling of the cathedral, leaving it in ruins. A devil pops out of the Kaiser's helmet saying, "Do I Hear Any Cheers?" and fries Wilhelm, who is immediately turned into a barbecued sausage. A British bulldog makes short work of that tempting morsel. Only six minutes long, it is a masterpiece.

Not only (or even principally) an animator, Speed was an illustrator of books, in particular the fairy books of Andrew Lang, done principally in a dramatic black-and-white, also the director of several silent films, a contributor to numerous periodicals, a cartoonist, and the set designer for the silent version of H. Rider Haggard's novel *She*, made after the war. All this with no formal art training.

She (1925) was a combined British-German production which starred Betty Blythe of *Queen of Sheba* fame.[15] Based on the 1887 novel, the film's opening credits claim the intertitles were written especially for the film by Rider Haggard himself. Haggard died shortly before the film was completed and never got to see it as a finished product. Blythe, who performed practically nude in *Queen of Sheba,* once again displayed her same talents in *She.*

Other animated propaganda shorts include *In the Clutches of the Hun* (1915), *Under the German Yoke* (1915), *John Bull's Animated Sketch Book* (1916), and *Britain's Effort* (1918).

John Bull's Animated Sketch Book is a series masterpiece of a different sort, i.e., a mordant wit. One of the sketchbooks begins with the British lion "awakening" with one eye shut—"How Britain Wages War," and "How Germany Wages War"—blowing women and children to bits. Another starts with the Kaiser turning a wheel for an endless belt across which march prisoners of war, then explains a "curtain fire" with an escaped spark from the fireplace lighting the window curtain, then depicts three comic Huns claiming they gained three meters (of land), as it shows them making off with three loaded boxes of goodies.

Much production was devoted to shorts that dealt with reality and necessity. The Women's Land Army was featured in a short appropriately titled *Women's Land Army* (1917). In *The Secret* (1918), a couple demonstrates how to eat well despite shortages; along the same lines, the public was exhorted to *Eat Less Bread* (1918).

Homes were also a priority in the United Kingdom. Munitions workers, many of whom were displaced from their neighborhoods and sent to remote locations where new factories were being built, were in dire need of housing. The Ministry of Munitions complied by providing 2,624 permanent homes. A fair percentage of these were detached or semidetached, and some even boasted bay windows. Since a fair percentage of the munitions workers were female, the idea of a real home was especially comforting. An Army corporal, H.V. Sawyer, recalled an incident during his service: "...I felt damned embarrassed when I walked into a pub ... one girl forestalled me saying, 'You keep your money Corporal. This is on us.' And with no more ado ... she produced a roll of notes big enough to choke a cow."[16] The corporal was exaggerating a bit, nonetheless, women did make more money in munitions than they were used to. Nevertheless, the well-paid job was also very dangerous and frequently caused serious life-long medical problems.

One of the innovations which spread from military use to civilian was the adoption of standardized prefabricated buildings. In 1914, Major Armstrong of the Royal Engineers, along with his team, created a new type of standard hut which became the model for the duration of the war.

Production a la Française

French film production for entertainment took a hit, naturally enough, when their Belgian audiences were deprived of films from that country after the German invasion. In suffering Belgium, which Kitchen refers to with such dismissal, many cinemas were closed entirely, or as necessary staff were conscripted or imprisoned, they were simply forced to shut their doors. In France itself, the filmmaker Marcel L'Herbier says it best:

> I was face to face with the awful reality.... Everything that was filmed passed through our hands ... we cut, we spliced, we chose what could be shown. I watched scenes of horror, I saw soldiers that had been eviscerated, cut in two, decapitated. That shock revealed to me that I had to become a filmmaker.[17]

As in most of the Allied world, with the exception of the United States, production declined precipitously. Filmmaking virtually ground to a halt until immediately after the armistice, when Abel Gance produced the anti-war *J'accuse* (1919), and the beleaguered Belgians released *La Belgique martyre* (*Martyred Belgium,* 1919), a film emphasizing the suffering of the Belgian people and the bestiality of the invaders.

However, what were the filmic attitudes of the opposing "bestial Huns" during the war years? Is the shoe on the other foot? Or do we see a surprising similarity in both intention and product?

Two Sides to One Coin: German Film Production

In a surprise turnup, German production actually stepped up. As we see from Kitchen's article, German film output mainly skirted the topic of the war problem entirely. Newsreels on the other hand devoted a good deal of time to one political leader or another, e.g., the Sultan of Turkey, or, of course, the Kaiser in full regalia, reviewing their troops, others showed infantry or machine gunners fending off attacks. However, no opposition is seen: equipment-laden trucks roll through the countryside unopposed; French graves are shown, the implication being that more of them have died; French prisoners of war are marched by the cameras by the dozens; the German Army digs up their guns from a beet field (rather hilarious); a cavalry attack which looks, for all the world, like a polo match; and the "Triumphant Germans Enter[ing] Brussels." The last, strangely, shows well-dressed, presumably Belgian, crowds lining the streets with a coterie of young men laughing and smoking, It makes us wonder.

There is no sign of defeat for the Germans—in fact, we never see them facing an enemy—and not a single German body falls. However, they do record the sinking by the Belgians, in the Scheldt river, of the German "liner," the *Gneisenau* (named for a 19th-century Prussian field marshal). Belgians are shown burning their own homes in desperation, as well as the bombing of a railroad bridge with a German troop ship on the tracks. All undoubtedly symbolic of the "treachery" and "cowardice" of the enemy.[18]

Much like George Creel's propaganda fodder intended to sway reluctant Americans, all of these heroic scenes served to lift the morale of German citizens who were facing a crisis of domestic food supply. This lack arose from an earlier lack of preparedness for a long war. A number of historians have suggested correctly that poor management contributed a great deal to the consumer shortages. Added to that, other factors such as the cut-off of wheat supplies from the United States and Russia, the sea embargo imposed by Britain, and the pressure on neutral countries to withhold exportation of dairy products, escalated the situation to that of desperation by 1915.[19] A number of unpalatable substitutes for essential foodstuffs, e.g., bread, were introduced. A substance known as K-Brot, made of a mélange of oats, barley, dried potatoes, and sometimes even pulverized straw, proved to be wildly unpopular with the citizens but given to prisoners of war (a souvenir slice is still extant).[20] Faced with the reality of the war in spite of the uplifting newsreels, it is no wonder the German public preferred to get away from it all. As he states in his article, Kitchen and the German officers seemed to be dining well—for the ordinary citizen, a different situation prevailed.

Film in the Time of *Kultur*

Oskar Messter was the most prolific producer of German films during the war. From 1911 to 1924, he churned out an astonishing 474 full-length and short films. A run-through of his filmography suggests that escapism was the tenor of much of his product. For example, *Er rechts, sie links* (1915), translated as *He This Way, She That Way,* but literally *He Right, She Left*, is a slightly risqué comedy about a doctor and his wife having marital problems and trying to solve them by little flings on the side. It was written by Robert Wiene, who would later direct *The Cabinet of Dr. Caligari* (1920); *Der Vetter aus Mexiko* (*The Mexican Cousin*, 1917), which introduced a bit of exoticism among a group of artists; also, *Edelsteine—Phantastisches Drama in four [sic] Akten* (*The Jewel—A Fantasy in Four Acts,* 1918). Again, written by Robert Wiene, *The Jewel* was more exoticism starring the very popular actress, Henny Porten, who was a favorite of Messter.

Porten (born Frieda Ulricke Porten in 1890) was one of only a few actresses to perform directly in film without any stage experience. Possessed of a haunting (and haunted) face, she was married to the director Curt A. Stark, who directed many of her early films. Matronly looking from an early age, she was never a fashion idol, but radiated a steady presence in her movies.

Widowed when Stark was killed on the Eastern Front in 1916, her career was established by then. Unlike most early actors in silent film, whose names were not known, Messter was forced to reveal her identity when she was acclaimed for her role in *The Love of a Blind Girl* (1910). This made her one of the very first movie STARS in capitals. Although many of her films were comedies, she excelled in playing women of submission and sacrifice, which inadvertently exposed the abuses of patriarchy and inequality between the sexes. Porten had an extraordinarily long career even though it was interrupted for a while. Married a second time to a Jewish man, she refused to divorce him during World War II, resulting in a hiatus of her film roles. Although she continued to live in Germany, she was boycotted by the Nazis. Even though well into middle age by this time, she resumed her career after the war until 1955.

Most of Messter's titles hint at the need to take the German population's collective minds off their empty bellies by filling their heads with fluff. The singularly oblivious Kitchen reads this partly correctly at least; nevertheless, he easily fills his stomach and seems to ignore shortages. A motion picture genius, Messter's contributions to cinematography were so many and varied, he was practically a one-man film studio. Among them are slow motion (1897); microscopic cinematography around 1900–1910; voiced projections (1903); films actually *spoken in English* at the St. Louis World's Fair in 1904; electromechanical synchronization of sound; and an early concept of "stardom" by his promotion of Henny Porten, just to name a few innovations from his copious list.

Germany was quick to realize the movie industry as a tool of propaganda. Newsreels, naturally, as Kitchen remarked. However, the Army Chief of Staff, General Erich Ludendorff, was not slow to realize the potential in the combination of film and entertainment as a war weapon. He wrote a letter to the Royal Ministry of War on July 4, 1917, stating "[the] war had demonstrated the superior power of images and film as a tool of reconnaissance and *means of influence*" (emphasis mine). He then persuaded the recently-formed Universum-Film-Aktiengesellschaft (shortened to UFA) to turn out pro–German films. One of which was the Max Landa movie referred to by Kitchen—*Sein Schweirigster Fall (His Hardest Case)*—intended to put Germany on equal footing, or supplant, the popular unerring detective, Joe Deebs, the British rival to Sherlock Holmes. Ludendorff also insisted on increasing the prominence of advertising in film, believing it strengthened the domestic industry.[21] Animation was also employed by the Germans to promote investment in war loans or other patriotic endeavors. Two examples are *Die Zauberschere* (*The Magic Scissors,* 1917) and *Der beste Schuss* (*The Best Shot,* 1917).

Since every combatant country was doing the same thing, it was a head-to-head battle to see who could misinform their audience the most convincingly.

Four

I Saw It in the Magazines

Many women who were not conversant with *Vogue* or *Harper's Bazar* (later changed to *Bazaar*) were avid readers of movie fan magazines such as *Photoplay* or *Moving Picture World.* At the same time as an army of females were thrilling to the latest news of their favorite—and newly acclaimed—stars, they were being brought up to date on the latest wardrobe trends—the war crinoline, for example. With regard to the crinoline however, the fashion news took a wider view and wasn't all bad. The April 1917 issue of *Photoplay* features Lillian Howard's article "Back to Babylon for New Fashions" which states that the "Princess Beloved" is "Inspiring the Modistes of Fifth Avenue." The Princess, of course, being the "Beloved" from the Babylonia segment of D.W. Griffith's *Intolerance.* The designs are lovely and anticipate the dropped waists and low belts of just a few years later. The author of the article, Ms. Howard, says "[they] had dabbled the past season in medieval inspirations of slashed sleeves, pointed bodices and *moyen-age* waist-lines but the real inspiration ... came when they gazed upon the filmed ladies of Belshazzar's court."[1] Of course, the influence on this fashion collection is still medieval rather than Babylonian, just as were the costumes for the movie, but the lady readers are not going to quibble. One example from the article is nearly a complete quote from saintly sculptures on the portals of Gothic cathedrals. With embroidered neckline, dropped-waist girdle, and hem, it's an altogether elegant recreation of the medieval *bliaut.* Although the skirt is full and pleated, the profile is narrow overall. The caption enthuses: "One-piece-street frock, which is nothing but an Assyrian garment slightly modified for the Fifth Avenue Girl of 1917." Well, a bit overstated, but it does have cuffs, dropped girdle, and fringed hem embroidered with vaguely Assyrian design, but the main influence is the Middle Ages. The length is mid-calf—a little shorter than the usual "street frock."

As is a sheer, shift-like evening frock of "mauve chiffon banded in spangles of a deeper tone—a true Chaldean inspiration" on the same page. The Chaldeans would be raising their eyebrows at this exaggeration. The spangles enclose a square bare-shouldered neckline, the dropped waist faux belt, and both the hem and a small train. Graceful and ethereal, the gown is gathered from the border of the neckline down, just barely contained by the implied belt. It does bear a distant resemblance to some of the gowns worn by Seena Owen in *Intolerance,* emphasis on the distant.

An advertisement for the Hamilton Garment Company, on the very first page of this issue, unfortunately negates the grace of the "Babylonian" examples inside, displaying garments that would make even the loveliest debutante look dowdy, drab, and matronly.[2] Two possible exceptions are the tailored jackets over the war crinoline skirt previously discussed. The garments are not all that inexpensive for the era, with a range from $5.00 to $22.75, so their dowdiness is all the more striking. There is a rather nice evening frock which looks as though meant for a late teens to early twenties young lady—an example of that frothy trend, nicely priced at $8.75. Otherwise, the advertisement seems to be pitched to what was called, at the time, the "odd" lady. Odd, meaning either an on-the-shelf spinster, a "bluestocking" intellectual, or at the very least, a spinsterish housewife, no younger than forty.

Another advertisement, from the same April 1917 issue, purports to be touting Burson Fashioned Hose, although only two inches of the hose are all that is in evidence. Instead, the ad displays Ethel Clayton ("The Girl on the Cover" as the caption calls her) wearing a velvet coat with enormous (possibly faux) chinchilla sleeves and at least a two-foot-wide band of the same at the hem. It's irresistibly over the top, disregarding any sort of wartime restriction with its yards of lavishly gathered velvet skirt. The hose, which the reader does not see, come in "Cotton, Lisle, Mercerized, and Art Silk," and are available in prices from 25 cents to 75 cents. Their "unusual comfort" comes from their being knitted in the shape of the "foot, ankle, and leg" rather than entirely straight. For those of you accustomed to the gossamer hose of today, the weight would be comparable to a pair of ballet tights—even in the "Art Silk."[3]

The young actress Mollie King is headlined in the October 1917 issue of *Photoplay* wearing a rather fetching satin and embroidery pajama outfit of "Oriental" influence—very *dernier cri* for 1917. Hip-length pullover-styled top of embroidered silk, trimmed in the solid satin around the neckline, three-quarter sleeve hems, and down both sides (ending in a slit), teamed with slightly blousy trousers of the embroidered silk, ending in six-inch hems of the satin tied at the ankle with bows. Ms. King, all of 19 in 1917 (or maybe 22, depending on the source), lives in the Ansonia apartment hotel, and "her English is as beautiful as she is."[4] Right-up-to-the-moment in her activities, she drives a car, has her own telephone (candlestick style), and looks down on Broadway from her window-seat. None of them well-known names anymore, her brother Charles and her sister Nellie were also actors. Sources put the birth dates of the siblings all in the same year, 1895. Since they were not triplets, the information is a trifle iffy. Molly seems to have retired from the films about 1924.

Frothy again best describes much of the evening and/or summer wear for 1917. Mary Pickford models enough lace and flounces to circle the globe, in the same October issue as Ms. King. Organdy, net, taffeta, satin, and yards and yards of lace decorate each piece; even an ermine evening cape is lined with pink brocaded satin and worn with a hair ornament of "ribbons, lavender, pink and gold."

The pannier look makes a reappearance in 1918 and 1919. A sampling of Lady Duff-Gordon's (Lucile) evening styles, sketched by one Marguerite Martyn for the *St. Louis Post-Dispatch* (Missouri) issue of April 6, 1918, demonstrates both the frothy look in a ballet-length frock, and also in a full-length gown of black and gold gauze stripes, with self-fabric shoulder straps (one shown daringly off the shoulder), a fitted bodice to mid-hip, and a blossoming of panniers below ending in a short train. There is also a faux sleeve adorning one arm. Definitely for a *femme fatale.*[5]

Martyn was both journalist and artist with the *St. Louis Post Dispatch* for many years and married one of the editors, Clair Kenamore. Along with fashion, Martyn wrote a variety of articles for the paper, including political conventions, ball games, and the Suffrage movement in which she took an active interest. Her sketches show both artistic talent and a gift for movement and character.

Frothy, sexy, tailored, elegant. Lady Duff-Gordon's (Lucile's) very desirable styles for spring 1918. Published in the *St. Louis Post Dispatch*, Missouri, April 6, 1918 (Wikimedia Commons).

The pannier look also appears for daytime in a *Franklin Simon & Co.* advertisement in the *New York Times* for Sunday, May 4, 1918—the "Betsy Wales" dress. This was paired with the flat-on-the-head hat styles popular for that year, but unfortunately, with a comeback appearance of the hobble-skirt hem.

Military styles are mostly absent from the 1918 issues of *Photoplay*. Although in the April 1918 issue, Anne Luther, a popular Keystone comedienne, is pictured in a double-breasted overcoat resembling an officer's coat and the frequent D.W. Griffith "juvenile" actor, Bobby Harron, is shown in full military kit for his movie role. The "officer's" coat, which was of heavy serge, was deemed by the military not suitable for all-occasion wear. An alternative was proffered in the form of the now-ubiquitous trench coat. Invention of this alternative has been claimed by both Burberry and Aquascutum, with Aquascutum's claim possibly taking priority as it dated back to the 1850s. Whoever may have been first, the final kudos go to Thomas Burberry, who invented gabardine in 1879 and presented his design for a trench coat to the British War Office in 1901. The individual fibers of the fabric could be waterproofed before construction of the garment, providing an effective water barrier. These were optional for Army officers for some years but grew in popularity during World War

I with the addition of shoulder straps and D-rings for convenient attachment of essentials.[6]

Finally giving in to the necessity of being practical, the British Army had relinquished their bright red uniforms, which had made them bull's-eye targets on the battlefield, and switched to khaki in the Crimean War. From then on, this was the requisite dress for common soldiers and officers alike. A felicitous choice, khaki was not only more practical, it made them look chicer and more professional while at the same time less visible. It did, however, take them a bit longer to realize that charging at machine guns on horseback was no longer a feasible option in the mechanized war of 1914–1918.[7]

Moving Picture Weekly for September 6, 1918, takes a more dramatic direction with seven pages in red and white declaiming "The Whole Colossal Drama of the War." This refers to the Jewel Production of *Crashing Through to Berlin.* The first page gives us Miss Liberty pointing the way for the doughboys with her sword. The second page is more frighteningly true to life. A full-page image of a doughboy in full uniform with gas mask, stands below a caption which says, "This Boy Used to Come to Your Theatre," making the point that this is every Mother's Boy. Even more chilling is a later paragraph in the text, "This is a War of Machinery." The next-to-last of the seven pages dramatically reveals "The Heavy Hand of *Kultur.*" The film is supposed to be seven reels of "authentic moving pictures," taking the audience behind the scenes of warfare to "see with their own eyes."[8] Since the war was still grinding on and would for another two months, one is tempted to wonder how many flocked to see this extravaganza, when so many of what would have been the audience was dead, maimed or gassed. The young man in the mask would have brought this fact brutally home to many a grieving mother or spouse. However, we can never be too insensitive if it might make money.

Unlike *Photoplay, The Delineator Magazine* for September 1917 does hint at military tailoring for women with a longish, gold-buttoned jacket over a full skirt. Gold stripes decorate the jacket and collar, and the ensemble is accessorized with gold-trimmed military style hat and gaiters. For home sewers, it recognizes wartime restrictions and also suggests "War Ways of Making," which include re-shaping old dresses, adding different fabric panels to pre-war dresses, or perhaps, a flounce. An undergarment article carols "First Line Defense of the Figure," displaying various suitable undies for a number of activities—golf, for one, but leaves the question of what to wear under one's uniform unanswered. A transitional period for the underneath lady, corsets are mainly confined to the waist and hips, and "bust confiners" (brassieres) are in. The cover of the September issue features a carefree lass wearing one of the offshoot styles of the war crinoline—a long-sleeved afternoon dress with hip panniers. A lovely shade of ashes of roses for the sheer sleeves and sheer bodice panel, it has an opaque faux vest effect in a deeper wine, which continues into the panniered skirt. Never a good idea on even the most sylph-like of figures, on most ordinary women more width at the hip was disastrous. There is a lovely day dress featured in another 1917 issue of the magazine, one of a trio of gowns of pictured day wear, which closely resembles the "Back to Babylon" styles already discussed.

As a contrast in tone, the cover of *The Delineator Magazine* for January 1919 features a moving painting, by an artist whose name has been lost to time, consisting of two male half-length depictions. The title of the painting, also moving, is "Behind the Men Behind the Guns—Your Letter," which presents us with something of an enigma. Both men are in full Army kit, and interestingly, both are bundled up in those newly fashionable trench coats. Nevertheless, one man crumples his letter in what looks like despair, while the other gazes hopefully into the distance. For the one man, was it a "Dear John" letter? Or is he simply beset with homesickness? The answer is as unknown as the name of the artist. What we do realize is that all the men are not home yet, and the war has not yet passed from the forefront of people's minds.

Strictly speaking, *The Delineator Magazine* was neither a film fan magazine nor entirely a fashion periodical. It could possibly be classed with *Ladies Home Journal* or *Good Housekeeping* (it even awarded a Seal of Approval from the Delineator Home Institute), although it catered a little more to the housewife of up-to-the-minute fashion. Founded in 1869 by the Butterick Publishing Company, the magazine appeared first as *The Metropolitan Monthly,* and then after 1875 under the *Delineator* name. In 1926, it absorbed a sister publication, *The Designer,* and leaned a little more in the direction of fashion. Usually featuring the latest Butterick patterns, along with sewing tips, home décor, photos and/or drawings of the latest fashions, as well as some fiction, it was issued monthly until 1937.

Snubbing from designers notwithstanding, there are serious looks at the war in the 1918 *Photoplay* issue, as represented by an article entitled "The German Curse in Chaotic Russia." In the backlight of history, the first sentence is chilling in the hindsight of a century later: "The world believes that Russia sold out her allies knowingly, but my camera will show that it was the German propaganda of lies that undermined this great country." The quote is taken from the statement of the director, Donald C. Thompson, discussing his war movie of the same title as the article.[9] Unfortunately, the photographs chosen to illustrate the article seem to indicate nothing of the sort. It is interesting to note the sympathy toward Russia in 1918, when just a few slight months later they are characterized as the "Red Menace," "Raving Anarchists," "Bolshies," and the like. An article by John Dolber from the May issue of *Photoplay* entitled "These Are Russians" lauds some screen newcomers, exclaiming "This is a Russian year" and featuring "real" Russians such as Vera

From *The Delineator Magazine,* January 1919. Enigmatic depiction of two soldiers still at the Front. One seems to despair, the other gazes longingly into the distance. We can only guess at their emotions. What we do know is that the war is not over for them (Wikimedia Commons).

Colodna and Vera Zovska. The actual meaning of the Bolshevik Revolution had yet to hit the nation's headlines, and even then, was not immediately understood.[10]

It may have been a Russian year, but it wasn't a German year with movies like *The Kaiser: The Beast of Berlin. Motion Picture World* magazine devoted four pages, in bright red ink and banner headlines, to advertising "The Soul of History's Maddest Murder-King." Unabashed propaganda, the movie depicts the maniacal greed of Kaiser Wilhelm who was, it cannot be denied, occupying another dimension. Then, with a quick run-through of the war up until that moment, imagined resistance of his saner soldiers and fantasies about the end of the war. The Kaiser becomes a prisoner of the Belgians, for example. It leans heavily on the entrance of the United States into the fight with the scenes of massive troop movement and the fast resolution of the war. The story is told through the eyes of Marcas, a Belgian blacksmith, played by Elmo Lincoln, better known as the first Tarzan (he was starring, at the same time, in the release of that first Tarzan movie). Rupert Julian, who wrote the screenplay, "stars" as the Kaiser.[11]

In contrast to the virtual reliving of the entire war in *The Kaiser*, the magazine advertises the early vamp, Louise Glaum, in *An Alien Enemy*, "The Picture that DOES NOT show the War but shows you the Reason Why!"[12]

Glaum plays Neysa Meyer, whose American parents are murdered by Emil Koenig, a Prussian officer. She is then adopted by the grandfatherly Adolph Schmidt (Charles Hammond), given a false last name (von Igel) and raised in complete ignorance of her real identity. When she is grown, she is recruited as a spy for the Germans but is filled with disgust for the work. Although she believes herself German-born, she falls in love with an American, David Hale (Thurston Hall). They soon marry and she renounces her intelligence work. She is blackmailed by the same Prussian officer who had killed her parents—he tells her that he will out her to her husband if she does not continue providing information. She agrees, but cleverly slips him only false data; nevertheless, her husband becomes suspicious of her and abandons her. Her supposed grandfather is nearing death and tells her the true story of her parents and birth. Discovering that it is the same man who is blackmailing her, she meets him alone, tells him she has been giving him nothing but false reports, and then stabs him to death. Unbeknownst to her, David has been watching and realizes her innocence. They embrace, and all is forgiven. After all, it's just a little killing, right? I'm not sure if the film answers the question of why there's an entire world war, but it answers the question of why Neysa has a personal one.

By comparison, there is *By Right of Purchase,* which is a war drama of sorts but takes place more within the battlefield of a marriage rather than the Western Front. Starring Norma Talmadge (of the Talmadge sisters) as Margot Hughes, she plays a "social butterfly" who flits from one man to another until she finds the highest bidder. She sells herself to him in return for marriage and money, but when he does not press her for conjugal "right of purchase," she believes that she is unloved and unwanted. To assuage the pain, she goes to war-time France to devote herself to serving humanity selflessly. There she and her husband-in-name-only meet again and work out the misunderstandings of their marriage. Love ensues as the audience knew it would.[13]

Reality Check

While *Photoplay* tended more to breathless reviews of movies, fashions, and the lives of the stars, there were American publications connected with the movie field which took a more sober tone. *Moving Picture World,* for one, which came out weekly, was less a fanzine than a newspaper, adopting a more journalistic style than *Photoplay.* While there were critical reviews of movies, fashion and acknowledgment of "women's interests," these tended to be muted in favor of quite a bit more space devoted to professional concerns connected with the war.

Articles, such as "How War Affects Pictures," with the subtitle "Board of Review Recapitulates Work of Manufacturers Since War was Declared," discuss the "two ways" production was affected. A "marked reduction" was declared by Cranston Brenton, the chairman of the National Review Board in New York City—in particular, single-reel features, according to the chairman. The second reason was the demand for pictures either with a war theme or played out against a background of war, as we see in *By Right of Purchase.* He emphasized the fact that the government had taken a marked interest in motion pictures, not only as a vehicle for propaganda but also the need for entertaining the troops faced daily with death. He ends by saying that motion pictures have been deemed educational, "morally healthful, pleasure giving and an instrument for reducing intemperance." Somehow, I doubt it reduced any intemperance if there were any intemperance that could possibly be managed.[14] The same issue proclaims the importance of the exhibitor in an article entitled "The Motion Picture and the War" which quotes Adolph Zukor, the powerful president of Players-Lasky. Feeling that it was the business of the exhibitor to "cheer" the public, he exhorts them not "...[to] let your patrons mope in their homes, but bring them to the attractiveness of your theater by systematic advertising." A bit self-serving, but he does add "[I]n times of war with the added mental burdens, the motion picture theater is more than ever a public necessity." Nevertheless, sounding like a narcotics pusher, his final statement is most revealing: "And when the war is over, and the country again filled with gladness, it will be a difficult matter to wean patrons from the theaters that established a clientele during the dark hours when entertainment was not merely a pleasure but a necessity."[15]

As a small bow to the ladies, an interesting little blurb, also in the February 2, 1918, issue of *Moving Picture World,* gives a short review of the first episode in an anticipated series centering on women in the world of work. Does this "first" discuss women in men's occupations—perish the thought! It deals with female perfumers. "Anne Haviland, a Southern woman, who has studied the production of perfumes in France," apparently "anticipated that there would be a shortage, and was prepared and willing to enter this pleasant occupation."[16]

In the meantime, *Photoplay* picked up the pace of the feminine trend. The overwhelming majority of the advertisers in the magazine, as I have noted, aimed their pitches at women. "The Secrets of Distinctive Dress," featuring Madame Petrova, occupied the right-hand page of the September issue, shoulder to shoulder with a call to "Women of America" to join the United States Student Nurse Reserve, adding a *soupçon* of patriotism at the same time that actresses in the *dernier cri* of fashion decorated nearly every page with less high-minded temptations. Alice Joyce in the February 1918 issue, for example, has two pages devoted to "Alice Joyce and Her New Clothes," where Alice models an eye-catching (understatement) evening cloak of silver, with velvet patches in a random pattern scattered over the skirt, and sporting a generous black-fox collar, along with a chiffon evening frock with a draped harem skirt, a faux tunic walking dress, and a second velvet evening wrap. Her expression in every instance is unexplained, since she bows her head and looks up with a pleading look on her lovely face. Is she, perhaps, hoping for a lucrative movie contract to pay for the wardrobe? Whatever the reason, she is undoubtedly going to be influential on the feminine readers.

Alice Joyce (her real name), one of the most stunningly photogenic actresses of silent film, began her working life at thirteen as a telephone operator. After her parents'

The lovely Alice Joyce in a possibly Grecian-inspired sleeveless gown. Her slender figure looked good in everything which made her a favorite fashion model and icon (*Motion Picture Classic*, Wikimedia Commons).

divorce she and her brother lived with their father in Virginia during her childhood, and then with her mother in the Bronx after her mother's remarriage. Once there, she was employed as a photographer's model, appearing in illustrated songs.[17] Her extraordinary looks garnered her a career in motion pictures beginning in 1910 with *The Deacon's Daughter*. In 1913, Joyce went to Hollywood, working at Essanay Studios and Vitagraph where she became a well-respected star, specializing in serene and dignified heroines. Between 1910 and 1930 with her final film, *Song o' My Heart,* she made more than 200 films. A favorite with fan magazines—she looked marvelous in everything—she was a style setter from early on and well into the '30s.

So too, is the lovely and graceful Irene Castle in the April *Photoplay* issue, "the slim princess of pictures," as the caption says. Castle, clad in a tutu-like gown, wears an amazing pair of buttoned-up shoes with the slenderest of curvaceous heels. In a dancing pose, with arms outflung, she also wears an equally amazing, feathered bandeau which rises like smoke rings above her head. Even though this is basically a dance costume, the shoes, bandeau and filmy skirt were certain to be copied by clever home sewers and thrifty shoppers.

Irene and her husband Vernon Castle were, to the teens of the 20th century, what Fred Astaire and Ginger Rogers were to the '30s. Starting with their triumphant success in Paris, shortly after their marriage in 1911, the ballroom pair were a sensation wherever they appeared.[18] Credited with making ballroom dancing not only a respectable art form, but a necessary adjunct to societal success, the couple not only performed the latest ragtime dances, but refined and re-popularized the fox trot. They went so far as to invent their own numbers and became the rage for their innovative "Castle Walk." Vernon had been born Vernon Blyth, and Irene was née Foote, but the Castle pseudonym which they adopted became world-renowned almost overnight. At the peak of their career, it was reported that they were able to ask up to a thousand dollars an hour for ballroom lessons. Ironically their twosome was "brief but spectacular." A military flying instructor, Vernon was killed

The graceful Irene Castle, c. 1914, in a romantic meringue of pastel chiffon combined with silk charmeuse. Her pose is pensive. Cinderella too long at the ball? (unknown photographer for Irving Berlin's *Watch Your Step*, Wikimedia Commons).

in 1918 in a training accident. Irene continued to perform solo, although she remarried three more times.

Even before Vernon's untimely death, Irene was already a fashion icon. Women devoured news about her and followed her wardrobe suggestions as though they were quotes from the Bible. Her penchant for shorter, fuller skirts certainly assisted the war crinoline's popularity. Wearing gowns designed by the designer Lucile, Irene was one of the first (if not *the* first) to bob her hair, as she appears in Irving Berlin's musical

Winter dark, 1917. Irene Castle in fur-banded afternoon ensemble, with lavish fur-trimmed sleeves and accessorized by patent court pumps with buttoned gaiters and a perky beret (Emily Burbank in *Women as Decoration*, Project Gutenberg).

Watch Your Step (1914). Wearing a sheer, full-skirted ballgown with a square neckline strapped on one side with a slim cord and the other with a slight frill, the bodice is satin to the waist. The gathered skirt is of the sheer material, closely gathered to below the hips and then billowing out to a satin banded, embroidered, bell shape. It's a veritable meringue of romance.

Irene's favorite designer, Lucile (née Lucy Christiana Sutherland, then Lady Duff-Gordon), had started as a simple dressmaker to support herself and her daughter after a brief early marriage. With a bit of savings and a few investors, she opened Maison Lucile and proceeded to call herself after her fashion house. One of her investors was Lord Cosmo Duff-Gordon, who quickly invested more than money, and the two married in 1900 after his quickie divorce. Unfortunately, even with Duff-Gordon's backing, the establishment was forced to close in the '20s due to financial mismanagement. During its heyday, nevertheless, Lucile garbed the rich and famous in lush fabrics—e.g., tissue lamé, satin charmeuse, embroidery-banded lace—and extravagant designs. The loss was felt deeply by society matrons and film celebrities, alike.

Generally speaking, to my mind, the clothing displayed in *Photoplay* for 1918 is really less than appealing (an understatement). "Jackie Saunders in Her New Togs," featured in the April issue, is a case in point (even Irene Castle is at something of a disadvantage in her costume). Ms. Saunders poses in a collection of distinctly unflattering and badly designed garments. One ensemble makes her look as though she has to sell apples on the corner. The skirt is ill-fitting with a sack-like jacket over it and flat shoes. The length is unfashionable at about two inches above her shoe tops. However, Ms. Castle is a vast improvement over *Photoplay*'s offerings in two ensembles, one for summer and one for winter. We see above her dark and mysterious winter ensemble.

Again, while it's evident that fan magazine articles were aimed at the housewife, advertisers were also heavily weighted in that same direction, occasionally with tone-deaf results. Catering to the woman of the house in the April issue, Eastman Kodak tries to pull in the ladies with a heart-tugging advertisement entitled "The Day of His Going." A uniformed father holds a little girl of around four, while a summery-clad wife and mother examines her camera. The text below ends with "Let the Kodak keep the dates." I'm sure Eastman Kodak must have been unaware, rather than just plain insensitive, to the negative effect this undoubtedly had on the hundreds of thousands of women whose husbands were either going or gone. However, one must wonder if the women so addressed were going to descend on the stores en masse for cameras after that painful reminder.

Kodak's seeming insensitivity was rare, even though by October 1917 many articles on the fanzines turned to focus on our doughboys. Still, the tone is nearly always sprightly and optimistic. This sprightliness was in tune with Creel's harmonious credo for movies.

A Private War

In antithesis to the perfumed fashionistas, the suffragists were out in force. From a distance of one hundred years—as of this writing, the 19th Amendment has just celebrated its centenary—these women seem like towering figures of Herculean strength, unbreakable will and indefatigable courage. Yet they came from every background, class, and educational achievement, joined and made one by the goal of equality under the law.

The bumpy story of women's march to the vote has been the subject of a number of books, movies, and television dramas, making it a fairly familiar one. The suffragists were led in England by the indomitable Emmaline Pankhurst along with her daughters Christabel (who was actually a barrister but forbidden to practice), Adela and Sylvia.[19] In the United States, their counterparts were Susan B. Anthony (until 1906), Carrie Chapman Catt, and Elizabeth Cady Stanton. Their travails, and even martyrdom, constituted nearly as much a pitched—and frequently violent—domestic battle, as those at the Front. Women had to contend not only with the censure of the government and the press, but also of their loved ones and even other women.

The women were continually imprisoned, beaten, force fed, and sexually abused. But, as with nursing, their devotion to justice made them press on throughout the most drastic of reprisals. A quote from Sylvia Pankhurst's stark recital of women's struggle gives us a slight idea of their suffering: "Meanwhile, four Suffragettes were suffering the torture of forcible feeding in Strangeways Gaol, [sic] Manchester. They had been arrested in connection with a meeting held by Mr. Runciman at Radcliffe, and sentenced to one month's imprisonment, with hard labour, [sic] on October 21st ... on Friday the doctors and wardresses came to feed them by force. Miss Emily Wilding Davison urged that the operation was illegal, but she was seized and forced down on her bed. 'The scene which followed,' she says, 'will haunt me with its horror all my life and is almost indescribable.'" This was repeated every day. At last, Miss Davison wedged planks against the door to bar it to the doctors, however, they forced a hose through the cell window and drenched her full force with the icy water until someone called out "Stop, no more, no more." They then took the door off the hinges, wrapped her in a blanket, dumped her into a hot bath and put her to bed. At 6:00 p.m. on Thursday, they released her after a week of such abuse.[20]

Nevertheless, even though beaten, force-fed, abused, and arrested, they did it stylishly, as the images of Emmeline Pankhurst demonstrate. Knowing the story, this is not a laughing matter—Pankhurst was always dressed in the height of fashion, feeling that it gave her cause more gravitas. Although her behavior might have been slightly less than ladylike, her clothing never gave her away. Even being carried away by the police, she is well-dressed, tidy, and doesn't even lose her hat. As Lucy Adlington has pointed out, the appearance of being a lady was paramount. She quotes an anonymous fan as saying that Pankhurst "dressed [with] the elegance of a Frenchwoman and the neatness of a nun." Some upper-class women, who were well-connected, actually disguised themselves as lower or working-class women in order to get arrested. Adlington also tells of Lady Constance Lytton who disguised herself as a member of the lower classes in order to protest the abusive treatment of that class in prison.[21]

Pankhurst, herself, was a figure of considerable controversy. Noted for her embrace of militancy, she made it clear that the time for patient ladylike waiting had passed, and action, even violence, was necessary. Small in stature, as we see in the illustration, and delicate in features, she possessed a will of steel. An indefatigable fashion plate, she defended criticism of her impeccable wardrobe with the rationale that suffragists had to always be at their best to be taken seriously.

Pankhurst was never clothed in anything but ladylike attire that was the complete antithesis of her personality. With her wardrobe she aimed to counteract the idea that she was given to rash and extreme behavior and never less than a lady. In this seated photograph, she poses as an ordinary woman of proper demeanor. In her demure shirtwaist and dark skirt, she projects the image of a woman who knows her place. Her expression—rather sleepy-eyed and dreamy—belied a will of steel and a volatile temper.

Pankhurst's passionate example inspired other women, who proved themselves the equal of any man in endurance, courage and sheer physical prowess, and yet, the struggle still goes on.

A secret photograph of a captive Lillian Forrester in the prison yard looks a little more dressed for whatever might come in kerchief and long overcoat. A militant suffragist, Forrester is noted for her attack on the Manchester Art Gallery in 1913 when she was 34. She and two other suffragists waited until the closing of the gallery and then broke the glass on as many of the most valuable paintings as possible. Four of the paintings were damaged in the fracas and Forrester received a prison sentence of three months.[22] One of her compatriots managed to convince the magistrate that she had not been there, and the other got only a one-month sentence. Lillian went to prison.

Theirs was not the silly endeavor that the demeaning epithet "Suffragettes" would have had it. The suffragists fought a private war, but it carried as much possibility of serious injury or even death as the more "patriotic" one being waged on the Continent. In the end, it led to a victory in just two years after the signing of the armistice. In America, the 19th Amendment was ratified on August 18, 1920. In the UK, the Representation of the People Act was passed on February 6, 1918, however it only granted voting rights to women over 30. It wasn't until 1928 that the Equal Franchise Act extended the franchise to women over 21 and granted the same terms as those of the men. France didn't fall into line until 1944, and the women of Switzerland had to wait until 1971. In the United States, 21st-century women are still waiting for the Equal Rights Amendment to be ratified.

Emmeline Pankhurst looking demure and proper. Her "just an ordinary woman" pose and rather sleepy expression disguises a steely will and a volatile temper (Library of Congress).

Suffragists were not the only activists fighting a war for women. One of the most notable, if not the richest, was Anne Tracy Morgan, daughter of J. Pierpont Morgan, thought to be the richest man in the world in the early 20th century. Born in 1873 and raised in the sheltered environment of private tutors and every facet of privilege, she threw off the traces to become an activist and dedicated advocate for women. Immersing herself in philanthropy, she traveled to Chicago in 1902 to meet Jane Addams, the founder of Hull House (a settlement home for immigrants, owned and managed by women). In 1903, she turned to the Suffragette cause, helping to create the Colony Club. This was a private club for women which imitated those exclusive institutions in which men brokered, dealt, and otherwise transacted "business," shutting women out of the process entirely. In this endeavor, she was following in the footsteps of Caroline Severance, an early feminist who has been called the "Mother of Women's Clubs." Before moving to Los Angeles, Severance had been active in the Suffragist cause and had been a co-founder of the American Woman Suffrage Association. After settling in LA, she established the first women's club there, with the hope of raising the level of activism among women in the area.[23]

In Chicago, Morgan was introduced to Elsie de Wolfe, one of the first professional interior designers, and her partner, literary agent Elizabeth Marbury. The three turned to worker's rights, in particular those of working women. They campaigned vigorously for the rights of the oppressed women at the Triangle Shirtwaist factory in New York and established a canteen for Brooklyn shipyard workers.[24] Morgan and the others were much criticized for their parts in advocacy for workers; owing to their very upper-class upbringings, however, what they hoped to achieve was a breakdown of the wall between rich and poor.

When the war broke out in 1914, the three were staying in Versailles, and immediately felt they should become involved in some aspect of the war effort. Thoroughly disapproving of the United States' isolationist stance, they made an effort to raise public awareness to the needs of the invaded countries. In 1915, Morgan, along with her friend Isabel Lathrop, put money into founding the American Fund for French Wounded (AFFW), later the American Committee for Devasted France (CARD), in order to raise funds for medical equipment for French hospitals and aid packages to wounded soldiers. On meeting doctor Anne Murray Dike after returning to the United States, the two started recruiting female volunteers to help civilian populations near the Front. At least 350 women joined the effort in the next seven years. They were forced to withdraw from Blérancourt, their base of operations, when the Germans mounted an offensive in the area, but redoubled their efforts as soon as the Germans drew back. Their efforts at assistance continued well after the armistice. In 1924, she and Anne Murray Dike were both awarded the *Legion d'Honneur* by the French government. By this time, she and Murray Dike had formed a romantic attachment which lasted until Murray Dike's death in 1929.

The two women wore well-tailored uniforms to look as official as possible, and certainly to blend in as much as possible. Morgan, in her photographs, looks almost identical to the photos of the Women's Army Corps in her belted, three-buttoned, masculine-styled jacket, with huge envelope pockets. Murray Dike adopts the new trench coat look with epaulets, and both women sport the slouchy, rolled brim, feminine, but military, hats—practical for both rain and sun.

From celebrity icon to society activist to stalwart Suffragist, the Great War fashioned fashion in a variety of ways. The most striking result is that—for women at least, even for those who did not serve—in one way or another it imposed a new variety of uniform on all.

Five

Post and Riposte

World War I War Posters

"For Every Fighter a Woman Worker
—Care for Her Through the YWCA"[1]

An interesting look into World War I fashion is provided by the spate of posters, produced by both allies and foes alike, exhorting the public in various ways to support the war effort: join up, grow food, buy bonds, save scrap.

A 1920 publication authored by Arthur K. Sabin and Martin Hardie, featuring a selection of war posters and released only two years after the war, is utterly fascinating—both in its choices and in its commentary. As it is an English publication, praise is lavished on the British public and their "good spirit,"[2] but it is surprisingly critical of the efficacy of the earliest posters. The editors feel the need to grudgingly admit the artistic (and emotional) superiority of the *German* product.

The Germans, at least in the examples provided by the British publication, tend to hark back to a mythical past, similar to the approach used in their filmic product. "Knights of Old" and Siegfried-like images predominate. On the other hand, women were depicted as strong and determined in their propaganda posters, while in reality their contributions to the war effort were cavalierly dismissed and there were far fewer German women working in the place of men than in other countries.

One of the mythic-oriented examples depicts a fully mailed and helmeted knight, armed with a huge sword and body-length shield, protecting a mother and child while spears bearing the insignia of Britain break against the shield. The artist is Erwin Puchinger, who treats his subject with as much care as he would a piece of fine art to be hung in a gallery. Powerful in composition and excellent in draftsmanship, it compels the viewer to "Subscribe to the 5½% Third War Loan."

Before the war, Puchinger had been part of the Austrian *Jugendstil* and *Gesamtkunstwerk* movements, the goals of which were to blur the boundary between fine and graphic art. He and other artists such as Gustav Klimt broke away from the academy and formed the Vienna Secession. Although he worked in London, Prague, and Paris, he remained in Austria through both world wars and died there just at the end of World War II in May 1944. His professed politics are obscure, but Hitler personally owned three of Puchinger's paintings. The content of Puchinger's works in oil would not have been offensive to *Der Fuhrer;* in other words, they would not have suggested the term "degenerate." Although his painting style was a bit Impressionistic, it was generally sentimental. And, certainly, Puchinger's graphic works were as German as Hitler could have wished. Most drew on mythical themes, such as the German eagle armored and bearing arms, German knights victorious (his war loan poster), or idealized Aryan-looking women also bearing swords and lances.

A wider look at German choices reveals some themes much closer to those of the Allies. "*Alles für Vaterland! Alles für Freiheit*!" (Everything for the Fatherland!

Mythic-style propaganda poster executed by German artist Erwin Puchinger. Very carefully balanced, classical composition, beautiful draftsmanship. Robed women with lance and sword—double eagle shield (Harry G. Sperling Fund, 2016; Metropolitan Museum).

Everything for Freedom!) depicts a German soldier holding his left arm high giving what looks like Churchill's "V for Victory" sign from World War II. Further analysis draws attention to lightning bolts descending from stylized clouds, suggesting the soldier might be calling on Thor the "Thunderer" instead.

More in line with Sabin and Hardie's selections is "*Un das deutsche Bolf!*" (Actually, *Un das deutsche Volk!* The script is written in the Old Gothic style where the V resembles an ornate B. The English translation: "Onward, the German people!") Dramatically depicting an armored Valkyrie brandishing a sword, accompanied by the German eagle with talons poised, leading a crowd of ordinary citizens into battle, it passionately combines the mythical with the realistic, suggesting that the past of Odin and his cohorts will triumph over *alles.* Another pictures a family of husband, wife and baby. It appears to be a sentimental view of common domestic life, until you realize the woman is crowned with a medieval circlet of braids, wears medieval dress and the man is clad in tunic and *hosen,* armed with a sword. Even portraying the commonplace, the emphasis is on a mythically heroic past. The title is a mixture of prosaic and poetic: "*Kriegsanleihe, helf den Hütern eures Glükes*" (War Loans help the guardians of your happiness).

One particularly well-executed example borrows exquisitely from Raphael Madonnas. Depicting a turbaned mother holding a baby in her left arm, while she clasps a slightly older boy with her right, it is presented in rondel form. The artist's tribute to the past is an almost direct quote from that bygone era. The title says: "*In unseren Kendern liegt Deutschlands Zukunft*" (In your children lies Germany's future). The artist is Ludwig von Zumbusch, and yes, it's kitschy, but the draftsmanship is outstanding. It strikes a chord with me still, as it must have done for the viewers at the time.

All About U.S.

Posters chosen from the United States, in a psychological similarity to the last two German offerings, sentimentalized women as either emblematic of Liberty or devoted mothers nursing their offspring, paying little attention to their practical occupations. This is peculiar, in the face of a probable two million women working in virtually every facet of the war effort. A notable exception to the editors' choices is Adolph Treidler's "For Every Fighter a Woman Worker." A full-length and stalwart young woman, clad in overalls, raises a biplane in one hand and a bomb in the other, proving her home front usefulness as well as courage. The subtext exhorts the viewer to show "Care for Her through the YWCA."

Oddly, another U.S. poster ignores American women entirely, concentrating instead on French women. "Four Years in the Fight" depicts coveralled young women doing men's factory jobs with resignation and grit.

In a number of cases, examples from the Library of Congress's large collection are not an improvement. Howard Chandler Christy, a noted artist, depicts a scantily clad Miss Liberty placing a laurel wreath over the diverse names of some of the fallen (Kowalski, O'Brien, Levy, etc.) with the title "Americans All!" Another scantily clad Miss Liberty graces the "Fight or Buy Bonds" plea for the Third Liberty Loan of 1918. A Fourth Liberty Loan example by John Scott Williams features a much more fierce and determined Miss Liberty, who carries a shield and waves a sword with a muscular right arm. A fascinating example of synchronicity with the above German depiction, she is accompanied by a screeching eagle with wings outspread. Both bear a similar open-mouthed war-cry expression. No shy violet or sex symbol here—a leader of men—but still giving no hint of what essential activities women were actually engaged in.

In a poster promoting homegrown farm projects, "Sow the Seeds of Victory" does show Miss Liberty striding along scattering seeds behind her. Nevertheless, we have only one example among these which portrays a realistic woman. This one is not exactly complimentary to the ordinary housewife. Clad in shirtwaist and skirt, she is being castigated for throwing out food (a whole banana, no less). The title calls her action "The Greatest Crime in Christendom." So there, ladies! Better to take up grand theft, it would be less shameful.

In fairness to the archives, there are other examples which are not either overly sentimental or slyly suggestive. For instance, a sturdy young woman holding a hoe shakes Uncle Sam's hand in a recruiting poster for the Woman's Land Army of America, Trenton, New Jersey Division. She wears a jaunty bloomer coverall with gaiters in patriotic blue and looks more than capable. Another from the National Archives depicts a middy-bloused, mature, capable young woman at the oars of a dinghy named The Victory. The caption pays tribute to the Victory Girls United War Work Campaign with the words "Every Girl Pulling for Victory." It doesn't say how in this case, but at least it recognized some sort of female war effort.

In jarring contrast, a recruiting poster, also by Howard Chandler Christy, features another middy-bloused female—this time one with a low-cut neckline—saying "Gee!! I Wish I Were a Man. I'd Join the Navy." I rather imagine the boys would have preferred her as she was presented.

A 1917 Red Cross poster by Harrison Fisher falls somewhere in the middle. An appealing young woman—in more than one sense of the word—stands in front of a unit of marching men and stretches her hand to us. She provides us with a glimpse of a real Red Cross uniform: turban-like cap with flowing tails; navy blue, brass-buttoned cloak; a white pinafore prominently adorned with a red cross,

Recruiting poster for the Navy by Howard Chandler Christie, c. 1917, suggesting fringe benefits for joining up. Probably more inspiring than Uncle Sam (Library of Congress).

as is the cap. Her right hand reaches to us in appeal, and her left points in a gesture over her shoulder, surely intended to direct our attention to the marching troops. Yes, she is an idealization, yet Fisher manages to make the pleading expression of her face both genuine and moving.

Another persuasive propaganda poster produced by the Salvation Army depicts a strong-looking young woman facing us with determination. Kitted out in full uniform and wearing a tin helmet, she balances a tray full of food on the tips of her fingers. In bold calligraphy, the poster commands "Hand It to 'Em." The sub-caption states, "The Salvation Army Gets It to the Boys in the Trenches." The determined young woman looks perfectly capable of doing just that.

Red Cross, 1917. The young woman stretches her right hand to us and points with her left both to her badge and the marching troops over her shoulder (Harrison Fisher, Library of Congress).

The artist signs himself J. Allen St. John. J. (for James) Allen St. John was a renowned American graphic artist and illustrator of books and magazines. Considered the "Godfather of Modern Fantasy Art," he is known in particular for his illustrations of Edgar Rice Burroughs' novels. The two were closely associated for many years until Burroughs opened his own publishing company and employed an in-house artist—his own son.

Born in 1872, St. John began his career as an artist around 1898, when he started studying at the Art Students League of New York, whose members included American Impressionist William Merritt Chase. Chase's sedate style would seem a far cry from St. John's lurid fantasy magazine covers. Nevertheless, in spite of their sensational content, St. John's graphics employed the most academic of figure types. His first commercial employment was with the *New York Herald,* after which he moved to Chicago in 1912 where he remained until his death in 1957, teaching at the Chicago Art Institute, as well as the American Academy of Art. Not just an illustrator but also a fantasy writer, he both wrote and illustrated one of his best-known novels, *The Face in the Pool* (1905).[3] During his long career, St. John produced covers for *Amazing Stories, Fantastic Adventures, Fate,* and *Other Worlds* magazines, among others. As the "Godfather of Fantasy Art," he garnered a number of acolytes; Frank Frazetta is perhaps the most famous.[4]

The comments on American posters from the authors of the 1920 War Posters publication, the very British Hardie and Sabin, are equivocal—respect is given but it carries a hint of disdain, and for every bit of praise, there is an equal dash of snark: "The nations needed posters, so the American bureaucrat [in all fairness, the authors inserted 'like his brother in Whitehall'] ... issued orders for posters to be designed—in much the same way as the British Food Controller ordered bacon to be provided, without a staff ... to see that it was first properly cured."[5]

British posters featuring women focused to a large extent on the Land Girls—the army of women conscripted to farm the fields now empty of men. Nurses were also featured, however due to the concerted lack of respect, as described in Chapter Two, the appeals were often rather muted. In one instance, a young woman in white holds open the door to "Opportunity," while, in her other hand, she holds a diploma. Above her, the caption reads "Be a Trained Nurse." Sadly, the whole composition is stiff, inert, and lacks any sense of the "opportunity" suggested. The rigid frontal pose of the young woman, her expressionless face, and the ambiguity of the background combine to discourage rather than the opposite. A small-print inset to the right details the qualifications, cost and length of the program in exceedingly dull prose.

A much better executed, and more emotionally appealing, poster, which promotes "Church Army Hut Day," pleads for needed donations that would supply recreation huts for the troops at the Front. These were small buildings that provided a semblance of normality, offering coffee, doughnuts, etc., and a few moments of sanity, even though still near the battlefield. The poster features a helmeted, Athena-like lady representing Britain, wearing a lion-headed breastplate and holding a British flag. The same lion head is emblazoned on the shield at her sandaled feet. She points to a nearby structure where troops mill in fair numbers. Although in full battle kit, they appear relaxed and engaged in friendly conversation, even while shells explode in the distance.[6]

A striking illustration, aimed mainly at a male audience, borrows from the emphasis on myth and legend we see employed by the Germans. An armored, helmeted knight, astride a noble white steed, pierces the heart of a fearsome dragon with his lance. The destrier rears, possibly adding the blows of his hooves to the attack. In large-font type, the caption proclaims, "Britain Needs You at Once." The underlying message implicitly compares volunteers to the gallant St. George hinted at by the image.

In a similar mythic style to the German propaganda posters, St. George thrusts his lance through the heart of a fearsome dragon. The patron saint of Britain calls tacitly for volunteers (Library of Congress).

An aeronautic example, which I found very compelling, pictures a twin-engine biplane in closeup with a more distant fleet filling the clouds. The caption also compels, simply stating "Our Aeroplanes [sic]. You Can Help. Buy War Bonds." Despite its non-retractable landing gear, double engines directly above the exposed pilot, who appears to be dropping *something*, it excites the viewer with its implication of speed, danger, and heroism. Again, one must remember, this was the first war to employ dashing, white-scarf-flaunting airmen with their glamorous repute. For young men with visions of glory, and confident of indestructability, it would have exerted a strong pull.

Posters were used to drum up recruitment business as well as to encourage the purchase of war bonds. Flying was the "new thing" in World War I as part of the compelling pull of the entirely mechanized new way of waging battles. Along with tanks and long-range cannon, planes appealed to the sense of adventure and glory felt by so many young men unaware of the reality of death. A special favorite was the Sopwith Camel which was pictured many times in posters and photographs to pull in the recruits. With their dangerous, romantic vision of speed, they promised excitement, soaring heights, and women.

Here, in restored splendor, is a Sopwith Camel held at the Cavanaugh Flight Museum at Addison, Texas. The front of the fuselage would never have been the bright red used in the restoration, of course, but a drab color to disguise the craft somewhat in the sky. As one can see, the Camel was a biplane, the cockpit was open, the machine guns pointed directly at the propellor—timing was of the essence—and the whole projected danger. If you're twenty, that's irresistible.

In the same area of the air, a poster from the U.K. betrays its sexist (to us) leanings by exclaiming "British Women!—the Royal Air Force needs your help—*as Clerks,*

A spiffy restored Sopwith Camel at the Cavanaugh Flight Museum, Addison, Texas. Originally posted to the Panoramio site, which closed in November 2016. The Camel was a favorite of poster artists (Eric Friedebach, Wikimedia Commons).

Waitresses, *Cooks* [emphasis mine], and [in *much* smaller font] experienced Motor Cyclists." Perhaps this answers our question as to whether they were in the driver's seat.

There is considerable evidence, in monies collected, that the efforts of the poster commissioners and the labor of the poster artists was not in vain. Patriotism was high in Britain and, once the United States finally joined in, the same patriotism was stirred in the States. Governments were careful to see that news was carefully filtered through an optimistic sieve, keeping the populace unaware of the true horror. As the blind, amputated, gassed, and wounded began to be shipped home, some of what had actually occurred began to sink in—but only some. Many citizens, not so personally involved, continued to manage total unawareness throughout.

Six

Aftermath and Fore(war)d

> "...neither an accusation nor a confession, and least of all an adventure, for death is not an adventure to those who stand face to face with it. It will try simply to tell of a generation of men who, even though they may have escaped (its) shells, were destroyed by the war."
>
> —Erich Maria Remarque. *All Quiet on the Western Front* (novel)

The "War to End Wars" was actually the War That Never Ended. The repercussions from the conflict were still being felt right up to the outbreak of World War II. American veterans were still pleading for relief—many were unemployed even before the thunderbolt of the Depression struck them. The Depression only deepened their misery. The German Weimar Republic played out the same fantasy as the Jazz Age, a false sense of prosperity and a delusion (rather than an illusion) of stability. As economic collapse spread throughout the world like the Spanish flu, those delusions all came crashing down. In a somewhat bittersweet happenstance, it boosted American film production.

There were two ironic developments which marched parallel with the increased American film output. As touched on previously, one was the fact that more compelling stories about World War I were released after the war than during. Second was the explosion of song-and-dance movies—oddly enough, even before talkies (one couldn't really call them musicals)—but particularly after the crash of 1929.[1]

The first film to venture a look backwards, after the traumatizing effects of the war, was the epic film *The Big Parade* (1925), starring John Gilbert as Jim Apperson, an American doughboy, and Renée Adorée as Melisande, the French girl with whom he falls in love. Directed by King Vidor, it was intended at first to be just a low-budget adventure/romance of little significance; however, as the film progressed, it developed into something much larger than even the director had anticipated.[2] The first of many realistic war films, *Parade* was a huge box-office success and may have been the "most profitable silent film of all time."[3]

Gilbert plays a spoiled, idle, rich young man, who joins the Army because his father threatens to kick him out of the house. He makes a couple of friends, and all are sent to France where the trio is billeted with a farmer who has a beautiful daughter, Melisande (Adorée). Naturally, all three of the boys are attracted to the girl, but she finally responds to Jim. She discovers he is engaged to a girl back home and runs away from him, only to return for a kiss when she realizes he is marching out to the Front. There is a lot of comedic camaraderie in the first half of the movie. The second half is something of a jarring juxtaposition. With a complete reversal of tone, the action now centers on the horrors of war—the battle scenes were much praised for their realism—where Jim's friend Slim is killed and Jim is wounded in the leg trying to rescue him. He is taken to a hospital, where he sneaks out to find Melisande, only to discover that the farmhouse is damaged and the family is gone. He collapses and is returned to the hospital. Sent home, Jim is told that his fiancée and his brother have fallen in love, which is fine with him, as the film now reveals that his leg has been amputated. When he finally tells his mother about Melisande, she is moved and tells him to go back and find her. Of course, he does. When Melisande sees him, she rushes into his arms, uncaring whether he has one leg, or any at all, as long as she has him.

Much praised as well, along with the realistic battle scenes, is a mustache-less Gilbert in the role of Jim. Without his facial hair, he resembles a young Jimmy Stewart, tall, gangly, and just a bit silly, very different from his Great Lover look when paired with Greta Garbo. The convincing evolution of his growth and maturation during the movie's length makes this one of his most acclaimed performances.

The wardrobe designer credit for this film is given to Ethel P. Chaffin, with the uncredited assistance of Robert Florey. Although, because the movie is mainly peasant garb and uniforms, there was little in the way of the stunning gowns Chaffin was known for executing.

Born Ethel Painter in 1885 in Pasadena, Chaffin had worked as a dressmaker for a department store following a very brief marriage. Returning home, she opened her own dress shop after a second marriage to George Chaffin. Word of her talents reached Famous Players-Lasky, and she was hired to head their wardrobe department in 1919. There, she designed for the studio's biggest stars, including Gloria Swanson, and Carmel Myers. Chaffin racked up 22 credits between 1921 and 1926 at the studio with spectacular designs, in particular her work for Gloria Swanson in *The Great Moment* (1921). In that film, Swanson wears a succession of evening gowns that can only be described as breathtaking. For one, a light-colored dress, sleeveless and narrow strapped, topped with an asymmetrical, beaded over-garment which flows, like a net of seafoam, down to an ermine banded train. Sensational!

She also wears a peacock-patterned showstopper which consists of another light-colored (so light as to appear nearly nude in some views) under-gown with an over-tunic which hangs from another asymmetrical strap. The peacock clings tightly to her body in the back while in the front the beaded panel sweeps down to a short, pleated train. These are only two of the continual parade of wardrobe changes which made the story of secondary importance. The reaction of the ladies in the audience must have been exactly like mine. Usually a woman of impeccable design knowhow, Swanson does don one unfortunate ensemble which makes her seem to be auditioning for Minnie Mouse. This concoction combines a sort of sari-like arrangement with two giant, Chinese-patterned mouse ears.

Ethel Chaffin, the designer, moved to MGM in 1924 where she continued to design for the big stars, such as Norma Shearer and Marion Davies. In 1927, while on an ocean voyage, her husband, George Chaffin, unexpectedly died. His widow, who never remarried, retired from Hollywood and spent the rest of a long life designing for private clients, dying in 1975.[4]

Another of the most heralded after-war movies was *Wings,* released in 1927 and winner of the Best Picture Oscar. With Charles Rogers (playing the character of Jack Powell) and Richard Arlen (David Armstrong) as the competing airmen, along with Clara Bow the "It" girl (Mary Preston), it tells the story of two rivals from a small town who join the aviation arm of the service to become ace pilots and continued rivals. Clara Bow, as Preston, does her part for the war effort as an ambulance driver. *Wings* also features a young Gary Cooper in a small part as Cadet White (the "small part" got his career off to a flying start). It also features Jobyna Ralston (Sylvia Lewis), who subsequently married Richard Arlen (David in the film). Jobyna had been a favorite co-star of the comedian

Gloria Swanson in *The Great Moment* (1921). One of a revolving door of showstopping gowns she wears throughout the movie. A mermaid of seduction (*Exhibitors Herald* Jul.–Sept. 2021, Wikimedia Commons).

Harold Lloyd and paired with him in six comedies. William Wellman, a veteran of real air combat experience, directed, which added verisimilitude to the air scenes—although Richard Arlen and John Monk Saunders, another cast member, were also aviators.

Formulaic in its love triangle story, *Wings* nevertheless is poignant and arouses our emotions with its tale of the two young men who go off to be heroes, fighting both the enemy and each other. David, in love with Mary, thinks she prefers Jack. He finds he is mistaken when Mary lets him know her feelings. David is shot down, but steals a German biplane, then Jack mistakes him for the enemy and shoots the plane down thinking he is avenging David, but fatally wounding David instead. As David is dying, Jack is persuaded to come to his side, whereby David forgives him and passes away. Jack confesses to David's parents that it is his fault that David was killed, but Jack's mother absolves him and says it wasn't his fault, it was the fault of the war. Mary decides that she loves him after all.

The film was controversial for its scenes of two men kissing and for its nudity. Nudity made a continual teasing appearance in silent film, so that this feature would stir up any debate comes across as a little hypocritical. The action scenes were particularly acclaimed, and in 1929 it won the Academy Award for Best Engineering Effects along with its Best Picture award.

No discussion of after-war films would be complete without a mention of *All Quiet on the Western Front* (1930). The original story was by the acclaimed author, Erich Maria Remarque (himself a German veteran of World War I), and adapted by Maxwell Anderson (*What Price Glory*). The story realistically focuses on the stresses of war and the psychological detachment from "normal" life when once at home.[5] In German, the title of Remarque's 1929 novel is *Im Westen nichtes Neues,* which actually translates as *Nothing New in the West*, West meaning the Western Front. *All Quiet* is a more lyrical expression of the same idea, meaning no movement, no change, just unutterable boredom broken only by horrific death. *All Quiet* reflects no "side" except, perhaps, truth.

A group of young men, inspired by hearing their professor speak about glory and "saving the Fatherland," are moved to join up. Their disillusionment begins almost immediately with their training under an abusive corporal. When they are sent to the combat zone, one of their group is killed even before they arrive at their post. There is no food available, and they are forced to resort to devious means. Once at the Front, after several days of conflict, they manage to take a trench. Another of their group is blinded by shrapnel and runs into machine-gun fire. Forced by bombardment to abandon the trench, the survivors get double rations back at the camp because so many companions are dead. All this happens almost immediately in the film. The rest of the movie records one after another of the boys being killed or maimed. In the end, the last young man (Paul) is shot by an "enemy" sniper while reaching for a butterfly. The synopsis does not do justice to the immediacy and painful reality of the film and to the unspoken lessons of the waste and uselessness of war on both sides.

In his breakout performance, Lew Ayres, later to gain fame as *Dr. Kildare*, plays Paul, the tragic "star" of the movie. Ben Alexander, much later co-star of *Dragnet* with Jack Webb, plays Kemmerick. Moved by the message of the film, Ayres was a conscientious objector during World War II; however, he served at the Front as a medic in the South Pacific and as a chaplain's aide (all under fire). After the war, he won one of his three Best Actor nominations for *Johnny Belinda* (1948) with Jane Wyman, Ronald Reagan's first wife. Married briefly to both Ginger Rogers and Lola Lane (of the '30s and '40s Lane sisters), Ayres' third marriage to Diana Hall lasted until his death in 1996 and produced a son, Justin, his only child. Throughout his long career he was always soft-spoken and understated, a quietly compelling actor, perfectly cast as the philosophical Paul.

In Britain, *The Battles of Coronel and Falkland Islands,* a 1927 docudrama, takes a fictionalized look at hostile encounters around the city of Coronel (Chile), and the Falkland Islands in 1914. *Battles* focuses on the sinking of the hopelessly outgunned, outmoded, and outmanned pair of British ships, *HMS Monmouth* and *HMS Good Hope.* Accompanied by the light cruisers *Glasgow* and *Otranto,* the battle resulted in the loss of 1,600 British sailors—there were no survivors from the *Monmouth* or *Good Hope*; however, the HMS *Glasgow* and HMS *Otranto* escaped with several casualties. Under the command of the aristocratic Reichsgraf (Count) Maximillian von Spee (whose name was later attached to a dirigible), the Germans easily sank the two light cruisers and severely damaged their escorts. Not just an act of war, but a terrible tragedy due to the circumstances: *Monmouth* and *Good Hope* were not only lightly armored and obsolete, but "manned" by teenagers *who had never been to sea before.* The shock and outrage felt in the United Kingdom moved the admiralty to send out a far larger force which included the heavy battle cruisers *Inflexible* and *Invincible.*

Vice-Admiral von Spee seemed to have had a premonition and was not optimistic about further easy victories of this sort. When the well-equipped battle cruisers *Scharnhorst, Gneisenau* and *Nürnberg* arrived in Valparaiso (a German stronghold), he did not join the predominantly German population in welcome. Nevertheless, with this new command he set off for the Falklands with the British fleet in hot pursuit. There, the *Scharnhorst*[6] was lost with all hands; only a few survived from the *Gneisenau* and the *Nürnberg.* Ironically, one of the surviving officers from the *Gneisenau* claimed to be a first cousin of the British commander. The entire set of ruinous debacles seems to have been the result of complete miscommunication.[7]

The movie, directed by Walter Summers and starring Hans von Slock as Vice-Admiral von Spee and Craighall Sherry as Admiral Sturdee, does dramatic justice to the action scenes. Its realistic presentation nearly fools the audience into thinking they are viewing a documentary rather than a re-creation. However, neither of the starring actors could match the aristocratic bearing of the real antagonists, especially Reichsgraf von Spee, who was the very image of a Count.

As demonstrated by the examples, most of the movies do not look back to the war with the prior sentimentality and illusions of glory which the government, hand-in-hand with the recruitment centers, attempted to foist on the public during the conflict. The possible exception might be *The Battles of Coronel and Falkland Islands,* which certainly glorified the heroism of the British Navy, but even then, the gripping scenes of the few German survivors flailing in the icy waters speak to the uselessness and tragedy of war, no matter the side. The dead and wounded spoke too loudly for the illusions of any glory to be maintained, well before the war ended. We do not know how long Karl Kitchen, with his air of detachment, could hold out.

The "Red Scare"

In one of the quickest turnarounds in history, the Russians, who had been treated sympathetically by the movie industry, became the Bolsheviks ("Bolshies") almost overnight in 1919 and a terrifying menace to the national security of the United States. Paranoia became the theme of many films. Steven J. Ross quotes a line from *Dangerous Hours* (1919): "Bolshevism has attacked America and we've got to fight that as hard as if it was Germany, and fight it to a finish...." The quote goes on to describe those malefactors as "filthy, *long-haired* (emphasis mine) degenerate murderers...."[8] Unfortunately, saving the country from those invidious types took the form of busting unions, to protect Americans from the working classes, rather than any real attempts to root out genuine enemies of the democratic way.

In defense of their livelihoods, the unions strove to produce pictures of their own portraying union organizers and members as modest, well-dressed, well-groomed (with short hair) and, above all, non-violent contributors to a smoothly run society. Ironically amusing, Russian films about union organizing use the same propaganda elements, e.g., short hair, tidy dress, as did American union-made films. In spite of their helpful, short-haired, neatly dressed, demeanor, they are still abused by the upper classes, from whence comes the violence. There is a little more frenzied milling around, in Sergei Eisenstein's *Strike* (1925) for example. But then, that was Eisenstein. In spite of his penchant for violence, Eisenstein's union members are still shown as the rational beings and the owners, as well as the Army, as bloated, greasy, sub-humans.

The mainstream filmmakers, on the other hand, portrayed the union members just as *Dangerous Hours* described them. *Photoplay* devotes two pages to the right way to portray Bolsheviks and the movie industry happily extended that stereotyping to union members, even to blaming the war deaths on them. In 1918, just after the armistice, the Fuel Administration made an outrageous film that blamed the union coal miners by having a dying soldier say: "The Germans did not defeat us. We were defeated by the miners at home."[9] This stunningly offensive accusation was patently false, but lapped up by members of anti-labor groups (it was determined that the fault was rather with the railroads).

What's in Your Closet?

Although the old guard was reluctant to admit it, the world had changed radically. In only two years following the armistice, one monumental goal had been achieved—votes for women. The suffragists had not starved, suffered abuse and ridicule in vain. Patriarchy was not down for the count, but it had taken a swift right cross.

In the world of fashion, women were freer than ever before. Trousers, as I have said, became a permanent part of women's wardrobes, and during the '20s were advertised—cautiously at first for "Outing and Sports Wear,"—even in the *Sears Catalogue.* Corsets gradually took a back seat to girdles and brassieres, although those items still look mighty uncomfortable, and the one-piece is still touted (with less severe stays).

By 1930, shorts and knickers for girls were seen everywhere. Bathing suits were actually swimming suits, rather than bathing ensembles guaranteed to drag the wearer down under the water at the first wave.

Sportswear became a major part of every woman's leisure wardrobe, frequently baring the back dramatically while keeping the front modest. Those who have seen

Bonwit Teller ad for 1916, published in the *New York Times*. Perky, but bulky. For the "we only wade" girls (Wikimedia Commons).

Downton Abbey remember Lady Violet plaintively inquiring, "What is a weekend?" With the advent of the forty-hour week, when the weekend was born, leisure wear turned into big business. Until then, the working classes would have had no answer for the dowager Countess.

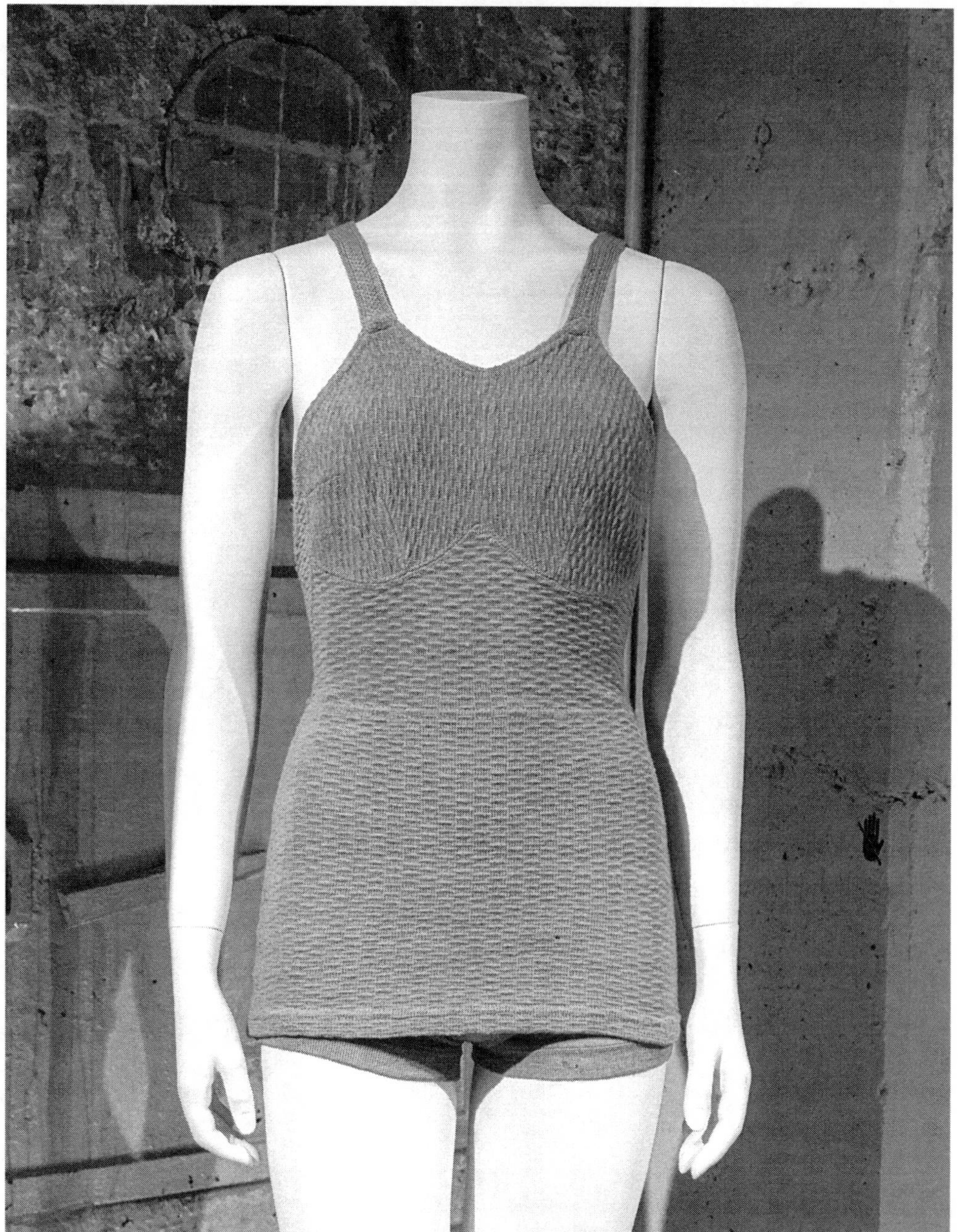

A two-piece bathing suit from 1930. Women could actually swim now, although the suit's cotton-and-wool combo would presumably be itchy and get soggy (photograph by user Daderot, Wikimedia Commons).

Hemlines, of course, had risen to the knee by the mid–'20s, and the Jazz Age had come roaring in. Rouged knees, rolled hose and the moment of the Flapper arrived, although the term itself actually goes back much further in time. But, like all moments, it had to end. In the last week of October 1929, it did. Ironically, as the stock market crashed, movies adopted the crashing cacophony of sound films to keep pace.

Do I Hear a Waltz?

We tend to think of the advent of sound in motion pictures as: a new thing of the late '20s; embraced with enthusiasm by filmmakers and the audiences to whom they catered, alike; and a great boon to the enjoyment of a film. Well, it was absolutely none of the above.

In (or Not) with the New

As already discussed, Oscar Messter, in Germany, was already experimenting with sound soon after the turn of the century. In the United States, Thomas Edison and his "chief" associate, William Kennedy Laurie Dickson, were already involved in the sound problem as early as 1894. There is actually a surviving test film, with Dickson himself appearing, which is dated somewhere between the fall of 1894 and spring of 1895. Dickson, of course, was the real inventive mind behind a number of Edison's claimed inventions. In this little fragment of film, we see two men dancing together, and a third (Dickson) playing a tune from an operetta, *Les Cloches de Corneville* (*The Bells of Corneville*). Long forgotten by modern audiences, the operetta was a hit at the time of its opening and was revived by the British in 1917 as a silent film. Since it was a musical play, presumably the libretto was substantial enough to warrant the silent treatment.

In 1919, Josef Engl, Joseph Massole, and Hans Vogt, three German inventors, secured a patent for the Tri-Ergon process, which converted audio waves into electricity. The electricity then powered a light which was photographed on a strip of negative film. A flywheel controlled the strip when played back, and the light was reconverted into electricity and thus into sound.

At the same time, Dr. Lee de Forest was also trying out one of his inventions, the Audion tube, in connection with film. He opened the De Forest Phonofilm Company in 1922 and produced a series of short sound films. His system was introduced into 34 theaters but failed to catch on in any permanent fashion, as did any of the other early experiments.

Are We on Sound Footing?

The opinion of filmmakers regarding sound can best be described as muted.

> "No, I don't think the talking moving picture will ever be successful in the United States. Americans prefer silent drama." Thomas Alva Edison. 1927.[10]

> "My personal opinion is that the silent film will never be eliminated, since certain stories are naturally suited for silent treatment and must be completely rearranged to serve as dialogue vehicles..." Nicholas M. Schenk (President of Loew's and MGM).[11]

And a rather long opinion from Monta Bell, a director for Paramount, which is representative enough to be quoted more fully:

> ["Its] value lies in its discriminate usage ... but I am afraid that our producers are rushing forward sheep like and embracing 'sound' as the panacea for all their ills.... Pictures give us a medium whereby we could put intimate stories in big theaters—the closeup allowing us to make our characters intimate. But not so with sound.... Basically, I believe it to be wrong for dialogues. Our writers will become lazy. It will be so easy to sit two characters down and let them talk instead of devising ingenious means for getting over points with pictorial action as

we do now ... for effects and occasional high spot speeches, yes. For entire pictures—well as far as I am concerned, silence is golden." Monta Bell. *Film Daily.*[12]

This particular issue of *Film Daily,* quoting Bell, was all about sound. One article was dramatically headlined "NOTHING BUT SOUND." That fact alone demonstrated the futility of fighting what was, by then, inevitable. Bell was grasping at straws while the floodwaters of sound were closing over his head.

We Had Faces in Those Days

Well, so much for the filmmakers. How about the actors? Of course, they may not have spoken for everyone, but here are two of the most celebrated, Lillian Gish and Clara Bow:

Gish: "...in the silent movies we achieved certain beautiful things. I mean that there were moments of beauty in pantomime and beauty in photography."[13]

Bow: Clara Bow has been repeatedly quoted as saying, when she heard about a major fire at Paramount in 1929, "I hope to Christ it was the sound stages!"

Burdened with a thick Brooklyn accent which contrasted sharply with her immense charm, Bow dreaded the advent of sound. Nevertheless, she made several talkies before retiring at only 26 to a ranch with her cowboy star husband, Rex Bell.

Consider also the case of Douglas Fairbanks, Sr. An incredible athlete, graceful and debonair, he was tethered by sound like a man sentenced to a chain gang. Microphones were literally placed in potted plants and actors were obliged to stand stiffly next to one, reciting their lines like Hamlet's ghost. Torture for a man used to bounding through his movies. Moreover, he would have to act—never his long suit. His appeal lay in his athleticism and his thousand-watt grin, not to mention unmeasurable charm. The only other actor who came close in that regard was Errol Flynn, Fairbank's counterpart in the '40s. Fairbanks' career declined precipitously after the adoption of sound, and he made his last film in 1934 after only four talkies.

Some actors took readily to sound—transferees from vaudeville, for example, like the Marx Brothers. The four Marxmen represented those comedians whose shtick depended on fast patter rather than pantomime. All except Harpo, that is, who never spoke a word. Nevertheless, as an accomplished harpist, Harpo still derived great benefit from sound in that regard.

In general, it would seem silent actors weren't all that enthused. Nevertheless, even John Barrymore was being wooed by Vitaphone to star in more films for them—he had already appeared for Vitaphone in the sound version of *Don Juan*. However, Barrymore's star was waning, due to both age and alcohol consumption, and he needed a boost, so he readily complied. Making several talking pictures, he grew increasingly unreliable owing to his alcohol consumption and many of the films were pitiful parodies of his actual condition.

On the enthusiastic side, an advertisement from *Variety Magazine* for October 2, 1929, screams in banner headlines: "Radio is Where it Belongs—Right on Top, and World's Greatest Showmen Now Demonstrating with Contracts Their Faith in Radio Genius." This exercise in hyperbole follows with a list of "Radio Smash Attractions" now clicking or shortly to grace the screens of the world: *Rio Rita, Street Girl,* Rudy Vallee—Greatest Individual Draw of Generation, and Richard Dix [in] *Seven Keys to Baldpate.*[14]

The fate of silent films was sealed, whether anyone acknowledged it or not. The studios fell in line and an era came to an end.

Am I Blue (or Amber, or Violet, or...)?

As many people have pointed out, the silent film had developed into a genuine art form over time. Intertitles had become less and less necessary—gesture, movement, wardrobe, all combined to create a symphony in pantomime. The ever-increasing sophistication of the audience schooled them to read the actor's subtle intentions without the need for interruption. Moreover, the movies were never really silent, in any case. There was always music to set the mood and to indicate changes in that mood. At the very least there was a guitar, in the larger houses usually a piano, a grand Wurlitzer organ, or on occasion, a full orchestra. The audience fathomed every nuance of the story from its accompaniment.

The Silents were not black-and-white either, as we are used to seeing them, but painstakingly tinted in various shades of color to reinforce the setting of a mood—hushed evenings, brilliant revealing sunlight, war, anger, despair—all so that dialogue was superfluous. There were protocols that were carefully followed for certain effects; these effects, of course, were what the audiences came to expect.

In his 1917 *Guide to Kinematography,* Colin Bennett provides a list of few guidelines for tinting, where the film was dipped in a colored dye:

> Early morning: Tint film lightly in one tenth per cent bath of crystal violet;
> Moonlight (night): Use one quarter per cent patent blue solution;
> Lamp or candle light: tint in half per cent orange brown (Mandarin) dye bath;
> Fire: Use bath containing one per cent each of brilliant yellow and rose bengal;
> Weird effects: Tint green in a half per cent naphthol green bath;
> Bright sunlight: Use half per cent brilliant yellow bath.

Even the names of the dye baths are romantic.

Toning required a more complex process, but achieved more subtlety in the final effect. Rather than the dye baths, tinting used more than one chemical method to produce its results. Using a variety of metals in conversion with the black-and-white image, a range of similar results were obtained.

Again, there were guidelines:

> Iron gives blue;
> Copper gives red to brown;
> Vanadium gives green;
> *Uranium* gives black to red; (emphasis mine)
> Selenium gives red-brown;
> Sulphide gives sepia.[15]

The results provided an enhanced atmosphere that gave great beauty to even the most mundane of movies. Restoration work is now being done on many of the extant silent films, to bring them back to their previous splendor—*The Sea Hawk* and *Snow White* are two lovely examples of tinted film, and really good movies as well.[16] The beauty of tinted film was not without problems, however. With regard to makeup, for example, red photographed as black against a blue tint, so that some actors used heavy white makeup in order not to look as though they had just come in from a coal mine. The same applied to fabric, and costume designers had to choose with care when dressing their stars. White and lighter colors were fairly safe, but darker shades frequently made the actors appear to be in constant mourning. Golden and amber tints were usually lovely. As late as the '30s and '40s, after tinted film was a thing of the past, Edith Head, the well-known designer, was still wearing tinted glasses to see how her color choices would photograph against black-and-white film.

Unfortunately, color tinting and toning interfered with sound movies, but multicolor systems were in place to pick up the slack, although they lost much of the atmosphere.

There were, as I noted, attempts at musicals. These, it goes without saying, needed sound. From the little I have seen of silent musicals, the few made were unsuccessful, at best, but this may be from a contemporary perspective. Some, such as *The Merry Widow* (1925), which started with a strong libretto, might have worked with a proper treatment. However, at the hands of director Erich von Stroheim, one would think the least musical person possible, the result was a nonsensical atrocity. The story was butchered, the acting was dreadful, and the whole appeared to take place within the confines of a Swiss cuckoo clock.

La Boheme (1926), directed by King Vidor, starring Lillian Gish as Mimi and John

John Gilbert, left, Lillian Gish, center, and the director, King Vidor, on the set of *La Boheme*, 1926. Opera in pantomime, but effective, nevertheless. Ms. Gish wears an Erté interpretation of a poor, consumptive Mimi (MGM Studios publicity still, Wikimedia Commons).

Gilbert as Rodolphe (Rodolfo), was a mite better owing to a much more sensitive director. Gish is playful and even dances, with the requisite fragility for Mimi's last days. The costumes are by Erté; however, he and Gish had a series of contretemps over her demands and his. Gish had a will of steel, and Erté was no slouch in that department either, which must have made for a lively time on the set. He is uncredited on the film, probably owing to his dissatisfaction with the unfortunate partnership. The costumes are outstanding, nonetheless, and for the most part, bear his signature attention to sleeves, these having a musicality just of themselves. Their bouffant presence almost steals the show, even as in this "simple," lower economic milieu costume worn by Lillian Gish as Mimi. The dropped-shouldered sleeves could contain Lillian and her sister Dorothy, as well.

They resemble the sleeves of the ethereal costume design on the cover of *Dress and Vanity Fair Magazine* for October 1913. The intrepid young lady balances uncomfortably on a stylized crescent moon clad in a frothy pink gown with a voluminous skirt and sleeves to match. Her small bag descends from the waist and seems heavy enough to pull her right off her perch. This design is by George Wolfe Plank, whom I discussed earlier, and although his style is markedly different, the voluminous sleeves are certainly the result of Erté influence.

In spite of the beauty of silence, and the above splendor, sound soon became a necessity, as voices were raised with the fall of the stock market. Sound musicals were just the ticket, so to speak.[17]

I'm Feeling Depressed

Sometimes referred to as "Black Friday," the stock market crash was more properly "Black Tuesday," "Black Thursday," and generally "Black Week." Beginning on Thursday, October 24 (Black Thursday), and continuing until October 29 (Black Tuesday), the Dow Jones Industrial Average dropped 24.8 percent. In a panic, investors sold 16,410,030 shares in one day. This led to a stampede of investors leaving the market, which resulted in the index falling nearly 90 percent. Affecting investors large and small, the crash wiped out businesses in a second. While there was some recovery, the overall trend continued downwards and by 1933 nearly half of America's banks had failed and approximately 30 percent of the populace was unemployed.

Not only the United States was affected—the Great Depression was felt in Europe as strongly as in the U.S. Strikes, by those both affected and disaffected on both continents, abounded. As always, the fan magazines carried on as though there was no Depression, just as they had carried on as though there was no war. The year 1930 displayed a schizophrenic fashion personality as demonstrated in the July issue of *Photoplay*. Skirts were only slightly longer than in 1929, but bosomy curves were starting to appear in evening wear. Bathing suits were actually cute and clung to the body with very low backs, and there were even rather daring faux two-piece items.

Variations of the cloche hat were still being worn; however, bobbed hair was getting a curl. In fact, an article focusing on Greta Garbo's latest movie, *Romance,* exclaimed "Garbo in Curls." One sign of the Depression—the lavish color photos, which had just started to appear, disappeared from the inside pages of the magazine with only the front and back covers remaining in color.

As the Dow Jones continued to fall, so did hemlines. In 1932, skirt lengths dropped from the knee and reverted to the four inches above the ankle of 1922. The jupe-culotte was reintroduced by Schiaperelli who was photographed in 1935 wearing her "own designed trousered skirt" in that mid-calf length.[18]

Nevertheless, even with an awkward hem length, frocks of the early '30s were among some of the most attractive and flattering in fifty years. The June 1932 issue of *Photoplay* gushed "Curves, Today [sic], are as important as complexions" and featured a sprightly Joan Blondell, one of Warner Bros. favorite musical stars, posing in bathing suit, evening gown and street suit. The text goes on to insist: "No longer can we dare ignore our figure. Dame Fashion has decreed that, feminine curves must show themselves—whether in sports-togs or in the clinging, revealing evening gown."[19] The curve-less, boyish silhouette had been swept away, to be replaced by the bias cut. For the majority of women, this demanded a tight girdle—busts were not a problem, tummies were. If you were Jean Harlow the platinum blonde bombshell however, an abundance of curves didn't detract for a second. If you were Jean Nobody, it didn't work nearly as well. Harlow figured prominently in ads for everything commercial: Lucky Strike cigarettes; Lux Toilet Soap; Coca-Cola—in ads for her movies, not so much. She did make the cover of *Time* magazine, for a 1935 issue, in little more than a charmeuse and marabou negligée. The negligée, of course, is nothing short of stunning, with its lushly feathered sleeves, so that lounging around like this was something I suspect every housewife, in their hearts, wanted to do.

What strikes us as rather peculiar nowadays are the advertisements for women proclaiming, "I am thirty-nine." This shocking confession is, naturally, for ads touting the right kind of soap (Lux), which, if used faithfully, will keep everyone from guessing you are tottering on the verge of senility. Other Lux advertisements are in the same ballpark as they ask, "Is 29 an age to Dread?" Esther Ralston and Anita Stewart assure the readers they know the "Secret of Keeping Youthful Charm." However, Palmolive soap has the *real* answer, Olive Oil! (Keep that Schoolgirl Complexion). Fears of aging banished at just ten cents a bar. This overemphasis on approaching deterioration at thirty is dismaying to those of us who do not feel the end of the twenties is the end of life. Yes, more mature actresses still find it a little harder to find work; nonetheless, there are constantly working actresses like Susan Sarandon, Meryl Streep, and certainly the active-to-the-end Cicely Tyson, who don't seem to need Lux.

The Depression had hit the bottom, and hemlines had dropped to their lowest, in 1934 when Jean Harlow posed for the August 1934 issue of *Photoplay.* Since it would have been almost impossible for "exotic" Jean to look anything but good in clothes, it is an added bonus that the ensembles are great looking, as well. A navy silk suit with white piqué cuffs and collar, featuring double rows of oversize buttons, is particularly nice, as is a white silk sports dress with sailor collar worn in the front "like a bib" as the caption says. For evening, more of that bias cut that Harlow did so well—in crepe with a long train trimmed in fringe. In the opinion of this author, 1934 takes the Oscar for best overall wardrobes.

It's still about age in the ads, so naturally, Kellogg's All-Bran claims to be part of "Woman's Ageless Weapons." "Youthful, rounded curves" are sure to be yours with cereal. Brunettes can quit worrying whether they look older than blondes with Lady Esther face powder, and Neet, which is still around doing its job as a stripper, is removing the arm and leg hair "problem" from your daily life.

The ultimately tragic, platinum-blonde bombshell Jean Harlow on the cover of *Time*, wearing not much (photographed by Harvey White, Wikimedia Commons).

Are You Going to Queen's Borough's Fair?

The Depression wore on through five more years, gradually easing but never quite releasing its grip. It can be said to culminate in the New York World's Fair of 1939. This extravaganza sang of "Peace and Freedom" just as the world was set to plunge headlong into another catastrophic war in September of that year. Represented by the iconic and still recognizable Trylon and Perisphere, the Fair spoke of the bright future of mankind—with fluorescent lighting from General Electric, television from Westinghouse and GE, and the World of Tomorrow with *everything.*[20]

On its opening day, April 30, 1939, in spite of the muggy heat, 260,000 visitors reportedly attended. That particular date was chosen intentionally because it coincided with the 150th anniversary of George Washington's inauguration. Over the course of the Fair's running, it attracted over 45 million attendees with a reported $48 million in revenue, even with a slight damper—in September 1939, Germany ran over Poland and World War II began.

The Fair did reopen for another six-month season in 1940; however, many theme pavilions had to be closed due to their relationship with Nazi Germany. As a result of the shrinking variety of exhibits, the emphasis was changed to the rides and entertainment rather than education and the future. After its final closure, many buildings were immediately demolished, and the future became the past almost overnight. That bright vision had held for two short years, for two short seasons—April until September—then dimmed for many years, possibly forever.

A Fair Flair for Fashion

Since the Fair began in April, even though the weather was warm on opening day, fashion rules of the time dictated that white shoes were not allowed until after Memorial Day. The most popular shoe for women was the laced oxford with a 1½ inch heel. Dark, of course, until okayed by the fashion police, then white for the summer months until after Labor Day when it was back to dark. Dresses, of course, no slacks, the length a modest just below the knee. In the fall, hats for both men and women. In the summertime, a few, generally younger, hatless women could be seen. Men were more casual when the Fair's muggy early summer heat arrived and a few rolled up, or short, shirtsleeves appeared, still mainly with those ties on, however. In the fall (which started right off the bat in September), it was right back to suits and fedoras.

Fall 1939 fashion images prove that those squared shoulders for women had not yet completely taken over in the magazines. *Photoplay* was leading the way with an article in the July 1939 issue, "Suggestions for Fall Formality," with a striking gown designed by Howard Shoup in a changeable blue/green metallic jersey. It's modeled by actress Brenda Marshall, who wears it in the movie *Espionage Agent,* and on whom it looks stunning. A shirred close-fitting, long-sleeve bodice, decorated at the neckline with silver leaves, is elongated to below the waist above a softly flowing, gathered skirt. The shoulders are of those soon-to-be widened-and-squared variety seen everywhere. Late in 1939, we see that trend to *Gone with the Wind* influence discussed later. It shows up in a Jeanne Lanvin–designed evening gown of spangled, deep brown silk, with a halter-style bodice and double-flounced skirt. Scarlet O'Hara would have been envious.

Nudity was the uniform of the day (month, season) for the many sculptures dotting the fairgrounds. Among them: *Time, Night, Golden Sprays,* two full-frontal young ladies representing ideal womanhood, executed by Leo Lentilli; *Fountain of the Atom* "with playful 'electrons'"; and stylized nudes in the Italian pavilion restaurant. Also included was Salvador Dali's grotesquerie *The Dreams of Venus.* Prominently featuring giant breasts, it was not renewed for 1940.

Jeanne Lanvin designed this evening gown with that *Gone with the Wind* influence, Fall 1939. Halter bodice with double-flounced skirt in spangled, deep brown silk. Stunning and ready for any ball (Metropolitan Museum).

Men were not excluded from the sculpted nudist brigade. They were represented in part by: *The Astronomer,* by the acclaimed Swedish import Carl Milles; *Samson and the Lion,* more familiarly known as "Man with a Dog by the Tail"; and *Morning,* which represents a nude man seemingly startled awake by the crowing of a cock (or possibly by another nude man forcefully blowing a trumpet behind him). The sculptures were, nonetheless, seriously beautiful and *moderne* examples of the Art Deco style which was the architectural theme of the Fair.

The reopening of the Fair in April 1940, now less a learning experience than an amusement park, with its changed character reflected the larger change in the character of the world.

Even though it lost money in the long run, the Fair was the last moment of hope for a long stretch into an uncertain future—in spite of the optimism promoted by the Fair builders. The 1940 season, although we were not officially at war, saw a noticeable increase of young servicemen in uniform photographed as visitors. Those young men presaged what was to come.

Seven

Peace and Promise Deferred

World War II

"Although the United States did not enter World War II until the end of 1941, the fairgrounds served as a window into the troubles overseas."
—"1939 New York World's Fair," *Wikipedia*

The (Reel) Time Wars: (John) Wayne's World

In spite of the section heading, it wasn't entirely John Wayne singlehandedly fighting the entire war, it only seemed that way. In movies like *Flying Tigers* (1942), *Fighting Seabees* (1944), or *Back to Bataan* (1945), the Duke punched his way through scores of enemies and came out victorious. He didn't stop when the war ended, either; *Sands of Iwo Jima* was released in 1949 and *Operation Pacific* in 1951 (there were more, but you get the point). Wayne was not the only one demonstrating his movie courage; for example, Robert Taylor, George Murphy (later Senator Murphy), Lloyd Nolan, and Robert Walker sacrificed themselves with equal heroism in the 1943 movie simply titled *Bataan*—before John Wayne went back there.

Nevertheless, stalwart heroines like Bette Davis, and understated heroes like Paul Lukas, fought on the home front, as well.

In the exceptionally well-done and well-received *Watch on the Rhine* (the title was taken from a patriotic German anthem), Bette Davis got top billing but played a supporting role to the strong performance of Paul Lukas, a Hungarian import, who played an anti-fascist German in a film that couldn't help but be good. Written by Dashiel Hammett from a 1941 play by Lillian Hellman, who contributed additional film dialogue, it was mature, literate, and profoundly moving. Lukas won his only Oscar for his role as a man of action, where he played against his usual type of wise professorial, although sometimes sinister, supporting actors. Painfully convincing, one watches him with surprising empathy as he kills an unarmed man outright, then says "I did it before, and I will do it again." You actually find yourself hoping he will.

Lukas's career began in 1915 with a short film and continued until 1970, an amazing 55 years and 135 credits. He is probably best-known to younger generations as the Professor in *Twenty-Thousand Leagues Under the Sea* which plays frequently on television.

Davis plays the American wife (Sara Muller) of the rather mysterious, German-born Lukas (Kurt Muller), who moves the family around Europe often (he claims to be an engineer), but who never seems to have a permanent job or enough money. They come home to her parents' house for a purported "holiday," however Lukas is, in actuality, on the run for helping a friend escape the Nazis' clutches. His friend is recaptured and Lukas is determined to return to Europe and lend his assistance another time. The husband (George Coulouris appearing as the ne'er-do-well Romanian count, Teck de Brancovis) of one of Davis's family's friends (Geraldine Fitzgerald as Marthe), is a Nazi sympathizer and threatens to out Lukas to the homegrown Nazi party, hence his death at Lukas's hands. Lukas heads off to Europe never to be seen again, and Davis is most moving when her eldest son tells her that if the war lasts much longer, he will be old enough to go and intends to do so. This is agony for her; nevertheless, she realizes she is powerless to stop him as soon as he is of age. It is all the more agonizing as she realizes that her youngest boy will want to emulate his brother and father and take their places if they do not return. The movie ends on that poignant note.

Watch on the Rhine was released in 1943 but set in the period shortly before the United States entered the war, as was Hellman's play. Although only the direct attack on Pearl Harbor moved President Franklin Roosevelt to declare war on both Japan and the Axis in 1941, he had been funneling arms to Britain *sub rosa*. Furthermore, coastal states like California were preparing for an attack by sea as early as 1939, with the establishment of military bases up and down the coasts. Those who foresaw the coming cataclysm were already active in anti–Axis pursuits; furthermore, many young American men had already joined the RAF or enlisted in the British Army as ordinary soldiers. Anti-German sentiment was not yet running high in this dramatized prewar period, however, so Lukas's acceptance in Davis's family and social circle would not have been exceptional. Nevertheless by 1943, emotions were such that making Lukas a sympathetic figure was an interesting choice. This, of course, at a time when that nationality would have been most suspect.

Davis is wonderful as always, using her enormous expressive eyes and spitting her words out between her clenched teeth. She plays against type as well, with her portrayal of a devoted wife and mother of three, rather than the usual steely-spined, a tad bitchy, woman of decided character, whether good or bad. She is convincingly softer and poignant in the role and actually insisted on taking a back seat to Lukas. According to film lore, she wanted him to take top billing but because she was the bigger box office draw, the studio refused.

Other heroines—those who were in fact at the Front and who got deplorably short shrift, both during and after the war—were depicted in the gripping story of a group of thirteen women in a Bataan field hospital. Two are servicewomen, Captain Alice Marsh (Fay Bainter), and Lieutenant Mary Smith (Margaret Sullavan) [sic], the rest are civilians which include Joan Blondell as Grace and Ann Southern as Pat, the troublemaker.

Desperate for help, and nearly out of supplies, especially quinine, Flo Norris (Marsha Hunt) comes back with a small horde of supplies and nine women refugees who are fleeing the inexorable march of the Japanese. The nine women are horrified at first with the dreadful circumstances of the hospital, but start to settle into the soul-deadening routine. All except Pat, who rebels constantly, and has to be constantly reminded not to light cigarettes outside and ignore other regulations. Furthermore, Pat becomes infatuated with an officer (unseen but heard), who has a "friendly" relationship with Lt. Smith (Smitty). Pat is warned off by others, but continues with her flirtation in spite of continued hints to back away. We hear the officer on the phone with Smitty and they sound very much in love. It turns out the two of them are secretly married; however, it is against the rules for them to serve together. To top it off, Smitty is also dying of "malignant malaria," and there are not enough supplies of quinine to medicate both her and the troops, so she sacrifices herself. In the end, the Japanese arrive before the women can be evacuated. Lt. Holt, he of the disembodied voice, is killed and Pat is overtly downcast. Misunderstanding her misery, Smitty asks if she "can't take it" and one of the others says that Pat's "boyfriend" has been killed. Smitty puts on her wedding ring and reveals their marriage; Pat is horrified and tells her that Holt never gave her a second look. She hands Smitty a half-empty bottle of quinine, and they walk out with arms around each other to face the Japanese.

Well, at the very least, and it is the *very least,* it acknowledges that women were doing something, although they were treated as Hollywood treated women. That is, caring for the sick and dying, putting their lives on the line, and being captured by the enemy were of secondary importance, because everyone knows that for women, life centers around that more important sexual jealousy.

Two of the stars, Joan Blondell (Grace) and Ann Southern (Pat), were both better known for their musical and comedy roles. Blondell had many star-turns in '30s musicals such as *Gold Diggers of 1933,* while Southern had her recurring role as *Masie.* They proved themselves equally at home with dramatic parts. The entire cast was star-studded. Others in supporting roles were Heather Angel (her real name), an English import and another star of the '30s, and Fay Bainter, who played Captain Alice Marsh and was an Academy Award winner for her supporting role in *Jezebel* (1938). In the same year, she was also nominated for her starring role in *White Banners.* Bainter was the first, out of only 10 actors in the history of the Oscars, to be nominated for dual awards in the same year.

The Avoidance Tact(ic)

> "I have always felt if you give a star what is most becoming, even if the style may be new to her, with tact you can usually win out. Tact, that nice clean four-letter word, what an important part it plays in the life of a dress designer."[1]

In another role where she plays against her steely-spined type, Bette Davis is equally wonderful in my personal favorite, *Now, Voyager* (1942). No matter that it is almost as melodramatic as *East Lynne,* the movie ignores the war in favor of being absolutely the *je ne sais quoi* of romance.

Wearing clothes that make her look the contemporary of Grandma Moses, Davis (Charlotte Vale) begins the film as a dowdy, unattractive, spinster aunt whom everybody makes fun of, in particular her abusive mother (Gladys Cooper as Mrs. Henry Vale). After a nervous breakdown, Davis's psychiatrist (Claude Rains) sends her off to a sanitarium to be rehabilitated and is she ever! She comes back 20 pounds lighter and with a wardrobe that causes amazed gasps—the first scene of her return focuses first on her feet and legs in fashionable heels, and then slowly pans up the latest fashions to her face. After this transformation, in which she has suddenly discovered good taste—sleek, upswept and gowned to the gnat's eyebrow—she catches the eye of Jeremiah "Jerry" Durrance (Paul Henreid, who will play the husband of Ingrid Bergman in *Casablanca*). Although technically a married man, he is long estranged from his wife, whom he has not divorced for the sake of their daughter. He and Davis fall in love on a cruise, miss a return to their ship in a car crash, spend five days together and decide to part forever. You know what's coming.

Once home, Charlotte (Davis) defies her abusive mother, who is determined to resume her domination, telling her she refuses to go back to what she was before. Mom has a heart attack at this evidence of a backbone and dies. Feeling desperately guilty, Charlotte returns to the sanitarium where Jerry's twelve-year-old daughter just happens to be in residence for depression. Knowing what it is to be unloved, she takes little "Tina" under her wing and Tina blossoms. This leads to the scene where Tina, done up and dressed up as fashionably as Davis, descends Charlotte's stairs in her new look and asks Jerry, "Do you like me, Daddy?" He takes her in his arms, looks up at Charlotte over Tina's shoulder with a face full of agonized longing, and answers, "I love you." What female could help but swoon?

Voyager is the movie with the unforgettable and much parodied two-cigarette scene and the line about the moon and the stars—"Oh Jerry, don't let's ask for the moon. We have the stars." Yes, it probably is over the top, but who cares? We'll all take the moon and stars, too. The movie is replete with scenes like these. For example, Jerry meets Charlotte at an airport, kisses her passionately, then proceeds to kiss her equally passionately every time they open another door (who knew airports had so many doors). It's another of those melt the nitrate moments akin to one of the silent ones with John Gilbert and Greta Garbo.

The film is based on a 1941 novel by Olive Higgins Prouty, whose name conjures up visions of the spinster aunt played by Davis. Prouty was also the author of the 1922 *Stella Dallas,* another melodramatic tear-jerker. The *Now, Voyager* title was taken from a poem of Walt Whitman, *The Untold Want*—"Now, Voyager, sail thou forth, to seek and find"—which most probably refers to Charlotte's psychological metamorphosis from caterpillar to butterfly. I do not recall that there has ever been a movie which could have told us more of the story with clothing than this one. The novel and the film were considered groundbreaking for their exploration of psychotherapy and Davis's costumes punch the message home in perfect synchronization. Between the romance and Davis's wardrobe, I'm not sure how many in the audience noticed the psychotherapy motif. Other themes may have engaged their attention.

After her makeover, Davis's wardrobe designed by Orry-Kelly is, of course, gorgeous. The designer favored large hats with shady brims that gave a touch of mystery to their wearer and were most becoming on Davis. Tailored suits with wide shoulders, along with evening wear, made up the bulk of her wardrobe, accompanied with (or accessorized by) elegant upsweeps of Davis's hair. One of the few women who could wear this style with a regal poise, she moved through every scene as one would have expected of Queen Victoria. Never just a "pretty" face, her obvious strength of personality, plus her enormous eyes, made her a beauty. The film ignores the rigors of war entirely in favor of utter escapism. Unlike *Watch on the Rhine,* the chemistry between Davis and Henreid would be enough to take one's mind off a submarine rising in the third row of the theater.

Orry-Kelly (né Orry George Kelly, 1897–1964) was originally Australian. After studying art in his homeland, he sailed to New York to become an actor. Fate seemed to have other plans. He first got a job, painting murals in a nightclub, which led to employment as a title designer for Fox East Coast studio. In 1932 he moved on to Hollywood,

Bette Davis and Paul Henreid in one of those lighting-your-cigarette scenes in *Now, Voyager*. She wears one of Orry-Kelly's large, shady-brimmed hats which emphasizes those wonderful eyes (Warner Bros. promotional still, Wikimedia Commons).

getting jobs originally with Warner Bros/First National Studios, then making the rounds of Universal, RKO, again Fox, and MGM. Everywhere he went, he designed for the biggest female stars in Hollywood at the time. Besides Bette Davis, Katherine Hepburn, Ruth Chatterton, and a host of others, Kelly also designed for Ingrid Bergman in the iconic movie, *Casablanca* (1942).

Who can forget *Casablanca*? The war was simply a supporting character when set against the romance between Ilsa Lund (Ingrid Bergman) and Humphrey Bogart as Rick Blaine ("*Everybody comes to Rick's*"). Although influential, I don't know whether her Orry-Kelly ensembles, elegant and beautiful as they were, changed the course of fashion since the styles were already in vogue, but they certainly told a story of their own. When she is shown in her apartment in Rick's company, wearing a lounging robe, it told you all you needed to know about their relationship. Naturally, the war separates them, leaving him confused and nursing a broken heart.

When she shows up in Rick's bar wanting help getting her husband out of the country, just letting slip that she has been married all the time, it doesn't go well. She asks Rick's friend and pianist, Sam (played by Dooley Wilson), to play *As Time Goes By* and no, she does *not* say "Play it again, Sam." Rick rushes over to admonish Sam and when he sees Ilsa, *he* says "If she can take it, I can take it." The film even outdoes *Now, Voyager* in quotable quotes: "Round up the usual suspects"; "Louis [Claude Rains], I think this is the beginning of a beautiful friendship"; "Here's lookin' at you, kid"; etc. To continue, Rick thinks he has been played for a sucker by Ilsa, as she finds it hard to explain her inconvenient husband. She finally threatens him with a gun to get what she wants—and the truth comes out. At the end, reconciled and still in love, they renounce each other and he tells her she'll always regret it if she doesn't leave with her husband, Victor Laszlo (Paul Henreid, Davis's lover in *Now, Voyager*), "Maybe not today, maybe not tomorrow, but soon and for the rest of your life." He reassures her with, "We'll always have Paris." While these quotes have been repeated to the ridiculous point where they have lost their meanings, when they were new, they only added to the atmosphere of an almost perfect movie. In addition, it had an almost perfect cast, which included Sydney Greenstreet, Peter Lorre and the compelling German actor, Conrad Veidt, as Major Heinrich Strasser. Veidt had gotten his start as the mesmerizing somnambulist in *The Cabinet of Dr. Caligari* (1920). By the way, in an ironic touch, the Nazis sing "Die Wacht am Rhein" ("Watch on the Rhine," used as the title of Bette Davis's movie, already discussed), in Rick's bar, but are shouted down by the French singing "Le Marseilles."

The designer, again Orry-Kelly, once more uses his, nearly signature, large, wide-brimmed hats on Ingrid, along with the tailored wardrobe he employed most often. A happy choice for both women, neither of whom could have brought off anything in the way of frills.

Akin to *Now, Voyager*, in that it is a movie that eschews the war in favor of an off-beat romance, was *Gaslight* (1944) starring Ingrid Bergman. Although more a study of psychological suspense, there is plenty of romance even though secondary to the suspense. It wasn't known for quotable lines, but the title has permanently entered the English language long after its origin has been forgotten. Starring Bergman (as Paula Alquist) as a frightened wife being slowly and deliberately driven mad by her Machiavellian husband, Charles Boyer (as Gregory Anton), she is rescued by the always debonair Joseph Cotton (as Brian Cameron). Even though mention of any war never enters this picture set in the late Nineteenth century, World War II was at its height in 1944. It seems impossible to avoid seeing a more sinister meaning behind the hypnotic power of Boyer and the original helplessness of Bergman which grows into defiance once she has an ally. The film was adapted from the British playwright Patrick Hamilton's play of the same name (1938) and had been previously made in Britain in 1940. In the United Kingdom, the Bergman/Boyer version was retitled *The Murder in Thornton Square* to avoid confusion with the earlier film.

The costume designer for the movie, or costume supervisor as the credits designate her, was the one-named Irene. Although the film is set in the 1880s, in the midst of the Victorian era, Bergman's wardrobe is more tailored than the usual unrestrained Victorian designs seen in fashion plates from *Les Modes Parisiennes*. Nearly always in dark colors and modified bustles, her gowns have just a white neck ruffle or other device to relieve the overall dark—and undoubtedly symbolic—look.

Irene, the designer, started as a small-part actress and ingénue using her birth name, Irene Maud Lentz. Playing opposite comedians such as Ben Turpin, she worked for Mack Sennett in half-hour shorts like *The Daredevil* (1922). Unfortunate in love, she married the director of her first film, F. Richard Jones, who died in less than a year of tuberculosis. After his death, and still needing to support herself, Lentz opened a dress shop displaying many of her own designs. She came to the attention of the prestigious Bullocks Wilshire department store which asked her to design for their Ladies Custom

Ingrid Bergman (seated), Angela Lansbury, and Charles Boyer in the psychological suspense drama *Gaslight* (1944). Bergman's dark wardrobe suggests the menace of World War II without any overt reference (MGM Studios promotional still, Wikimedia Commons).

Salon. This exposure led, in turn, to attention from the studios and her future was made. She dropped the Lentz from her name and billed herself simply as "Irene" from 1933 on with her first film *Goldie Get Along*. Her career continued on an upward arc until her death in 1962.[2]

Let's Face the Music and Dance

On the other side of the coin from drama, in a reaction similar to that of the Depression, musicals resembling those first talkies of the late '20s were popular, i.e., a mélange of diverse performances tied to very little story. With a patriotic twist this time around, movies such as *Thank Your Lucky Stars* (1943), which sought to raise money for the war effort, crammed as many stars as possible into an almost plotless plot "starring" a painful-to-watch Eddie Cantor as he mugged outrageously, being even more painful in a double role. *Lucky Stars* even convinced Bette Davis into doing an excruciating rendition of "They're Either too Young or too Old" ("What's good is in the Army; what's left will never harm me"). In an equally excruciating performance, tough guy John Garfield crooned a romantic ballad. The fact that these stars were willing to make themselves look really silly, is a tribute to their patriotism and their generosity. It's hard to sit through today, because it looks as though the director coached the actors to look as hammy and uncomfortable as possible. The one bright light is a young and talented Dinah Shore who rose to even more heights of stardom on television ("See the USA, in your Chevrolet").

The "gowns" credit went to Milo Andersen, noted for his costume designs for Joan Crawford in *Mildred Pierce,* in which she gave an Oscar-winning performance and so did her wardrobe. Crawford, by the way, epitomized the broad-shouldered, aggressive, no-nonsense look of the '40s. In their hefty tome, *Creating the Illusion,* Jay Jacobsen and Donald L. Scoggins quote Crawford's own anecdote regarding her screen test for *Pierce* and the reaction of the director Michael Curtiz: "He said, 'I hate you.' He tore the dress off me. Thank God I had a bra on. He said, 'My God, they're hers!' Not these (pointing to her breasts). These! (pointing to her shoulders)." The director was reportedly embarrassed beyond words.[3]

Stage Door Canteen, directed by Frank Borzage, followed in the same year (1943) with an almost identical concept to *Thank Your Lucky Stars*—this time using virtual unknowns mingling with the glittering list of stars including (Dame) Judith Anderson and the renowned stage actress Katherine Cornell in her only film role. William Terry, in his first big role, is a young soldier on a pass in New York City, who visits the famous Stage Door Canteen. There, he meets a pretty hostess played by Cheryl Walker and romance grows. Newcomer Terry, born in 1914, had a short career and never really achieved stardom before his premature death at 48. Cheryl Walker, his newcomer co-star, had a more successful run as an actress, however, like Terry, never quite making it to stardom.

Known mainly as a stage tragedienne, Katherine Cornell was noted for turning down film offers, so it was a feather in Borzage's cap to win her for *Stage Door.* Amusingly enough, she did appear on television in an adaptation of probably her most famous part, that of Elizabeth Barrett Browning in *The Barretts of Wimpole Street,* and in Robert Sherwood's *There Shall Be No Night.* She was also the narrator, while not appearing, for the movie documentary [*Helen Keller*] *Her Story,* which won her an Oscar. Possibly television, being more spontaneous, as was the theatre, made her feel more at home.

The wardrobes were credited to Albert Deano, known mainly for costuming Lou Costello, of Abbott and Costello comedy fame (Who's on First?), and Donald O'Connor, as well as a fair number of "B" movies. Not really a designer, he amassed 24 credits for "wardrobe," and only three for costume designer. The *Stage Door* costumes consist mainly of military uniforms and aprons worn over undistinguished dresses, so Deano didn't have much opportunity to showcase his own designs. The garments on the famous may have been his (doubtful), but more likely, either from a general wardrobe supplier or from their own closets and their own designers.

Hollywood Canteen, following up in 1944 with the identical concept and practically the identical story, was made with slightly bigger stars interspersed with the *big* stars, and is actually pretty good. Robert Hutton as Corporal "Slim Green," is the young G.I. on a pass who visits the Hollywood version of the Stage Door Canteen, and Dane Clark is his oblivious buddy. The story gets even more fantastical when the G.I. meets Joan Leslie (the real Joan Leslie) and they immediately fall in love. A doubtful premise, and criticized for its improbability, *Hollywood Canteen* is, nevertheless, charming, feel-good, and probably gave a lot of soldier boys some hope. Milo Andersen again takes the credit for Jimmy's wardrobe, as he did for *Thank Your Lucky Stars.*

Resembling Jimmy Stewart in his tall, lanky, and self-effacing persona, Robert Hutton was another of those workmanlike actors who never quite make it to the top. Nevertheless, he had a career lasting over 40 years with 89 actor credits, as well as credits as producer, writer, and director.

In 1942, Bing Crosby and Fred Astaire sang and danced their way through the semi-patriotic and ingenious *Holiday Inn.* Filled with Irving Berlin's songs, even one from the First World War, "Oh, How I Hate to Get Up in the Morning," but including "Song of Freedom" and "Let's Say It with Firecrackers," as well. Remembered primarily for one thing, *Holiday Inn* also introduced the song that has become a holiday icon, "(I'm Dreaming of a) White Christmas." The movie is lighthearted, full of melody, and displays Crosby and Astaire at their best—it also contains possibly the most embarrassing and insulting blackface number in movie history; it's even worse than Al Jolson and that's saying a lot. Not only is it insulting to adults, it exploits two small children outrageously throughout the entire movie, but most especially in the blackface segment. Moreover, the movie features the intelligent and multi-talented Louise Beavers (she garnered an Oscar nomination for her portrayal of Delilah in *Imitation of Life*) doing a Stepin Fetchit [sic] routine that makes you want to weep ("Is You's Names Mamie?"). Delightful as the movie is in many respects, it is acutely discomfiting to watch. Nevertheless, it is a significant part of the allusion-to-the-war-without-showing-it genre.

In most of the above examples, with their skirting of any serious issues, people die or are killed, and you know more are going to die or be killed. However, with the more dramatic films, the action happens off-screen, as in *Watch on the Rhine* or *Casablanca.* In the musicals, the action *doesn't* happen with an unreal joviality, as in *Holiday Inn,* which is supposed to buoy up everyone's morale. In point of fact, as it did in the Great Depression, the unreality simply underscores the seriousness of the situation which people are facing. Although, with their avoidance tactics, these movies would have made the aforementioned Mr. Creel happy.

On some heartwarming occasions, the tables were turned and the actors, who portrayed servicemen on the screen, stepped off to bring the action of diversion to those who were seeing action of a different kind.

EIGHT

On the Home Front

Let Me Entertain You

To their everlasting credit, the stars who were, for one reason or another, not in the armed forces—over the age limit, female, or not classified 1A—were unstintingly generous with their time and talents at the Front. Under the auspices of the USO (United Service Organizations), stars went forth with considerable bravery to the hot spots on the globe where our service people were stationed.

Formed in 1941, the USO is a nonprofit organization which brought together six separate civilian service organizations: the Salvation Army; the YMCA (Young Men's Christian Association); the YWCA (Young Women's Christian Association); the National Catholic Community Service; the National Travelers Aid Association; and the National Jewish Welfare Board.

Their service actually began a bit before the United States entered the war—October 1941—with "camp shows." At first these stuck fairly close to home, e.g., touring the Caribbean, but by April 1942, 36 overseas units had been formed. Only one month after D-Day, camp shows were already in Normandy. Similar organizations were set up in Britain (ENSA; the Entertainment National Service Association), Canada (*The Army Show,* a review), and New Zealand (the Kiwi Concert Party).

The icon of icons in the entertainment travel regard was, of course, Bob Hope. He traveled so many miles to entertain the troops, wherever and whenever he could, that one fellow comic quipped that Hope was gone so much of the time that when he was home, his four children called him "Sir." He often traveled in company with his longtime friend, Bing Crosby, who nearly equaled Hope in mileage.[1] Naturally, they always had at least one beautiful girl—Dorothy Lamour, for instance, their companion on many of the *Road* pictures. Bob Hope was active from World War II to Desert Storm—50 years of that laughter for the benefit of three generations of servicemen and -women.

Not to downgrade Hope's contributions, nevertheless it would be good to remember that the secondary singers, dancers, and bands, who were much less heralded, were also putting their hearts and lives on the line to be part of the show, logging as many miles as the headliners.

In the Heat the Fans Come Out

Throughout the years between the wars, fan magazines had been just as active in promoting fashions worn by the stars, but went into overdrive with the advent of World

War II. Their aim was, certainly, to make a profit but, at the same time, they strove to provide reassurance, diversion, and yes, admittedly, a rosier version of war news than was realistic, in the hopes of keeping lonely families' metaphorical chins up.

The overall format was very little changed from the earlier issues, e.g., focusing on one star posed in a variety of ensembles. Occasionally, something new was added. In the July 1943 issue of *Photoplay*, rising starlet Janet Blair appears with a "reader-model" Virginia Symmes, in "Have a Good Time," which suggests to *Photoplay* readers, "Look as Smart as a Star While You're Having It." The blurb continues: "Janet Blair, who knows how to have fun, picks these play clothes with an eye for budget and an ear for applause, for reader-model Virginia Symmes, of Kew Gardens, New York." Ginny then wears the clothes—a half dozen leisure wear outfits: tee-shirt and shorts; "spectator" dresses; and blouse and slacks. One spectator dress example is a little puzzling. The caption says the "skirt unbuttons down the side to disclose well-tailored shorts." What, then, does one do with the skirt? Toss it away? Leave it hanging? A second example partially answers the question: "...when you shed the charming full skirt, you'll be cool as a breeze in trim shorts." The price is $8.00 and the *smallest* size is a 10.

One coy advertisement depicts a nervous young woman being appraised by two G.I.s, and asks: "Should an unmarried girl go *alone* to an Army camp?" The ad turns out to be pushing underarm deodorant—*Etiquet*. We don't find out whether she should or shouldn't, but we do know she needn't worry for one to three days.

The July 1943 issue also emphasized the number of stars in the services. Among others: a full-page photo of John Payne in Army Air Force uniform; an article by Brenda Marshall about her loneliness since hubby, William Holden, has been away; and Alan Ladd in uniform talking about his devotion to his wife, Sue Carol Ladd (they *were* devoted). Humphrey Bogart, too old for the service, sees fictional *Action in the North Atlantic,* along with Alan Hale and Raymond Massey (also too old). Top lady stars give sugary tips on how to entertain servicemen. And, for the folks at home, comfort is assured with the use of "Unguentine Rectal Cones," "Dr. Scholl's Kurotex" foot relief, and "Dermoil" for their psoriasis.

Rather jarringly, the 1943 issues featured a continuing series of articles called "What Should I Do? Your Problems Answered by Bette Davis." Considering the continuing series of newsworthy exploits headlining Ms. Davis, this seems like satire but was presented quite seriously. Those dealing with the most common problems were printed in the magazine—with names changed for privacy purposes. For skeptics, the claim was made that Ms. Davis read every word and answered personally. Count this author with the skeptics. The letters did, nonetheless, provide a sort of (comedy) relief from war news.

(Mis)information, Please

> "The essence of propaganda consists in winning people over to an idea so sincerely, so vitally, that in the end they succumb to it utterly and can never again escape from it."
>
> —Joseph Goebbels, Nazi Minister of Propaganda

Keeping the civilian population happy and confident, in the face of what they could see for themselves, took a government tightrope walk. Movies were not the only pervasive influence on either attitudes or fashion, as we saw in World War I. Patriotic posters again played their part in more than just promoting styles or reminding the home front that they needed to support the war effort. They served a larger purpose than met the eye where either patriotism or fashion were concerned. Marching along in

Bill Mauldin's 1944 editorial cartoon depicting weary and disaffected G.I. Joes. They saw the war as it was, thus offending the brass who wanted to cover up the *real* war (Wikimedia Commons).

lockstep with them like a unit of infantry were the advertisers, the filmmakers, the animators and radio.

Advertisers hit the theme of patriotism hard and often, launching all-out promotions for war bonds, lauding efficiency among factory workers, quashing rumors, and above all, keeping morale at a high level. Some of the claims bordered on the ridiculous: Lucky Strike cigarettes boasted that changing the color of their packaging from green to white saved bronze for armament. Coca-Cola (and other soda manufacturers), not to be outdone, implied that defense workers and members of the armed forces performed at a higher level because of soda pop.

Little Orphan Annie, Terry and the Pirates, and other comic strips frequently included war themes in their stories. Drawn by Milton Caniff, *Terry,* for example, a teenager at the inception of the strip in 1934, grows up, becoming more and more rugged as he goes along, and becomes a United States Army pilot during the war. After the war, *Terry* continues in the service and, in his last appearance in 1973, is an Air Force officer helping to break up a heroin smuggling ring. *Superman*, of course, was, and still is, always fighting for "truth, justice, and the American way," and *Annie,* along with her adopted father, Daddy Warbucks, reflected contemporary wartime events.

A different, world-weary, voice came from the two-time Pulitzer Prize–winning Bill Mauldin's more downbeat approach. The cartoons were not universally accepted, and were not syndicated until 1944, only after being praised by the celebrated war correspondent, Ernie Pyle. Pyle, also a Pulitzer Prize winner, lost his own life at the battle of Okinawa. Mauldin's main characters, Willie and Joe, were tired, unshaven infantrymen, who saw no glamor in war, simply soul-deadening routine. Just the opposite face that the government wanted to put on the war, since it put the lie to the uplifting effect the government was trying to generate. Mauldin's captions were always ironic, sardonic, and sarcastic, and gave the top brass fits.

Serving with the 45th Infantry Division, Mauldin worked with the unit's newspaper creating the Willie and Joe characters. In 1944, he was transferred to the Army's newspaper, *Stars and Stripes.* Supported by the War Office by then, but still much criticized by several officers, he had his own jeep and traveled the Front looking for material for his cartoon. General George Patton, who was among the most important officers who were offended, called Mauldin an "unpatriotic anarchist," wanting to "throw his ass in jail" and ban the *Stars and Stripes* magazine. Only the intervention of General Eisenhower saved both the publication and Mauldin's weary G.I.s.

Radio, animation, and leaflets dropped over Allied as well as enemy territory, all played their persuasive roles in the propaganda barrage. Radio, unfortunately, could take a more sinister side.

"Axis Sally"

"Sally" was possibly two people, Mildred Gillars and/or Rita Zucca, an Italian American, who broadcast from Rome using the name Sally, and the two are frequently confused.

A restless sort, Gillars was working with the German State Radio (Reichs-Rundfunk-Gesellschaft) after moving to Dresden in 1934. She became engaged to a naturalized German citizen, who refused to marry her if she returned to the States; however, she did not leave even after he was killed in action. Coming under the influence of Max Otto Koischwitz, her previously apolitical broadcasts turned to the dark, earning her the nickname of "Axis Sally." When she was captured at the end of the war, she had the dubious honor of being the first woman to be charged with treason. Sentenced to 10 to 30 years in prison, she served her sentence from 1949 to 1961.

Zucca was an American-born daughter of a successful restauranteur and was sent to Florence as a teenager to attend a convent school. In 1938, at the age of 26, she returned to Italy and took a job as a typist, renouncing her American citizenship at the same time. In 1943, the Mussolini Facisti hired Zucca as a broadcaster in the style of Mildred Gillars. Paired with a German broadcaster, she performed in the program "Jerry's Front Calling," also calling herself Sally. Zucca's programs were always more damning than Gillars, but attempts by the United States to prosecute her after the war were frustrated by the fact that she had renounced her citizenship. An Italian military tribunal then brought charges of collaboration against her, and she was sentenced to four and a half years in prison, but only served nine months of the sentence. In 1946, the Italian government offered general amnesty for all collaborators; nevertheless, she was barred for life from entering the United States.

"Tokyo Rose"

A Japanese-American citizen who had been trapped in Japan after the Pearl Harbor attack, Iva Toguri (aka "Tokyo Rose"), was also convicted of treason and served six years of a 10-year sentence before being released and returning to private life.

Because she had no way to leave Japan when the war began, Iva's position there was precarious. Always maintaining her innocence, her story was that the Japanese had tried to force her to renounce her United States citizenship and swear allegiance to Japan. When she refused, she was classified as an enemy alien and monitored. Moving to Tokyo, she met an Australian major who wanted to use her as a sort of comedy radio announcer. Occasionally warning the audience that the show was complete propaganda, she performed on "Zero Hour" as Orphan Ann starting in 1943. Extant recordings and transcripts of her programs demonstrate that she never threatened Allied troops or suggested their wives were carrying on with someone else.

By the end of the war, Toguri had married a Portuguese-Japanese man named Filipe D'Aquino with the expectation of returning home. Money was tight, however, and she accepted an invitation from two American reporters to tell her story. At first, things seemed to go well, and a government investigation deemed her broadcasts harmless entertainment. Nevertheless, at the constant urging from the broadcast journalist Walter Winchell, who never missed an opportunity to ruin a reputation if he possibly could, she was rearrested and charged with eight counts of treason. Found guilty, she received a 10-year sentence. On January 19, 1977, she was granted a presidential pardon by Gerald Ford, exonerated of treason and had her citizenship restored.

Toguri was not the only "Rose" who rode the airways. Servicemen used the same nickname for several women who read propaganda, some with far more menace.

The Other's Side: We Have Allies

However, in service of this discussion it is also necessary to take the same look, as in World War I, at how others where wartime restrictions were more stringent—friends and foes alike—treated similar issues. Were either the ends or the methods the same?

Mais oui, nous sommes Françaises

Due to the German occupation of Paris, filmmaking in France during World War II was extremely difficult. The best-known, as well as most well-received, movie to come out of occupied France was Marcel Carne's *Les Enfants du Paradis (The Children of Paradise)*. Or alternatively titled, *The Children of the Gods*. The title is actually a pun. *Paradis* refers to the second balcony in a theatre where the common folk sat and who were sarcastically nicknamed "the Gods." However, this movie, although made during the war, was not released until 1945. Running nearly three hours and told in two parts, the historical romance was set in 1828 and tells the story of a beautiful courtesan, Garance, and her four lovers (naturally, it's a French movie, after all), a mime, an actor, a criminal and an aristocrat. The three hours are divided into Part One, *Boulevard du Crime* (*Boulevard of Crime*) which begins around 1827, and Part Two, *L'Homme Blanc (The Man in White)* which takes place about seven years later. The "Boulevard of Crime" was the nickname of the Boulevard du Temple, so-called because of the number of blood-soaked melodramas staged there. With its epic scope, the film has been compared to *Gone with the Wind* (1939).

The characters of Garance's lovers are cleverly based on genuine historic figures: Baptiste Debureau, a famous mime; Frédérick Lemaître, a famous actor; Pierre Lacenaire, an infamous criminal; and the Comte Ėdouard de Montray, a fictitious character based on the Duc de Morny. The writer, Jacques Prévert, had to be virtually bribed to write the scenario, owing to his purported detestation of mimes. However, when he conceived of the inclusion of the criminal, Lacenaire, who fascinated him, Prévert was inspired. This was a bit of subversion on his part, because the Germans disapproved of celebrating "criminals"—any but themselves, that is. It is impossible to prove whether the film was sly propaganda or art for art's sake. Because the movie was not released until immediately after the war, it is futile to guess.

Designed by Mayo (real name, Antoine Malliarakis), the costumes frequently borrow from the *Commedia dell'arte* (e.g., Pantalone). Full-skirted and nip-waisted, the beautiful women's gowns are lush, sensual, and romantic, displaying no concession to lack of wartime materials. Over the course of a 20-year career in movies, Mayo was also known for production design for the New Wave success *Hiroshima Mon Amour* (1959), which has been considered one of the most influential movies of that movement. Shocking for its time, that story was of the affair between a Caucasian woman and a real Japanese man, rather than just another Caucasian in "yellow face." In the '60s, the exceptionally talented Mayo left film, moving to Rome to concentrate on his studio art, a decision which evolved into a good living.

With a Stiff Upper Lip

Devasted by the "Blitz," British films of the 1940s frequently employed bucolic English country scenes to ease wartime tensions in movies such as *The Tawny Pipit* (1944) and *A Canterbury Tale* (1944).

Tawny Pipit is a sentimental tale of the response of an English village to the discovery of a pair of rarely seen, nesting tawny pipits. The discoverers are a fighter pilot just released from the hospital and his erstwhile nurse, now his girlfriend, who are on a country walking tour. When they report their find to the locals, the villagers respond with enthusiasm and collaborate to protect the eggs. A plot by an unscrupulous dealer to steal the eggs is foiled and they hatch unmolested. The villagers are overjoyed at their success and that of the pipits.

The charming story is symbolic of the average Englishman's devotion to his/her country, and unity against a common threat. It was not shown in the United States until 1947, after the threat was over, but was still an instant success due to its "Englishness."[2]

A Canterbury Tale (1944) is a rom-com/mystery which obviously borrows its title from Chaucer. Its engaging story has been described as a combination of British realism combined with cinematographer Erwin Hiller's brand of German Expressionism. *Tale* centers around three young people—a British Army sergeant (Dennis Price as Sgt. Peter Gibbs), a Land Girl, Miss Alison Smith (Sheila Sim), and United States Army Sergeant Bob Johnson (who was an actual Army sergeant, Sgt. John Sweet). All three stars were unknowns before the film. There is also a narrator, Esmond Knight, who reads an extract from *Canterbury Tales* and a Chaucerian-style piece.

The three are thrown together by circumstance: Peter is arriving to take his place at his new assignment; Alison is about to start work at a nearby farm; and Bob has gotten off the train by mistake thinking he was in Canterbury, his destination. They chat and leave the station together when suddenly a mystery man in uniform attacks Alison and pours glue in her hair. They find out that this has become a regular incident in the town and decide to investigate. Their investigations lead them to a gentleman farmer, Thomas Colpeper (the veteran actor, Eric Portman). They discover that his motive is to keep servicemen from the distractions of women and keep women faithful to their men. When the trio get to Canterbury, they are "blessed" with good luck: Alison finds out the boyfriend she had thought killed is alive; his father, who had been reluctant, gives his blessing on their marriage; Bob finally gets a letter from his sweetheart, whom he thought had failed to write; and in something of an anti-climax, Peter, who had been a cinema organist, is allowed to play the organ at Canterbury Cathedral. Colpeper, the sticky wicked (pun intended), gets off scot free. This may be a "happy ending," nevertheless the message here is dismaying. The movie was not released in the United States until after the war, when Raymond Massey was added as the narrator and Kim Hunter was added as Bob Johnson's girlfriend. However, not all the English version was included in the American version when it was first released in the States—the original version ran 124 minutes and was cut to 95 minutes for the U.S. A modest success when released, the film has been fully restored to its original length and is now considered a "masterwork."

One of the most English of "English" films was actually an American production directed by Mervyn LeRoy taken from a novel by the English author James Hilton, *Random Harvest* (1942). A romantic tearjerker, the movie starred the genuinely British actors, Greer Garson and Ronald Colman (two of the most beautiful people in films), as star-crossed lovers. Set in 1918, it hints at the ongoing war in Europe by only referencing World War I. Colman plays a shell-shocked, amnesiac soldier who had been gassed in the trenches and confined to an asylum. After the armistice, Colman ("John Smith") simply wanders away and encounters Paula Ridgeway (Garson), who manages a traveling group of performers. They fall in love and are married, even though "Smithy," as she calls him, never regains his memory.

Smith goes to Liverpool for a job interview, where he is immediately struck by a taxi, wakes up in the hospital, and remembers all his early life but not Garson—he is now aware that he is Charles Rainier. His brother's stepdaughter (the tragic Susan

Peters) becomes infatuated with him and he proposes.[3] However, it becomes evident that he loves someone else and she calls off the engagement. In the meantime, Paula has seen his picture in the papers and gets a job as his assistant, using another name. Not even that jogs his memory, nevertheless, he comes to admire her and proposes (for the second time). She accepts, feeling that a business proposition is better than

Greer Garson and Ronald Colman in a Japanese publicity poster for *Random Harvest* (1944). A hint of the tweedy Mr. Colman and the gorgeously elegant Ms. Garson (Wikimedia Commons).

nothing. Uncertain about her acceptance, she decides to go abroad without him to clear her head. Nevertheless, shortly before the liner sails, she goes back to the village where they had lived when he was "Smithy." By filmic coincidence, Charles is summoned to the same village to mediate a strike, and while wandering through the village, his memories start to resurface. Paula (now Margaret), hurries to the cottage and finds Charles outside the door. He recognizes her; they rush to each other and fall into each other's arms. It sounds corny when recited but played by Garson and Colman, two exceptionally convincing actors, it causes a real emotional response.[4] Oddly, all things considered, the movie seemed to be very popular in Japan, if a Japanese poster advertising the film can be believed.

The costume designs are credited to Robert Kalloch, who had started with Columbia Pictures in the '30s. Ronald Colman is generally tweedy throughout the movie with the exception of his soldier's uniform and one appearance in formal white tie and tails. However, Garson is never less than elegant and beautifully turned-out, even in her very short-skirted costume as a show girl (her legs aren't too bad, either). She seems to have an endless wardrobe of enviable fashions, even in the cottage. In one scene she wears a large-brimmed hat similar to an Orry-Kelly design. In this instance, it is pushed back farther on her head, framing her exquisite face. With it, she wears a dark suit, relieved with a triple-notched collar of a sheer material. From catalog illustrations, such as Sears, and street photographs of the period, one can see that this tailored look was certainly popular with the ladies of the viewing public.

Prior to his movie career, Kalloch had worked as a sketch artist for the designer, Lucile, where he had designed gowns for the ballroom dancer, Irene Castle (Castle, during World War I, was considered *the* fashion maven of fashion mavens, and had elevated ballroom dancing to not only respectable, but elegant). Staying with Columbia until 1941, Kalloch then moved to MGM for only two years, before retiring from studio work. After that he did only occasional freelance commissions. Suffering from chronic ill health, he died in 1947 at only 54, with a filmography of 152 movies to his credit.

The cinematography of *Harvest* is beautiful, the stars are beautiful, the clothes are beautiful, the story is incredibly romantic, and it's from a great novel. Altogether, it's irresistible.

For propaganda purposes, even when the stories are set against war as a backdrop, the atmosphere is one of "Keep calm and carry on," with a happy ending to round everything out.

The efforts of the British people themselves were celebrated in another American-made movie, *Mrs. Miniver* (1942), starring Greer Garson and Walter Pidgeon, who portrayed a comfortable middle-class housewife and her husband, now facing the reality of war. They have lived well, have three well-behaved children (one at Oxford), a cook and a maid, and a dock on the Thames with a boat.

The oldest son, Vin (Richard Ney), has fallen in love with the local aristocrat's granddaughter, Carol (Teresa Wright). He proposes to her and she accepts; however, he feels he must do his part in the war and enlists in the Royal Air Force, succeeding as a pilot. Kay (Garson) discovers a wounded German soldier in her garden, he demands food and a coat at gunpoint, then he collapses. She disarms him with aplomb and calls the police. Vin and Carol marry in spite of their youth and over the protests of her grandmother. They are determined to have as much life together as is possible with death facing Vin in the skies. The family drives Vin to join his squadron, and on the way

Kerrybrook suits shown in *Sears Catalog* for Fall 1943. Sears' own brand, these sold from $9.98 to a whopping $16.98 depending on fabric quality and are just as stylish today (courtesy Dover Publications).

home they can see RAF and Luftwaffe planes in a dogfight. A German plane crashes, but Carol is wounded by stray machine-gun fire and dies just after they reach home. Kay is broken-hearted, and Vin cannot fathom the irony of his being the survivor and Carol the victim. At her funeral, the vicar gives a sermon so powerful that President Franklin Roosevelt had it printed in several languages and dropped as leaflets over enemy and occupied territory. It resonated just as powerfully in Germany, prompting Joseph Goebbels, the Propaganda Minister, to write:

> [Mrs. Miniver] shows the destiny of a family during the current war, and its refined powerful propagandistic tendency has up to now only been dreamed of. There is not a single angry word spoken against Germany; nevertheless, the anti-German tendency is perfectly accomplished.

The prolific, and supremely talented, Robert Kalloch is again credited with Ms. Garson's wardrobe, and again, she is beautifully tailored, impeccably turned out, and unflappably gorgeous. In one publicity shot for the movie, Garson wears a Kalloch design consisting of a full-sleeved day dress, with a vee neckline, embroidery on the blousy sleeves—caught with a tight cuff at the wrist—a large button at the closure of the vee and slim skirt. She is posed with Walter Pidgeon and Teresa Wright, who wears another Kalloch design displaying an uncollared bodice, large button closure which folds over to the left shoulder, and three-quarter length sleeves above a gathered skirt.

Gile Steele, no slouch as a designer in his own right, is responsible for the men's wardrobes. Sadly, his career was cut short when he died suddenly at 43.

Mrs. Miniver has been called silly, artificial, and stilted by several of today's critics, but that is because we cannot recapture the time period, or even imagine the daily horror of the Blitz, and the need of the British to see themselves as stalwart in the face of the unimaginable. If even the urbane, and upper class, Franklin Delano Roosevelt, a member of America's royal family, was impressed, who are we to disdain?

Britain also made good use of radio as a medium for propaganda. Winston Churchill was the force behind the creation of the British Political Warfare Executive (PWE) in 1941, the object of which was to broadcast propaganda to lower enemy morale. These were German language broadcasts set out from more than 40 false German radio stations, which ironically, employed powerful American transmitters. Along with radio, the PWE dropped postcards and leaflets behind enemy lines, as did the United States.

The Other's Side: And Then There Were Foes

During World War II, the German film industry was under the control of the Propaganda Minister, Joseph Goebbels. Beginning in 1940, movies with a militaristic theme made a small intrusion in the list of dramas, historical, crime, or comedy films. However, short propaganda documentaries were already popular. Some displayed aircraft, weaponry, or tanks with smug self-congratulation. Others were more sinister in tone, such as *The Eternal Jew,* which depicts the Jews as depraved, degenerate and abnormal. Manipulative and uncivilized, the Jews supposedly conducted depraved religious rituals, preyed parasitically on the "superior" Germans, and so on. One has to wonder, if the Jews were able to accomplish this so easily, how superior could the Germans have been?

In a fascinating twist, Hitler was a devoted fan of Fritz Lang, the director of *Metropolis,* evidently because he saw it as a parable of his own life. A peculiar delusion, because it depicted the overthrow of fascism and totalitarianism which Hitler must have taken to refer to the Kaiser. Hitler presumably identified with the hero, who is not subsumed into the faceless masses, but offers freedom and equality. Lang later said Goebbels had told him (Lang) that Hitler exclaimed, "Here is a man who will give us great Nazi films."[5] Lang, whose mother was Jewish, hated everything that Hitler stood for and fled for his life to America, taking his great films with him.

Hitler found his "great Nazi" filmmaker in Leni Riefenstahl and her *Triumph des Willens* (*Triumph of the Will,* 1934/35). Riefenstahl co-wrote, produced, directed, and edited this unabashed hagiography of the already murderous chancellor. An outstanding director, and genuinely talented filmmaker, she used marvelous technical innovation to make probably the greatest propaganda film of all time. Her use of moving cameras, aerial photography, long-focus lenses, along with stirring music and genius cinematography, combined to make it a symphony of what we now see as horror. Hitler, carefully edited to seem a giant figure and supported by shots of the roaring crowd, gives the performance of his life, starring himself. Surrounded by bemedaled and ornately uniformed subordinates, he wears a plain, unadorned uniform decorated with only the Iron Cross, awarded him from his service in World War I. A man of the people, never mind that a few of those people were missing since they had already been murdered on the Night of the Long Knives.[6] It would appear from the style of the film that Riefenstahl may have been heavily influenced by the "City" films of the Silent era. She had previously used a similar style for her first propaganda film *Der Sieg des Glaubens* (*The Victory of Faith,* 1933).

The "City Symphony" was a popular genre during the Silent era—the most representative of which would probably be *Berlin: die Sinfonie der Grosstadt* (*Berlin: Symphony of a Great City,* 1927). The movie, although silent, is arranged to simulate the movements of an orchestral piece. Beginning with a calm sunrise, the tempo slowly accelerates along with the arrival of a train which proceeds into the city as it gradually wakes up. We see a piece of paper blowing in the empty street, then a slight speed-up of the tempo as people start to fill the streets with activity: streetcars, trains, workers heading for factories where machinery starts to whirl and produce. We go from andante to almost allegro. This is the end of the first movement.

The second movement focuses on the activities of the workers in all fields, typists, telephone operators, machinists, dogs fighting in the streets—all building to a crescendo. Generally speaking, there is scarcely a hint of high fashion, the inhabitants are clothed in the most ordinary of attire—shapeless dresses and bowler hats.

The third and fourth movements continue in this vein, whipping the tempo up into a frenzy with newspaper headlines spouting "Mord" (Murder), "Krise" (Crisis), and especially "Gelt" (Gold), until the frenzy begins to subside and night falls. Early on, we do see mannequins in a shop window but, by day, they are as anonymous as the crowds until the evening when they reveal more upscale gowns. Occasionally, a touch of couture is glimpsed, and we even see a style show. The up tempo seems to bring out the *bon ton* and we have more fashion; a lot of militarism; and girls, a la *Cabaret.* The final moments concentrate on these people at night, ending with the spin of a roulette wheel and the spin of the city.

Also a propaganda film, well before the rise of Hitler and his minions, it portrays the "Great City" of its title with love, but with a realistic eye, as well. Unlike Riefenstahl, it doesn't manipulate the truth just to paint a pretty picture—the grimmer sides of city life are portrayed unsparingly—intimations of lust, murder, poverty, longing, all take place under the eye of the camera.

Germany's suppressed militarism was not a new phenomenon between the defeat of the Kaiser and the rise of Hitler. The suggestions were already there in film straight through the Silent era. A case in point is *The Haunted Castle* (*Schloss Vogelöd,* 1921). The English title gave the impression that one was going to see an outright horror movie. The actuality could not have been more different. The "haunting" is all psychological—locked in the hearts of the protagonists, who each hide a secret which governs their behavior. The action of the characters, in their rigid isolation even when together, reveals their inner torment, and their wardrobes provide a chilling hint of what is to come. Chilling is the right word—the sets, with their obviously faux painted doors and architectural elements, the ambiance, the behavior of the inhabitants—all are as icy as a wind from the North. The Expressionistic treatment and deliberate pace only add to the overall chill.

Much of the time, the women wear severely masculine apparel, e.g., men's shirts and ties, with militaristic overtones or dark dresses only relieved by white collars. Only occasionally do they break free of the somber mood, most often in flashback. The men are buttoned up in suits or in hunting dress very similar to Army uniforms. One slightly comic character, a visitor to the *Schloss,* wears a pair of pajamas so like a fancy-dress military uniform that he appears to have fallen into bed straight from a review of the troops.

A melodramatic gem which sustains its icy atmosphere throughout, *Haunted Castle's* scarcely repressed resentment echoes that of the German populace and is apparent in hindsight. There is just a flash of sardonic/ironic humor in the final scene, like a touch of O. Henry or Jonathan Swift, capping the film off beautifully.[7]

To underscore my point, in his pessimistic study, *From Caligari to Hitler: A Psychological History of the German Film,* Siegfried Kracauer looked back from 1947 saying, "I told you so." A Jew who had to flee Germany with the rise of Hitler, Kracauer had been a prominent film critic in Germany until then. In exile, he pointed out that all the earmarks were there for the rest of the heedless world to discern. While he may have overstated a bit, on the whole, his assessment is persuasive. It must be remembered, nonetheless, that while he is not wrong—the signs were there—Kracauer is assessing the past through the filter of his own rage. Not all German filmmakers were simmering under the strictures of Allied reprisals. Nor were all bent on vengeance to the point that their product was continually affected.

Nonetheless, these subtle but noticeable hints in German movies which Kracauer discussed must have acted as subliminal propaganda, preparing the German psyche for the appearance of a charismatic demagogue like Hitler to prey on that resentment and set the stage for conflagration.

Nine

Keep Me Posted

World War II War Posters

> "...we here highly resolve that these dead shall not have died in vain.... REMEMBER DECEMBER 7th!"
>
> —World War II poster commemorating Pearl Harbor

Propaganda posters in support of the military began appearing even before the war. Rumblings of the coming conflict had been felt for some time and recruiters were already calling for young men to join up. An exceptionally attractive 1938 poster for the United States Army pictured Lady Liberty holding high a laurel wreath before a billowing American flag. Below, a receding wedge of fighting men going all the way back to the Revolution face toward an unseen enemy with bayoneted rifles held at the ready over their shoulders. A similar billowing flag is clutched in the hands of Uncle Sam who points his finger sternly at us, like God giving life to Adam, as he strides through the clouds below a convoy of bombers and above a contingent of charging Yanks. The work is undated, but it seems to be early in the war, because the fighters are still wearing World War I helmets and carrying out-of-date rifles. The bombers, however, look like B-17s. Large capital letters order "BUY WAR BONDS."

A poster for Westinghouse was the basis for the unforgettable *Rosie the Riveter* image, which has become the most recognizable icon, next to the raising of the flag on Iwo Jima, of World War II. The Westinghouse poster is titled "We Can Do It" and depicts the defiant pose of a strong young woman rolling up her sleeve and flexing her muscle.

The model for the image had several claimants: Geraldine Hoff (Doyle, 1924–2010) who was later dismissed as the model; Mary Doyle (Keefe, 1926–2015) who has been much disputed; or Naomi Parker (Fraley, 1921–2018), all of whom were touted as the possible inspiration taken from factory photographs. Mary Doyle had a very brief career as a factory worker owing to her fear of injury to her hands. As a cellist, she knew this was a well-founded possibility and it led to her leaving the factory after only two or three weeks. In her youthful photographs, there is a distinct resemblance to the woman in the poster, including the definitive cleft in her chin.[1] The final claimant to the original "Rosie the Riveter" title was Naomi Parker, whose photograph operating a piece of heavy machinery has also been the basis for her assertion. Unfortunately, she is only seen in profile and not full-face, so determination of a resemblance is more uncertain, however she is wearing the same bandanna as the poster girl. Parker (or Fraley after her marriage) spent her life trying to substantiate her claim. Although the dispute has never been fully resolved, with supporters on both sides still carrying on the rivalry, Parker's January 2018 obituary awards her the crown.[2]

A possible outgrowth of the bandanna fad, as well as another way to keep one's hair out of the machinery, was the snood. Considered a more stylish way to confine one's coiffure than the tied-up bandanna, the World War II version rapidly moved from the factory to the office, dinner-club, and theater; it was advertised by even well-known designers such as Lily Daché, the prestigious hat designer. Consisting of a band that could be tied over the top of the head a la the bandanna, or simply slipped over, it also boasted a draped sack-like section attached at the bottom into which the ends of the hair were tucked. This section was more often crochet or net but fabric on occasion. A rolled pompadour frequently completed this ensemble.

J. Howard Miller's inspiration for Rosie the Riveter. Several women claimed to be the model for the image; however, the real Rosie is still in doubt (War Production Board, National Archives).

Snoods were actually quite attractive, as glamorous as you might want when you wanted, and disguised a really bad hair day with style. While the turban-tied bandanna spoke of utility, the snood hinted at nights at the Ritz.

The snood already possessed a long history—the first mention of the word was seen before the Twelfth century in reference to a band (or fillet) for women's hair. Since then, the name has been applied to various articles of head and neck-wear—male snoods, worn over the face to keep beards and moustaches under control, particularly in the food industry; doggy snoods to keep the little pooches warm; and tubular scarves similar to infinity scarves, which sit high on the neck and can also act as hoods. In the end, however, it's the '40s image that comes to mind in connection with the name.

For the Seventh War Loan, the already iconic image of the Iwo Jima flag-raising on Mount Suribachi was the chosen image on a poster entitled "Now—All Together." The speed with which this poignant image became the *leitmotiv* for the war was astonishing.[3] Especially because the photograph was not taken until February 1945, although published in the newspapers two days after taking. This was only five months before the end of the war. Moreover, by the publication date of C.C. Beall's poster version in May 1945, the war was over in Europe, and victory was at least in sight for the Pacific theater. Nevertheless, the end was still uncertain, because the Japanese were determined to fight on to the last man. Beall's images seemed to do the trick for the Seventh War Loan, because it raised over $156,000,000,000.[4]

Racism was rampant during the war, with hostility toward people of color, be they Asian,[5] Hispanic, or African American, and was demonstrated time and again. Oddly, however, it was just a little easier in the armed forces than at home—not much, but a little. In one instance, African Americans in the Air Force had to fight to be pilots against the prevailing opinion that they were less coordinated (!). When they won out, they were then forced to do more than the Caucasians. Rather than flying 50 combat missions, e. g., they were required to fly seventy-five, a punishing amount. Nevertheless, their performances proved their abilities, especially among the Tuskegee Airmen. Finding posters celebrating their achievements, however, was not easy. One of the few, but an excellent example, shows us a half-length pilot who faces us, with his hands wrapped around his parachute straps, as he looks to the sky. His goggles are pushed back from his forehead for a clear vision. Captioned "Keep Us Flying!" it reaches out to all to "Buy War Bonds." In fact, the Tuskegee Airmen get most of the poster glory, while images of the heavyweight boxing champion, Joe Louis, are exceptions to the racism rule.

Powerful image of a Tuskegee Airman—probably Lt. Robert W. Diez (1943). The lieutenant is a perfect model for a War Bond appeal (National Archives).

Seemingly unconscious sexism was rampant, as well.[6] Depicted on a 1941 Royal Canadian Air Force poster, a woman in a well-fitted uniform with sergeant's stripes stands out in front of a line of airmen in flight clothes. The title states with evidently no sense of self-parody: "*She* Serves That *Men* May Fly" (emphasis mine). No mention is made of the fact that *she* might possibly be a test pilot, an aircraft ferrywoman, or an instructor of other pilots, herself.

Yes, women freed men for combat, but only by putting their own time in the air as a Women Airforce Service Pilot (WASP) or in the Royal Canadian Air Force Women's Division (RCAF).

In the United States, these intrepid ladies were not an official branch of the military but federal civil service employees who performed all the above duties. The idea for a women's branch was the concept of two skilled pilots—Nancy Harkness Love, the youngest American woman to earn a license, and Jackie Cochran, an accomplished pilot who had already flown a lend-lease bomber to England to prove that the idea was sound. In September 1942, the idea became reality with more than two dozen

She **might also serve by being a pilot herself. No mention of the women who tested planes, ferried planes, or instructed other pilots (Ted Harris, McGill University Special Collections).**

female pilots reporting for training. At first, it was just at New Castle Army Air Base in Delaware, but another program was established in Houston at Howard Hughes Airport. The programs merged in 1943 with Jackie Cochran as director. At least 25,000 women applied, and about 10 percent were accepted (there were rigorous physical requirements).

The female pilots dressed exactly as did the men in most cases: for high altitude, fleece-lined jackets, caps with goggles, trousers and heavy gloves (with a chic parachute); for every-day wear, waist-length jackets ("Eisenhower" jackets) with matching trousers; and for dress, a fitted jacket with a belt, matching skirt and beret. WASPS were the only women to wear berets.

When I said garbed exactly as the men, I meant it literally in many instances. Just as in World War I, for mechanic work, e.g., they were issued men's coveralls (nicknamed "zoot suits") in size "small"—this was a 44 long—and were forced to roll up the sleeves and pants. The same was true for open cockpit or cold weather flying, the leather suits and/or fleece-lined jackets came in men's sizes only.

Philip Zec, *Daily Mirror* cartoonist (1941) and noted socialist. His poster closely models Russian Marxist style (Wikimedia Commons).

Otherwise, their various uniforms were styled and sized for women. To show how times have changed only on the surface, this situation has still prevailed with female astronauts—space suits, which need to be a perfect fit, are only just beginning to be made for women. They have been wearing men's smalls.

It wasn't until recently that these servicewomen were recognized as veterans, even though 38 of them were officially recorded as having lost their lives in service and the fate of a 39th is still unknown. In 2009, President Obama awarded all of them the Congressional Gold Medal.[7]

A 1941 British poster, executed by the artist Philip Zec, exhorts the ladies "Women of Britain, Come into the Factories," with a grey, overall-clad female raising her arms to a fleet of bombers passing overhead. It bears a strong similarity to one from World War I. Zec was a Jewish Socialist, whose work has been compared to Soviet propaganda posters extoling manual labor, however this poster could be classed in the same genre with the Canadian example "She Serves That Men May Fly."[8]

An interesting twist, however, is that in the same year, the British National Services included women in conscription by decreeing that all unmarried women from twenty to thirty had to go into some form of war industry or serve in the women's auxiliary forces.

A striking example of "sex sells," a Harold ("Hal") Forster poster from 1942 warns, "Keep mum—she's not so dumb." Besides a curvaceous blonde on a sofa, it features good-looking representatives from three branches of the United States Armed Forces. Garnering both praise and blame, the poster draws more attention, at the very least, with its suggestiveness.

Forster was best known for his advertisement illustrations for "Black Magic" chocolates which depicted high society ladies but was affordable for the average housewife—2/10 a pound. The suggestion, of course, was that one was indulging one's sweet tooth in exactly the same way as those of the upper echelon.

Another example, where women are worker bees rather than *femmes fatales,* depicts three aproned women with laden arms—one holds a banner shouting "Up Housewives and At 'Em" with the interesting request "Put Out Your Paper, Metal, and Bones (!)"—a stalwart Scottie carries the latter which, one assumes, were used for fertilizer. The poster conveniently overlooks the fact that it was "housewives" who were keeping the planes flying, the munitions blasting, and the food coming.[9] Part of Britain's propaganda campaign already discussed, these posters were aimed at the home front with as much vigor as that aimed at the occupied countries.

From Australia, we see an attractive 1943 example, aimed at the ladies as well, featuring an oblique line of smiling young women representing the various branches of the women's military services, plus a nurse and a land girl, and urging "Join Us in a Victory Job," and suggesting "apply at your nearest service office." The land girl wears the ubiquitous polka-dotted bandanna already mentioned on "Rosie the Riveter" with her overalls, and the servicewomen wear smart uniforms with becoming hats. The bandanna, which turned into a world-wide fashion phenomenon, although already in use, was almost certainly spurred on by the Rosie poster. What is odd is that the style is lifted entirely from shameful "Mammy" caricatures such as the earliest depictions of "Aunt Jemima," polka-dots and all.

Aunt Jemima was originally taken from a minstrel show character, who had been seen by Chris Rutt, the originator of self-rising pancake batter. He and his partner, Charles Underwood, decided to use the character as their marketing ploy. Rutt, in turn, sold to the R.T. Mill Company which decided to use a living person as their marketing ploy. The first "real" Aunt Jemima was Nancy Green, who had been born a slave and was recruited by the baking flour producers to impersonate Aunt Jemima, which she did until her death in 1923. She appeared at the 1893 Chicago Exposition, performing as a white-fantasy happy Black, talking and singing about the Old South as a great place to live. Fortunately—well, in a way—she had, at least, a sympathetic and more engaging persona. Earlier, Aunt Jemima's image had appeared on Rutt's boxes of pancake flour as a dreadful minstrel show blackface caricature, prominently wearing the red polka-dot bandanna tied on top of the head, just as Rosie does in the iconic poster. The irony seems to have escaped the female white community.[10]

Continental Efforts

Two posters from occupied France present a study in contrasts: From the files of the *Affiche de propagande* (Archives of Propaganda) comes one issued by Vichy France. Under the identifying heading of the Fascist *Parti Populaire Français* (founded in 1936 by the Communist Jacques Doriot) is the symbol of the German-backed party surrounded by blazing rays of light. Strangely, the party was violently anti–Marxist and increasingly anti–Semitic, regarding Marxism as "Jewish." It hovers over what appears to be a flower-bedecked anvil, against a background of factories belching smoke. The second, a product of Free France, simply places a cameo of *La Liberté* against the French tricolor and says "*pour la France—les libertés pour les Français*" (Liberty for France—liberties for the French).

Hungary, although part of the Axis, issued a number of posters saluting the International Red Cross and their services. One heartwarming depiction shows a white-clad nurse supporting a wounded serviceman on her left arm while she attempts to give him a drink of water. The title states "*A Magyar Vöröskereszt*" (The Hungarian Red Cross).[11] Others aimed at women exhorted *Jelentkezz* [sic]; the literal translation would be "come forward," which we can assume could be loosely translated as "join up," or "contribute." For example, saving your wastepaper, rags, etc., was an activity of international concern, and one Hungarian example pictures three stylishly clad women—in dresses, covered hygienically with aprons, heels and hose—throwing wastebaskets full of paper products into a large bin as a little girl does her little bit helping them. Generically housewifely, they could come from anywhere: the United States, Britain, Australia. The only giveaway is the very Eastern European man who stands to one side. There are a number of these *Jelentkezz* issues, some others of which are definitely in the German style, i.e., militaristic, mythical, and menacing.

Anti-Semitic, anti–Soviet poster from Germany. Kills two birds with one image. Bestial Jew wearing Russian red-star cap (United States Holocaust Memorial Museum).

German posters are considerably more menacing overall, e.g., a 1943 horror from the contested areas of Poland and Ukraine depicting what we are to assume is a Jew—only incredibly bestial—wearing a Russian cap and pointing a gun straight at us. He looms above a group of mourning women gazing sorrowfully down at scores of bodies strewn like cordwood. This example kills two birds with one image—it manages to be economically anti-Soviet and anti-Jewish together.

Many are directed at the Russians, such as the "Down with Bolshevism!" example, written in Cyrillic, meant for the occupied Soviet territories. Dramatically composed, with strobe-like streaks of light partially illuminating a fist which tears down a hammer and sickle flag, it is an unapologetic depiction of conquest. For more irony, a Soviet poster shows the Soviet/Nazi joint occupation of Poland before the relationship went south. Starring an enormous red (in color) soldier knocking over a parade-uniformed, presumably Polish character with the butt of his gun, he accomplishes the "liberation" of two peasants by this action.

Trying to tie Germany for menace is an Italian poster featuring the Statue of Liberty as a grinning skull rising in a cloud of fire and smoke over a helpless city—a burning building prominently displays a red cross. While Liberty waves her torch with a skeletal right arm, she holds a serene mask in her left. The caption screams in red "*Ecco i 'Liberatori'*!" (Behold the Liberator).

A disingenuous sample from Poland (c. 1939) is chilling in its understated menace, celebrating, as it does, the Soviet/Nazi occupation of Poland as the liberation of the peasants. With mealy-mouthed mendacity, a long text in Ukrainian says, "We held out our hands to our brothers for them to straighten their backs and to throw the despicable kingdom of whips (*pans*) into the darkness of the ages." The depiction is of a stalwart Russian soldier with a red-starred helmet, who knocks over an officer wearing a parade uniform, and holding a whip, while two mustachioed peasants break their bonds.

What We Wear Depends on Where

On the fashion front, particularly from the English-speaking Allies, the evidence presented shows that it was not entirely the movies that drove the bus of fashion. Posters had a wider influence than just spurring the populace to perform their patriotic duties. Although it was within a rather restricted range for women and, in many cases, simply reinforced stereotypes—for housewives, apron-covered dresses worn with heels, come to mind. However, the posters did include overalls and bandannas for factory workers, angelic white for nurses, and uniforms for service personnel. Maybe the last category is the most telling, uniforms for women did exert an undeniable influence on styles for women at home.

It must be acknowledged that posters, however much they presented a meta-message, were not crafted with clothing in mind. As we know, they were intended to carry a powerful influence of a different sort, even as they may have secondarily exerted a fashion influence. As a last word in that arena, here are two contrasting examples from the United States: The first depicts a woman in Army uniform and helmet, with what might be a lieutenant's bar on her collar along with her nurse's insignia. She sits before a plasma container, which she has hung on a rifle, and wipes the sweat from her forehead. With her brow creased in desperation and overwork, she holds out her hand to us in supplication. The caption chides us with "More nurses are needed!" The poster compels us to understand the actual *need* for women in service, and demonstrates the fact that many of those women, nurses in particular, served at the front under fire.

This movingly exhausted appeal to our assistance contrasts with another example which depicts a white-clad nurse in an almost identical pose to the Hungarian example discussed above. She supports a wounded soldier in the same way with her left hand, while her right is laid gently on his cheek. The terse caption tells us, "Fighting Men Need Nurses." The first poster carries the more powerful message but unwittingly contributes to women's leisure wear. Her uniform translates easily to a casual sports ensemble of open collared men's styled shirt with slacks.

Recruiting poster for the U.S. Army Nurse Corps appeals to emotions of sympathy and empathy while also paying tribute to nurses' exhausting efforts (National Archives).

While all were a part of the propaganda machine, all carried that secondary influence which reached further than the intent of the issuers.

TEN

Walking the Streets

"World War II...[E]ven though just over half of the decade was marked by conflict, the entire period was influenced by its actuality or aftermath."
—Emmanuelle Dirix and Charlotte Fiell, *1940s Fashion: The Definitive Sourcebook*

Once again, we must ask questions: How do the examples given in the above chapters translate into everyday life? What wider effect do patriotic or historical movies have on the movie audiences? What about the posters we have seen?

A Trend to Shame?

Released in 1939, just at the start of the European conflict, although before the United States became involved, *Gone with the Wind* saw an upsurge of sweeping, romantic evening wear a la Vivien Leigh as Scarlett. For home-sewers, the most popular pattern was a dress modeled on one Leigh had worn to a picnic in the film. An interesting psychological facet of this trend is that women seemed to want to be Scarlett, who was defiant, willful, outrageous, and generally naughty, rather than Melanie (Olivia De Haviland), who was well-mannered, a perfect Southern lady, and most of all, married to Ashley Wilkes (played by Leslie Howard), the guy Scarlett originally had her eye on. Furthermore, Scarlett seems to get a final comeuppance at the end of the movie, as Rhett utters his famous line, "Frankly, my dear, I don't give a damn." I would wager there hasn't been a single woman who believed that line. All know he's going to come back and they're going to be bedeviling each other for a lifetime. Unfortunately, as popular as the movie has been, by inference it makes the South noble and the North ravaging marauders in the same way as did D.W. Griffith's *Birth of a Nation* or Buster Keaton's *The General*. Slavery is represented as just background to more important things, e.g., gala balls. Furthermore, the destruction of Atlanta is played for sympathy.

Another movie in this (to us) puzzling trend is the 1940 release, *Santa Fe Trail*, starring Olivia De Haviland again. This time she portrays a much feistier "Kit Carson" Holliday, paired with Errol Flynn in their seventh outing together (like Ronald Colman and Greer Garson, two of the most beautiful people in movies). Directed by Michael Curtiz, the film purports to be about John Brown (Raymond Massey) and his passionate—and admittedly rather violent—dedication to the abolition of slavery. What the film actually does is make the abolitionists sneaky, treacherous and cowardly, in the form of Van Heflin, as the dishonorably discharged West Pointer, Rader. The fancy West Point graduates

Jeb Stuart (Errol Flynn) and the misfortunate George Armstrong Custer (Ronald Reagan) are taken, with a great deal of "artistic license," from the real-life Confederate officers. Custer actually graduated from the Point at the bottom of his class, not much like the heroic image in the film, but they serve as the South-supporting "heroes." It is true that John Brown, although a passionate abolitionist, was also an erratic zealot and careless of lives, but the rest is pure Hollywood fantasy. The movie is appalling to watch nowadays, but was an all-time top grosser when it was released. A trailing, but almost too late, entry in the Scarlett trend, it most certainly lent a larger influence to the treatment of African Americans under the "Jim Crow" laws rather than to fashion.

About Face in the Closet, America!

Happily, the Scarlett trend in fashion with its ruffles and bonnet-styled hats was a brief one. Wartime restrictions had gained a foothold even before the United States was directly involved. By 1939, skirts had risen to just under the knee and shoulders were just beginning to assume the militaristic look they would carry throughout the war—broad and squared. In fact, shoulders were squared to the point where they began to look as though women had forgotten to remove the hanger. Joan Crawford in *Mildred Pierce* is a case in point.

Waists were very much in vogue—fashion illustrations of 1940 pictured women's suits with nipped-in waists and slightly expanded shoulder line. Jackets most often ended just at or a tad below the hip, however an occasional tunic length cropped up. Skirts, for both dresses and suits, tended to be flared or pleated (box or all-around). A publicity photograph of actress Martha Vickers, for example, posed her in a Travilla (who preferred to use just his last name) designed, smartly tailored, gabardine dress of a soft pink, with a fly-front bodice that continues below the belt, ending in a box pleat. Two darts on each side culminate in box pleats as well, and the seams of the belt loops continue in a curve delineating flat pockets on either hip. This is a sophisticated design, flattering to most figures. The gentle pink of the gabardine softens the masculine tailoring, but in no way makes the woman who wears it look less than in charge.

William Travilla, he of the single name, began his film career in 1941, after being turned down by the Army owing to flat feet. He was just 21 at the time and not an overnight success, although he had studied at Chouinard Art School in Los Angeles, California, was a precocious talent, and was selling his fashion designs from the age of 16. Nevertheless, he remained second-string until 1946, when actress Ann Sheridan saw some of his sketches and became a fan. He designed her gowns for the 1947 movie *Nora Prentiss* and went on from there, winning an Oscar in 1948 for *Don Juan,* dressing many big stars until his contract ran out at Fox. He then proceeded to design under his own label, as well as freelancing for television.

The masculine, almost military look of shoulders continued in popularity throughout the war, paired with the tailoring seen in Orry-Kelly's wardrobes for Bette Davis and Ingrid Bergman. It is not only possible, but probable, that this trend reflects women's more active roles in many formerly masculine pursuits.

Ensembles, consisting of dress and matching coat or jacket were popular and so were furs. PETA was far in the future and fur coats and/or accessories were ubiquitous. For the less affluent, mouton (sheared lamb intended to look like beaver) as well as dyed marmot, was seen everywhere and at every length. Boxy was the thing, however, whether one preferred long or hip-length. In an unfortunate choice of possible trends, the furs of the '40s are generally bulky and unflattering in contrast to the graceful styles of the '20s and '30s.

Prices are eye-openers for today's customers, used to amounts hovering at or nearly ten times those of the past. The *Sears Catalog* for 1940 advertised its "1940 Edition of Sears Famous *Miss America* Polo Coat" at a whopping $12.98 for its "best" camel hair and wool number. Double-breasted, princess line, with a broad, wing collar, the graceful style was remarkably flattering to women's figures. It was also available, for the "young Miss America" ages 10 to 16, at $8.98. Sizes were eye-openers, too—starting with size 12 for misses and size 11 for juniors. Women of the period would have laughed hysterically at the idea of a size 0 for anything but a newborn.

For boys, the "Knicker" suit, almost identical to the plus-four style of the '20s, was very *au courant* according to the 1940 *Sears Catalog,* and ranged in price from $7.50 to $9.75. Plus-fours had been introduced to the States in 1924 by Edward, Prince of Wales, the later King Edward VIII—he of the rapid self-dethroning. They caught on quickly for men and boys, not losing their popularity for several decades—most of all in sports such as golf and baseball. Men wore "swagger" overcoats which were wool variations of the World War I trench coat, but full militarism seems to have been ignored, in the main, by Sears. Where it does crop up, it is only for the little people, miniature Army and Navy uniforms sizes 4–10. The boys have a wide range of styles including "Admiral"

From left to right, Mrs. J.A. Holton, Colonel "Sonny" Sonnkalb, Mrs. Sonnkalb, and Mr. Holton, c. 1940s. Boxy sheared mouton fur jackets, "roller" hat on both ladies (author's costume collection).

and "Aviator," however, the girls have WAAC and WAVE, and that's it. The boys are officers, the girls are non-coms.

In that earlier trend, hats in the 1940 *Sears Catalog* jumped on the *Gone with the Wind* bandwagon, with bonnet styles for young and old. The examples were accompanied with a breathless blurb that stated: "The bonnet's back—prettiest fashion of the 19th century gets a royal welcome along with Clark Gable...." Fortunately, for anyone over the age of five, those were quickly supplanted by, well, different fashions—I hardly know what to call them. Some perched on the sides of the head rather like a bird alighting on a branch, exposing the entire face. These were particularly cute and attractively flirtatious, adding a touch of gaiety to an otherwise somber era. One such was even worn by the then Queen of England, who was also an Elizabeth, but as just the wife of the King, and a commoner to boot, was not included in the queen count.

The era also saw the introduction of the "roller," as in the group photo of the two dressed-up couples we see above. Wider-brimmed and turned up all the way around, it created a sort of halo effect around the wearers—*very* flattering to almost any facial type. And, again, there were the turned down broad-brims, in the Orry-Kelly style, which provided a hint of mystery to the women wearing them. (See *Now, Voyager.*) Another popular style was the turban. The *Sears Catalog* for 1941 enthuses "Turbans 'Certain to Charm'" giving the "Little Lady" a hint of the exotic East and the *Arabian Nights.*

Slacks for women were definitely in, especially after women began joining the assembly lines, and hundreds of "Rosie(s) the Riveter" took to the factories. Ladies' coveralls started appearing in the catalog by 1942, addressing the reality of women's employment. Beginning, as discussed, as far back as World War I, and made particularly popular by screen icons such as Katherine Hepburn and Marlene Dietrich, trousers for women definitely came into their own during the wartime years.

The bandanna and the snood, as previously mentioned, became fashion necessities after their first appearances in the factories. Keeping one's hair out of the machinery made them necessities on the assembly lines, but they soon spread to day and evening wear for the general female public. Snoods, worn with a rolled pompadour in front, were elegant even with a soldering rod in hand.

Bandannas, on the other hand, spoke of real work. Unfortunately, they also bore that hint of racism, copied as they were from images of "Aunt Jemima." All too frequently, they were red with white polka-dots exactly mimicking Aunt Jemima's advertising headwear.

As the war wore on, little changed in the fashion department, for the duration. Shoulders squared a bit more, nevertheless, skirt lengths remained just about the same as in 1939, waists and bosoms remained defined, and evening wear continued to be glamorous. Think Bette Davis in *Now, Voyager,* appearing in a veritable carousel of exquisite gowns. In one especially scrumptious example, for a scene set at a concert, Davis wears a full-length evening coatdress of off-white, decorated with what resembles an EKG printout of glittering beads, accessorized with a faux-modest scarf and sparkling brooch at the plunging neckline. Davis carries it off as she carried off most things, with confidence, authority, and elegance. Sadly, most people at a concert nowadays look like they've just come from the gym and hadn't bothered to shower. The wide shoulders of the day gave an air of in-charge competence to all females. Whether they were Bette Davis or not, women wanted to look like *that*!

"Dependable! On the War Front—on the Home Front!" shouts an August advertisement for *Fashion Frocks.* "Parachutes for our 'Soldiers of the Sky.' Dresses for our 'Soldiers of the Home.'" The illustrations are of a paratrooper reining in his parachute, contrasted by a pert young woman in a long-sleeved checked bolero with wide collar and squared shoulders, paired with a flared, pocketed skirt in a solid orange. The cuffs of the jacket, her gloves, and her little hat match the skirt color. With the exception of the stiffly padded shoulders, this is cute, timeless, and wearable today for younger women.

Whip-Test Lipstick and *Special Drene* [sic] *Shampoo* at least acknowledge that not all women are "Soldiers of the Home." *Whip-Test* dedicates a series of ads to various branches of the women's forces—one month, WAACS, one month, WAVES, and so on. *Special Drene* addresses servicewomen in general. Both products, nevertheless, focus their texts on the women's appeal for men, rather than on their service. In contrast,

"Eisenhower" jacket actually worn by General Eisenhower during the war. His endorsement created a whole new fashion trend for both the man and woman of the streets (National Archives and Records Administration).

"What the well-dressed soldier writes about..." isn't what one would expect. It turns out that he doesn't write to wife, girlfriend, or Bette Davis—perish the thought! No! It's to Fels Naptha because his long johns aren't "tattle tale gray!"

Men were not excluded from restrictions. Suits, which before the war were generally three-piece and double breasted, were now produced in the "Victory Suit." Single breasted, minus cuffs, no pocket flaps, and narrowed lapels, they were boxier, less fitted, and were mainly two-buttoned. Wartime necessity gave rise to the mismatched jacket and trouser trend, although dark jackets with white trousers were popular in the late '20s and '30s. Trousers eschewed pleats in favor of flat front, although rather wide legged. Evening dress, for those who could afford it, was still elegant even in the face of war. A 1942 advertisement depicts two natty gentlemen in top hat; white wing-collared shirt with stiff front and white tie; satin-faced shawl collars; pleat-front trousers; and full tails. These were worn with white gloves, and on chilly evenings, a black overcoat also with satin-faced lapels—very Fred Astaire-ish. For lesser folk, the tuxedo jacket paired with white shirt, black tie, and black trousers satin-striped on the outsides, would suffice.

There was one outstanding male fashion innovation, however, which suited the restrictions, namely, the "Eisenhower" jacket. Made popular by General Dwight D. Eisenhower, the "M-44," as it was labeled, was a result of the Army's search for a more practical, all-season jacket that could be worn under a heavier outer layer. General Eisenhower had already requested something of the sort, and it soon became standard Army issue in late 1944 and remained standard until 1956. The stylish waist-length jacket caught on with civilians almost immediately, for both men, women, and children. A similar style can still be purchased from such diverse stores as Hammacher Schlemmer, Dickies, or Target. It looked really sharp on Ike.

Stiff Upper Girdles

In Britain, where restrictions were much more severe, the garment industry was carefully regulated by the government throughout the war. Designers and advertisers were featuring so-called "Utility" wardrobes, which were also subject to strict regulation. Raw materials to be used for producing Utility wardrobes, for example, were under the complete control of the government, which also encouraged manufacturers to produce limited stocks at low prices. However, 85 percent of their manufacture had to be devoted to Utility garments—the remaining 15 percent could be given over to creating non–Utility wear *but* it had to meet the same style regulations, which were: no more than two pockets; five buttons; six skirt seams; two inverted or box pleats or four knife pleats; and 160 inches of stitching.[1] Garments were tailored, unadorned, and practical; however, even prestigious designers such as Norman Hartnell got into the patriotic act, but with better tailoring and design, similar to this shirtwaist polka dot day dress. Overall, his designs were still utility but utility with cachet.

Price control was imposed upon these outfits so that civilians could dress fairly well without breaking the budget. Labelled with a utility mark—CC41—the image of the stylized brand looked like Pacman gobbling up opponents.[2]

Utility garments extended to underwear as well. The descriptions sound less than comfortable but warm—wool and cotton shorts, vests (like tank tops) and socks. Women's and girl's undies varied little from the men's outfits. Consisting of wool panties,

Rayon Utility dress. Scarlet red with white polka dots and white buttons. Shirtwaist style, accessorized with white gloves and popular turban (Wikimedia Commons).

which cost 3/11 and 3 ration coupons and must have been excruciating to wear, or rayon lock-knit, which was jersey, more comfortable but not nearly warm enough for British winters. These, of course, were paired with the ubiquitous vests and, for adult females, that absolutely necessary girdle underneath the panties. Serviceable, and nobody's looking anyway.

Shoes tended to be as utilitarian stylistically as the label suggested. Two-inch heels, sometimes wedges, and closed toes, because open toes were actually prohibited as impractical and especially unsafe. Not so far off the mark since the experience of the Blitz made walking as risky as climbing Everest and nearly as athletic. Mounds of smoldering debris clogged the sidewalks—more than could be cleared away with any speed or facility—and tended to make everyday life an Olympic event.

Some Utility fashion advertisements suggested ideas for repurposing or restyling garments, which Madame Housewife could borrow for/from her own closet. Models

Splendid example of repurposing whatever was available. Bridal gown made of collected parachute silk with simple bodice—sleeveless and gathered—flounced skirt. Gown could tell several stories we wish we could hear (Museum Rotterdam).

would pose wearing pre-war clothing that had been dressed up with different accessories or the jacket from one suit paired with the skirt from another to make two ensembles. One such restyled outfit detailed the touches which had been given to a dinner dress. The model wore a black chiffon blouse made from a pre-war evening gown, a black

Repurposed evening wear. Black chiffon blouse from one gown, skirt from another, and accessorized with turban, pearl necklace and dressy belt (Wikimedia Commons).

skirt from a friend's old gown, dressed up with a white turban, pearl necklace and dressy belt. The accessories are all suitable for day wear, as well.

A unique and very clever use of repurposing can be seen in this bridal gown put together from reclaimed parachute silk. The design is simple but festive, with its flounced skirt, and sleeveless, high-waisted (almost Empire) bodice. The bride must have felt a kinship with those valiant parachutists who bequeathed it unknowingly to the cause of romance. We feel we are there with her and can only hope it was a long and happy marriage, with no shadow of tragedy.

With war right in their kitchens, in a fairly literal sense, British women made do with as much good grace as they could. If wearing "Utility" garments eased the burden of those fighting, they sacrificed with pride.

The Continental Touch

The outgunned and outmanned French had surrendered Paris to the Germans with little resistance. So many Parisians had fled to the countryside, that, when the Nazis entered, they found they were occupying a near ghost town. After the occupation, in a strange reversal, the residents started to straggle back to the city, only to meet with even more severe shortages of food, heat, and clothing. A thriving black market was soon in place, making the plight of the residents even harder.

Stringent curfews were imposed immediately. From 9:00 at night until 5:00 in the morning citizens were confined to their homes. Moot, because there was no electricity and the city was dark. Finding the conditions increasingly intolerable, the populace began to return to the provinces where life was a bit easier—more to eat and fewer oppressors. Under the Nazis, Jews were, at first, only forced to wear yellow Stars of David, plus they were banned from some occupations and places. However, on the infamous days of July 16 and 17, 1942, over 13,000 Jews, nearly 10,000 of which were women and children, were rounded up and sent to Auschwitz—*The Velodrome d'Hiver.*[3]

Resistance began with students starting in November 1940. Most certainly meant to be symbolic, the first demonstration erupted on November 11, Armistice Day for World War I. Localized disruptions continued even in the face of German reprisals, which were exceedingly cruel. After D-Day on June 6, 1944, a concerted uprising occurred on August 19, because hope of deliverance seemed imminent. The hoped-for liberation came true on August 25. On August 26, General Charles de Gaulle led a victory parade triumphantly down the Champs Èlysées and swiftly headed up a new government.[4]

French fashion almost disappeared, for the rest of the world, in early 1942, a bit over a year after the June 14, 1940, fall of Paris to the Nazis. Germany, ever ready with self-marketing, claimed in the first edition of *Die Mode* (January 1941) that "...the German victory over France has an incisive meaning for fashion." The Nazis purportedly planned to move the entire fashion industry, lock, stock and designers, to Berlin and Vienna. Owing to the considerable persuasive skill of Lucien Lelong (plus the Battle of Britain and the entrance of the Russians) this did not happen, and the French couture industry continued in a somewhat reduced condition—about 60 of the more than 90 houses remained open, such as Jacques Fath, Marcel Rochas, and Nina Ricci, who continued to exhibit. For his efforts, Lelong was tried for collaboration at the end of the war but acquitted—ruled to have saved jobs and France's cultural heritage.[5]

An early 1940 illustration for *Très Chic* even depicts an adorable military-styled ensemble consisting of a short-sleeved dress with all-around pleated skirt, teamed with a matching cape and hat which borrows from a military cap.[6] *Idèes (Manteaux et Tailleurs)* for Winter, 1940, has some of the same military-suggestive touches that were shown in *Très Chic*. For example, three very feminine skirt suits paired with garrison-styled caps—I hate to use the word adorable again, but they just *are*. The skirts are flared, or knife-pleated, and the closely fitted jackets are to the waist or just slightly at the hips. The perky little garrison caps have a contrasting band, flying ribbons, or no

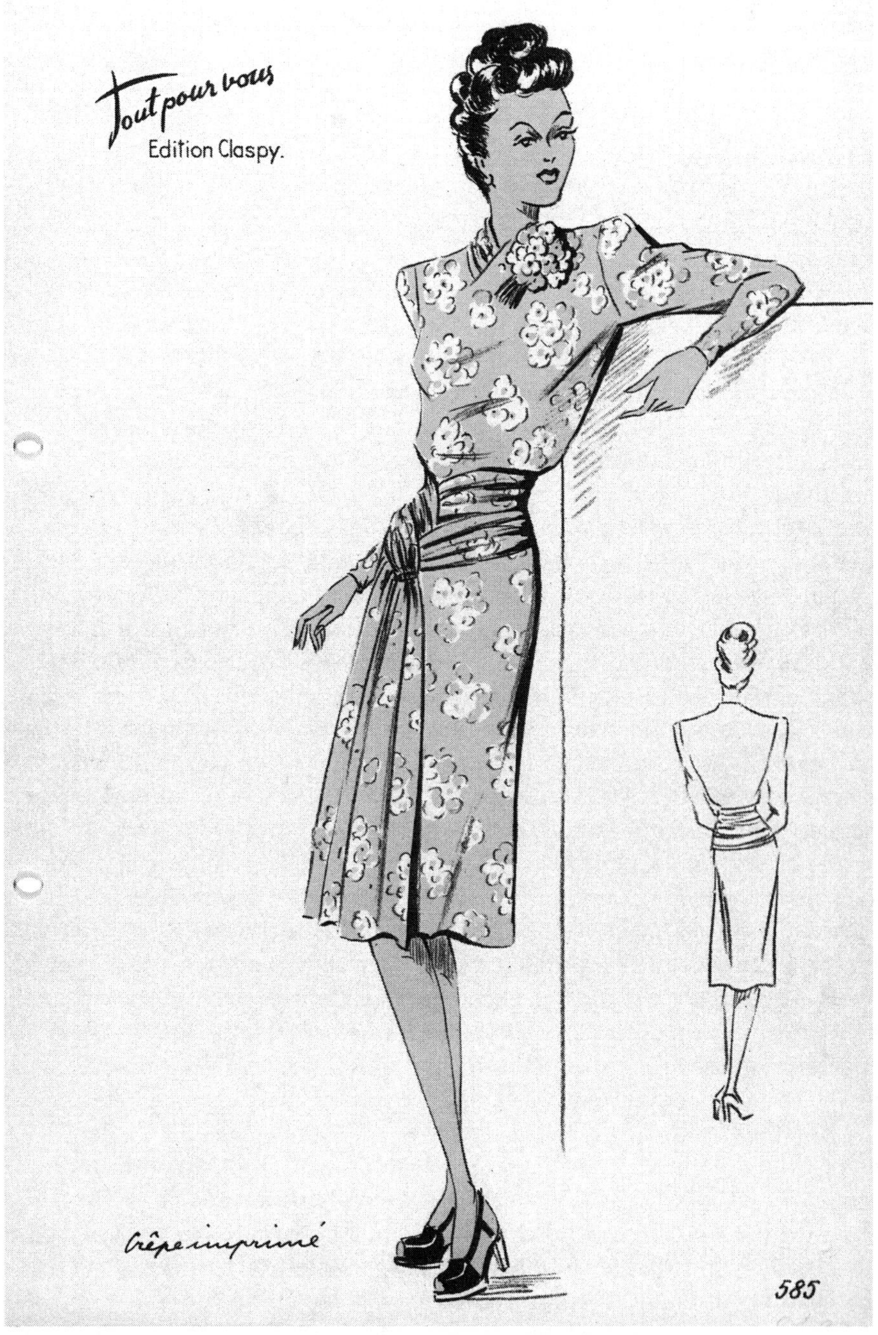

***Edition Claspy,* French/German publication. "Tout pour vous" ("All for You"). Printed crepe, wide shoulders, draped waist, blousy bodice, drape to hem (Rijksmuseum).**

adornment at all. Most of the hats shown for 1940–43, no matter the country of origin, tended to perch in that perky manner on the front of the head, even those with a wider brim. Evening wear in *Idées* featured much of the same fitted jackets over long skirts or billowing skirted ballgowns in luscious colors. In the cruel light of hindsight, these examples are more than sobering, as representatives of an era's end. A telling merger of French and German "co-habitation" is this illustration from *Edition Claspy* entitled "*Tout pour vous*" ("All for You"). Of printed crepe, with the wide, square shoulders of the period, it features a draped waist which wraps around the hips and descends in another drape to the hem. The skirt is slim, but the bodice is just a little blousy. The shoes are slight platforms with open toes.

Just as in World War I, knitters in all countries were much in demand. Yarn companies such as Estway Knitting, which advertised in magazines like *The Star Weekly,* a Canadian publication, suggested the most appreciated articles of knitwear: socks! It goes without saying, those were particularly welcome, as were balaclavas again for those in the North Atlantic; vests, scarves, sweaters and gloves for everywhere; for airmen, much needed extra layers of warm woolies to wear in frigid airplanes which were often below freezing temperatures. My Air Force pilot father-in-law, who was a participant in the actions on D-Day, could (and did) attest to that.

According to some advertisements, knitted caps in gaudy colors, topped by pom-poms, were very popular. Some sweaters came with a knitted-in hood which needed no separate cap, but if things were especially frosty could be supplemented with a jaunty pom-pommed number.

Hats indeed, both knitted and couture, turned into more than a way to keep warm. Headgear blossomed into a high-spirited way to thumb one's nose at the invaders. As one writer has put it: "Hats, maybe more than any other accessory, are able to confer a certain presence on the wearer." Knowing this and knowing their customers, French milliners fought back against Nazi seizure of materials, and restrictions on fabrics, by concocting innovative and stylish headwear from whatever scraps they could find. French milliner Paulette, for one, needed a head-covering for dining out one evening and created a turban from a black jersey scarf and gold pins. Receiving many compliments, she put out a turban collection which proved to be very successful. These, in turn, became a badge of defiance among French women. With only a scrap of fabric wrapped around whatever would work, they could mimic a flaunting of Nazi restrictions with only the slightest of efforts. Frustrated, and aware of an ulterior motive, in 1943 the Germans cracked down with a ban on "fantastically voluminous" hats.[7] We have seen the power of hats—and knitting—in recent years. In 2016, knitted pink "pussy" hats made a powerful propaganda statement for feminism.

For those propaganda purposes in World War II, important people, First Lady Eleanor Roosevelt for example, had themselves photographed knitting or at least carrying knitting bags to promote the activity. Newspapers and magazines did their part by adding their own propaganda blurbs. *The New York Times:* "The propaganda effect of hand knitting cannot be estimated in terms of hard cash, but it is considerable." Unfortunately, the paragraph continues dismissively, referring to the knitter: "[And] she herself feels that she has an active part in this vast conflict, she is not useless, *although she can do nothing else to help win the war*" (emphasis mine).[8] Other periodicals took up the cause. Even the prestigious *Life Magazine* devoted an entire article to learning how to knit, complete with patterns.[9]

Seattle, Washington, seems to have been a hotbed of knitters. Just as in World War I, "Seattle area knitters jumped to action." There were competitions among auxiliary groups to determine who was the fastest knitter, and who could turn out the most items in the least time. Enumclaw, Washington, knitters produced—between January 1, 1943, and March 9, 1944—sixty-five sleeveless Army vests, nineteen women's service sweaters, twenty-five Army helmets, three Navy helmets, one Navy vest, four Army scarves, ten heavy coat sweaters, four afghans, fifty-six children's sweaters (for children in war-torn countries), eight turtleneck sweaters, five pairs of Navy gloves and one Navy scarf! The mind boggles.

Service*women* were not left out by the knitting brigade. Copley Smith & Sons, Ltd. devoted much of their Leaflet No. 1170 to necessaries for females. Socks, gloves and scarves, certainly, but some quite chic sweaters with decorative ribbing made an appearance, along with hooded examples and collars with attached hood. Also included were knitted one-piece "step-ins," with spaghetti straps, which must have been itchy enough to win jitterbug contests.

When the end of the war put the balaclava knitters out of business, designers went with much the same styles for the next two years. Hemlines stayed pretty much just below the knee and shoulders were still squared.

Then ... fashion took an unexpected U-turn back to a late '40s version of the Scarlett O'Hara trend—the "New Look."

Eleven

After(war)ds

By 1946, things were back in full swing, almost literally, with a number of swing-back coats being featured. The boxy look was also in, vying in popularity with the enduring tight-waisted redingote. The Americans had already been showing the boxy (and, for the most part, unflattering) coat styles in 1945.

Before Dior launched his "New Look" in spring 1947, skirts were still being shown at just-below-the-knee length and shoulders were still wide, as stated. Dior, in an eye-blink, dropped skirts to ballerina length with swirling *Giselle*-style skirts. *Idées (Manteaux et Tailleurs)* for winter 1947 was still picturing a number of short, boxy, mid-length coats for day, while Dior models were already wearing coats almost to the ankle in a variety of styles.

Although one would not think the fashion would be popular, there was still a hint of military fashion in the *Croquis Elegants* stylebook for summer 1946. A white summer dress boasts an almost trench coat–look on the bodice front and back, paired with a side-pleated skirt and faux short jacket. A companion figure couples a taupe, side-pleated, box coat over a khaki-brown pleated peplum dress with a faux two-piece appearance. Both display that hint of military uniforms that one would expect to be avoided, considering the circumstances so recently escaped. Early 1947 saw some skirts which had lengthened to just above mid-calf but had not yet reached their longest. "*Photoplay* Fashions" for August 1947 was still displaying several demure examples at that length, very soon to be out of style. The most appealing is an attractive plaid ensemble with a flared skirt and short capelet in a red and black on white; large-scaled, plaid accented with solid red; and three-quarter length sleeves. There is also an advertisement for a "Skirlotte," which is described by its name, recommended for all sporty pursuits.

With 1947 came the stunning "New Look," out of the house of Christian Dior. Owing to the suffocating difficulties of the war, Dior had had a spotty fashion career up until then. After the armistice, however, in December 1946 he founded his own fashion house and presented his first collection, called by the poetic name of *Corolle* (referring to a circlet of flower petals), in February 1947. He, along with his collection, were both "New."

The emphasis of the New Style was on the bust and as small a waist as possible. Iconic images of the suit which launched Dior's New Look have been reproduced innumerable times. With its rounded shoulders, tightly nipped waist, shawl-collared, hip-length jacket, and full-circle skirt, it created a stir not seen for decades. It graced the cover of the August 1947 issue of *Vogue,* sporting a red jacket, rather than the dramatically contrasting light jacket and dark skirt seen elsewhere. Called the "Bar" suit, it sent women back to the 19th century, emblematic of the retro attitudes of the entire '50s. As retro as it may have been, it was also beautiful, with an elegance, grace, and rhythmic flow that made it an instant success.

"There's the rub," as Shakespeare said. The "Look" *was* beautiful, and young women in particular loved it. One could look like a princess in a black, rayon faille, circle skirt, and a sheer, white nylon, Victorian-imitation blouse. An image from a *Sears Catalog* for 1949 pictures this exact skirt model, which the caption describes as "The Wasp Waist with Boned Girdle." The opposite page displays the perfect "Gibson Girl" blouse to go with it. The swirly skirts were elegant and the nipped-in waists were sexy.[1]

Nevertheless, it wasn't popular with all segments of society. "Coco" Chanel had nothing good to say about either the look or the designer. In another instance, models in a

A trio of swirling ballerina skirts and nipped-in jackets, c. 1889. Elegance, grace, utter impracticality. I'd take the one on the right—a Ceil Chapman design—any time (Wikimedia Commons).

photo shoot were attacked just for wearing the clothes, the rationale being that there were still government-imposed shortages and the insensitive extravagance shown was enraging. Once the restrictions were lifted, though, Dior's revolution swept the fashion industry.

According to the Dior website itself, *Elle* magazine printed a photograph of Marlene Dietrich's calves, stating that the "most beautiful legs in the world" might never be seen again since Dietrich had ordered 10 "New Look" dresses which would completely cover those fabulous legs. Well, so they did for a decade and a bit, until the '60s when women decided to display them again.[2]

In an even more "Scarlett" touch, as the '50s were ushered in, the "Look" would add ruffled petticoats to the more tailored Dior, *Giselle*-ballet-length, skirts. The men were back and "bringing home the bacon" while the girls were in the kitchen gushing over their wonderful labor-saving appliances. Naturally, as we have seen previously, the "girls" were in heels and aprons over their swirly skirts.

This vision was particularly emphasized at the 1964 New York World's Fair. The marvelous world of the future, conjured up by those astute businessmen, was one where the little lady could get more housework done than ever. As I said, bosoms were prominent, waists were as tiny as possible, and *My Friend Irma* celebrated the dumb blonde in film and television. Sad to state, the "New Look" appears to have been a male response to the wartime situation where women proved they could do men's work.

Fan magazines, naturally, did their parts to reinforce the idea that women had to be decorative, smooth-skinned, divine-smelling, and well-dressed even when stoking the furnace. A token semi-exception to this mindlessness is an article in the July 1947 issue of *Photoplay*. It features Joan Leslie as the voice of wisdom asking, "How Beautiful is Your Mind?" According to Ms. Leslie, one should supplement her high school diploma by "taking college courses." Not only that, Joan reads at least one newspaper a day, one news magazine a week and house or fashion magazines only once a month. On top of this she goes to at least one lecture, concert or play every month. Now she can take part in any conversation!

As they had done in World War I, in World War II women did "men's" work, with the same efficiency and dispatch they had previously, and wore clothes that fit those roles. With the cessation of hostilities, and with men expecting things to be as they were before, the psychological effects were even more dramatic than in the previous post-war era. Stringent protocols were established where women were concerned, for which their "uniforms" turned into aprons, heels, and eye-makeup.

In far too many high schools and colleges, certain courses were reserved for males only, such as physics, calculus, advanced algebra, and various other science-oriented studies.[3] In the workplace, women were told flat-out they would not be considered for advancement to even middle management positions. Credit was denied them without a man to sign for them, and they couldn't buy a house, a car, or even a dress in their own names. Needless to say, birth control was out of the question except for married women and then only with a doctor's prescription. Men, of course, could always get condoms with little problem. That unequal situation eased somewhat in the '60s, but it wasn't until the '70s that those restrictions were (almost) entirely lifted.

The societal changes of those decades, when they came, turned the world upside down with the advent of the Vietnam War and the arrival of the hippies.

Twelve

The Indo-Chinese Conflict

Vietnam

"Anyone who isn't confused really doesn't understand the situation."
—Edward R. Murrow, newscaster

Napalm in the Morning

How do fashions, fads, or trends, come about? Against what background do people seize upon a certain way of doing, wearing, or being? We cannot always answer that question wholly, but in the case of the Vietnam years, the above quote by Edward R. Murrow probably says it best.

It cannot be said that wars are ever popular—except, perhaps, with those who do not fight but are happy to send those who do. Vietnam, however, stands out in modern times as the most controversial and unpopular war of the last hundred years. Those who felt it a duty to fight were vilified as "baby killers" by those who did not fight but conveniently forgot that those who did were dead, dying, or maimed by the many thousands. This unfairness persisted for many years; nevertheless, Vietnam veterans finally received some of the recognition due them, much after the war, as we struggled through another unpopular and controversial war in Afghanistan. Those who had been severely affected by Agent Orange, for example, were finally able to realize their G.I. benefits and be treated.

Twenty-twenty hindsight, based in part on subsequently disclosed government communications, has proven that those who protested were partially in the right, at least politically. This was an egregious war which should not have come about but was inevitable in view of the errors of judgment, and inability to see the actual facts of the situation, by those in charge. That having been said, while the war itself may have been a mistake, the truth was that more than 50,000 of our young men died and making cruel mockery of their sacrifice was unconscionable. Nonetheless, whatever one's opinion, and whatever the reality, it must be said that the effect on fashion was the strangest and most surreal one of them all.

Are You with Me?

The roots of the war dated all the way back to 1945, when Japan was defeated and withdrew its forces from the country. Of course, Vietnam ("Indochina" at the time) had been seeking independence for much longer, having been under French colonial rule since the 19th century. After the withdrawal of the Japanese forces, France hoped to regain control and backed the French-educated Emperor Bao Dai against the Communist sympathizer Ho Chi Minh. Both wanted a unified Vietnam; however, Bao Dai wanted close ties with the West while Ho wanted a Vietnam modeled after China and other Communist countries. The war erupted in 1954 at the Battle of Dien Bien Phu in May 1954, resulting in the defeat of the French and the end of colonial rule in Indochina. The country was more disunified than ever with Ho as leader in the North and Bao in the South. Unification elections were to be held in 1956; however, before those could take place, Bao was pushed out of power by Ngo Dinh Diem, a devout Catholic and fanatic anti–Communist. The fuse was now lit.

Who's Up for Dominoes?

As far back as 1954, under the Eisenhower administration, the domino theory was first offered as a certainty in Indochina. In the course of a speech made on April 7 of that year, Eisenhower argued:

> Finally, you have broader considerations that might follow what you would call the "falling domino" principle. You have a row of dominoes set up, you knock over the first one, and what will happen to the last one is the certainty that it will go over very quickly. So, you could have a beginning of a disintegration that would have the most profound influences.[1]

This concept was repeated *ad nauseum* during the Vietnam war years as a rationalization for the continued efforts in the area which were fast proving to be futile. Again, 20/20 hindsight has proven that this argument was, in essence, more right than wrong, as the Pathet Lao and Khmer Rouge quickly grabbed power in Laos and Cambodia, led by those who previously had been part of the Vietminh.[2] These were brutal dictatorships on their own, nevertheless they drew, in the major part, from a base of Communism.

The Summer of Love was still in the future when the Summer of Hate saw the United States' public entry into the Vietnam War. This unwinnable conflict had already been covertly in progress for a decade by this time,[3] but came out in the open with the torpedo boat attack on the destroyers *Maddox* and *Turner Joy* in August 1964. By this time, there were already around 23,000 United States troops stationed in Vietnam and we had lost about 400 of them. Before the last of the United States military would leave the region, nearly another entire decade passed and more than 58,000 United States' troops were killed. Civilian deaths numbered around 2,000,000 including more than 200,000 South Vietnamese and possibly more than 1,000,000 North Vietnamese (statistics on North Vietnam are uncertain). Australia, New Zealand, the Philippines, South Korea and Thailand deaths amounted to another 7,000, approximately.

The United States entered the fray after the Gulf of Tonkin incident, when North Vietnamese torpedo boats attacked two of the United States destroyers at that location. President Lyndon Baines Johnson ordered retaliatory bombing over military targets in the North—as yet there were no acknowledged boots on the ground.

In March 1965, Johnson made the fateful decision to send United States troops to Vietnam, and by June there were 82,000 stationed there. At first the American public stood solidly behind Johnson. Very soon, however, there was a groundswell of public opinion against the conflict. Particularly after 175,000 more troops were needed by the end of the year.

Johnson, who was elevated to the presidency with the assassination of John F. Kennedy, refused to even try for a second term. Although an ambitious man, with considerable ego, he could see no way out of the morass into which the United States had been trapped through two administrations—and would be for a third—and so felt certain that a run would simply have ended in a public rout. Rather than risk humiliation, he chose the "better part of valor" and bowed out of the position with his ego intact. The Paris-located peace talks with North Vietnam, in spite of the inclusion of South Vietnam, were unsatisfactory to say the least, and the 1968 United States election was a bitter one which awarded Richard Milhous Nixon the presidency. Those who imagined a better outcome with Nixon at the helm were doomed to disappointment. Although the Paris peace talks continued, progress was nonexistent. The North Vietnamese insisted on unconditional United States withdrawal to which the U.S. refused. The war dragged on and on through the next four years, with more "peace" talks, more bombing and more death. A peace agreement was reached between the United States and North Vietnam in January 1973; however, the North and South fought on until April 1975 when Saigon fell at last to the North Vietnamese.[4]

Has the Vietnam War ever really reached an end? Was it worth it? The tens of thousands of veterans who suffered permanent damage from PTSD, Agent Orange, along with the unwarranted contempt of those who did not fight, would answer with a resounding NO! Those who opposed the war would answer just as vociferously. Some of these adamantly, and sometimes violently, held viewpoints were reflected in what we chose to wear, or not wear as the case may be.

Are We Hip? Far Out!

> "Confusion is the best form of communication. It's left to be unexplained."
> —Twiggy (fashion supermodel)

Trying to pin down a starting point for the hippie movement is nearly impossible. Although, to be strictly accurate, the beatniks (offspring of the late '40s Beat Generation) were already much in evidence in the '50s. That Beat movement centered around two main characters—Jack Kerouac, author of the phrase "Beat Generation" which he claimed meant beatific, and Alan Ginsberg. Their louche way of dressing—black turtlenecks, berets, ankle boots or sneakers—certainly lent its influence on the hippie style.

Whenever and however, it probably started as a reaction to the societal strictures of the post-World War II 1950s. Civil unrest was definitely in the air by 1960. For example, even following *Brown v. Board of Education* in 1954, desegregation was a still a sore point. In the South, schools did not even pretend to comply. In California, where segregation was less an issue, people of color still faced institutionally based discrimination, culminating in the Watts riots of 1964. Disaffected, affluent, white youth, unofficially headed by the psychedelic drug guru, Timothy Leary, were encouraged to "turn on, tune in, drop out," along with the rest of the population, if they so desired. Designers evidently got this last message, as fashion broke out in what frequently could have been mistaken for a bad trip, a trend that was gleefully adopted by those we now refer to as "hippies."

Like the Flapper phenomenon of the '20s, even those more "mature," both male and female, fell into line, garbing themselves in fringed vests, miniskirts, beads, and flare-legged hip-huggers. In a psychologically fascinating reversal, fashion proceeded from the streets to the big screen. This time, "Your Clothes *Went* to Hollywood."

Along Came Mini

The invention of the miniskirt has been attributed to Mary Quant, a London designer, who was not shy to take credit, although the idea was in the air. Both Courrèges and another British designer, John Bates, have also been suggested as parents of the idea.

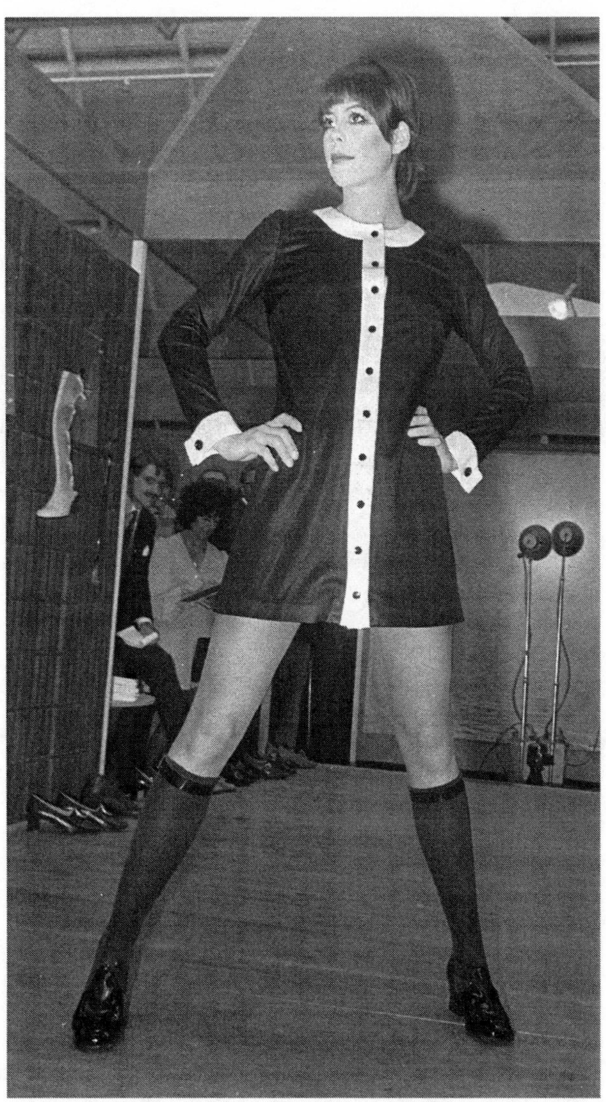

A Mary Quant design worn with knee socks and Oxfords. Cute, actually, if a bit girlish (Dutch National Archives).

Born Barbara Mary Quant in 1934, her parents were Welsh teachers. Marrying the man who would become her business partner as well, Alexander Plunket Greene, she opened her first shop, called *Bazaar,* in 1955 in Chelsea and a second one of the same name shortly thereafter. Quant's original concept took off like a wildfire, her skirt designs becoming shorter and shorter, to the point of needing an extra something for the office worker to avoid arrest for indecent exposure. Brightly colored and patterned tights filled that bill. In the later '60s, hot pants joined her "liberation" line of short skirts and tights. Worn often with knee-high boots, or conversely, knee-high hose, these, too, advanced to the office. Every stenographer looked like a *Star Trek* extra.

Quant later claimed that it was her customers who insisted on lifting the hems to the just under the derrière level, saying "Shorter, shorter," and that she merely followed their lead. Not just a fashion designer, she also designed wardrobes for the films *The Haunting* (1963), *Georgy Girl* (1966), and *Two for the Road* (1967). In 2015, tribute was paid to her tremendous influence on world style, and she was named Dame Commander of the Order of the British Empire.[5]

Down to the Sea in Hips

And then there were hip-huggers. An Irene Kasmer design first seen in 1957, they came into their own in the late '60s to early '70s. Sporting flared legs (or "bell-bottoms"), they borrowed from traditional sailor's uniform trousers in a way not foreseen by the military. Kasmer was a California fashion designer and founder of the Museum of Fashion Designers and Creators. Biographical information on Kasmer is slim to none. However, the *Los Angeles Times* featured a 1990 article on her stating she was "on a roll" with a new collection and praising her attention to precise detailing of hems, darts, seams, etc. In the article, although she refused to reveal her age, she admitted starting her design business in 1951.[6] Her daughter Lauren, a textile designer in her own right, has carried on in her mother's footsteps and has offered a collection of reinterpretations of her mother's designs. There is a short blurb regarding her mother on Lauren's website; otherwise, biographical information seems to be unavailable.

Hip-huggers are still with us, now transmogrified into skinny-legged versions. Combining, if I may be allowed an opinion, the worst of two fashion mistakes.

On the Fringe

Fringe tended to drip from many items of clothing circa late '60s into the '70s—most especially from vests. The hip(pies) seemed to feel that resembling Buffalo Bill Cody made a statement of wild rebellious youth. However, it actually spoke more of their social sidelining. Nevertheless, again like the Flappers, much of the population who had never been hip in their lives adopted the uniform of sideburns, fringed vests, flared hip-huggers and synthetic fabric everywhere. Vests came in lengths from cropped to maxi, with fringe running the entire length. There were bell-bottomed jumpsuits—those awkward-in-the-lady's-room, one-piece ensembles—which often boasted fringed sleeves, or capelets of fringe, fringed minis, fringed jackets, and entire dresses of nothing but fringe, which made the wearer resemble a walking cheerleader's pom-pom. The sort of pirate look, with long fringed vest over a full-sleeved, ruffled-cuff blouse was actually attractive and fun, imparting a swashbuckling look to its wearer. In truth, a lot of it still looks like fun today and was revived a bit by the fashion houses for spring 2020.

However, fringed clothing was only part of the story, there were other fringes of a more peculiar sort.

Just One of the, uh, Whats?

The "androgynous" look began to be popular in the late '60s. It was best epitomized by the desperately thin supermodel Twiggy. Since there was little to differentiate her from a boy, her tweeny frame was perfectly suited for unisex dressing. Unfortunately, too many teenagers adopted her as a role model and attempted to reach unhealthy weights, with the goal of achieving that waif-like image. Luckily, the "boyish" appearance of the '20s did not catch on as a trend in the '60s. On the other hand, the unisex look did and is more popular than ever. Clothes for men or women can hardly be told from one another in either tailoring or style. The staying power of this trend may be due to the increasing presence of women in the executive suite—not nearly enough, but still an improvement. In a peculiar juxtaposition, the style is now paired with necklines cut down to the navel and a lot of exposed busts. Nothing *uni* about that sex.

Twiggy (née Lesley Hornby in 1949) was one of the first of the parade of supermodels which followed. Second only to Jean Shrimpton, her face was everywhere from 1965 to 1970. Giving up her modeling in 1970, she then embarked on a successful show-biz career on the stage, in film, on television and as a recording artist until 2009. She is probably best known for her part in *The Boy Friend* (1971) but has also appeared in many diverse roles right up until the present. However, she released what she claimed was a final musical album, *Romantically Yours,* in 2011. For her services to fashion, the arts, and charity, she was appointed a Dame Commander of the Order of the British Empire in 2019 under her married name, Lesley Lawson. Her pert, large-eyed visage became an icon of the era and will be remembered when many others have been forgotten.

Tripping the Light Fantastic

Psychedelic and mod were two of the most (over)used words of the period. The psychedelic camp was certainly encouraged by the above-mentioned renegade guru, ex-academic Timothy Leary. Under his dubious endorsement, the "Heroin" style as it was called in the '90s, actually had begun much earlier. As I alluded to at the beginning of the chapter, it became, inexplicably to me, the rage. Models skulked and slouched around like an early zombie apocalypse, wearing very little except mask-like makeup which hollowed their cheeks and enlarged their eyes, like victims entertaining Dracula. Case in point is a John Bates shift-dress design for the fashion house Jean Varon. Constructed of tiny rows of pink-edged ruffles falling from a modified mandarin collar to just below the derrière, the frothy baby-doll appearance of the dress is negated by the giant panda eye shadow, and the blank, stoned-to-the-eyebrows stare on the model wearing it.

Jean Shrimpton, a noted "supermodel" of the '60s, epitomizes the look as she was caught unaware at a 1965 party in the Netherlands. She displayed the same big-eyed, blank, stoned stare as the fashion model, only in reality and not for playacting. Again, I emphasize, the blame for this trend to idiocy can be placed at the feet of Leary, that ex-PhD turned advisor of children. His motto, "Tune in, turn on, drop out," became the mantra for a generation of sheep who baaed their way to fried brain-hood. Astonishingly, it didn't just fade away, it was revived, a generation later, with the same results.

When it was revived in the '90s, it was also accompanied by extreme emaciation, dark red lipstick, and angularity, epitomized by Gia Carangi, a supermodel in the late '80s, who ironically died of AIDS-related complications resulting from heroin addiction at the age of twenty-six.[7]

With a foot in both mod and psychedelic categories, brilliant, neon hues appeared everywhere and for every occasion from beach to bistro. A favorite combination was dayglow orange paired with an acidic apple green. This combo showed up in plaids, prints, and piping on solid colors. John Bates does one of these in the same shift style as the ruffled example above. Very short, sleeveless, and an almost perfect triangle, the solid apple green frock is set off by trim in the eye-catching orange around the neckline and armholes. Also falling under the mod umbrella were Mondrian-inspired shift

Dr. Samuel B. McKinney's striking church robe and hat. Emulating African textiles, the robe is outstanding, not to mention super cool, c. 1970s (Joe Mabel, Creative Commons).

dresses for anytime wear. Mainly black and white with random color blocks, they closely imitated the geometric works of the Dutch artist Piet Mondrian. Sweater knits worn with patterned tights made a frequent appearance. These made the wearers look a bit chunky, so were better worn by the very slender.

Cat suits, and those unappealing strap-under-the-foot trousers for women (stirrup pants), were just dreadful on almost every figure. The so-called cat suits delineated every bump, or lack thereof, on thin, fat, young or old, alike. Stirrup pants, an evolution from jodhpurs, did well as ski wear, but unless a woman had an exceptional figure and was as tall as a model—no, no, no.

For the slightly more traditional, although avoiding the "square" designation, were cocktail frocks in more subdued hues. Often in rayon faille which imitated silk, it made those designer knock-offs available to the office worker. A mini-dress from 1972, for example, in lavender rayon faille—not quite A-line but somewhat unfitted, long-sleeved, and the only adornment a row of ruffles in the same fabric down both sides, from collarless neckline to hem (not a particularly long distance).

Even some more daring church pastors got into the mod act. During the 1970s and into the '80s, the Reverend Samuel B. McKinney of Seattle's Mount Zion Baptist Church wore this striking orange cope. Woven of African cloth, the robe was embellished with an all-over geometric design. This was interspersed with a vertical stripe, edged with circles, which emphasized the center back pleat and the front opening, as well as the sides from the shoulders down. A matching beretta completed the formal, and strikingly attractive, ensemble.

There were other exceptions to the extremes of either length or color, proving that traditional could still be hip. A yellow chiffon evening gown by the French designer Jean Dessès is an enticing example. Nearly invisible, narrow straps gave a strapless impression, above a tightly fitted bodice embellished with narrow fan-pleating, which dips in the back to just above hip length. The same narrow pleating, similar to Fortuny pleating, flows in a waterfall down the columnar skirt where it twists in a complex, knotted-train effect.

French designers were as popular as ever with the rich: Dior, Givenchy and Yves St. Laurent went on designing beautiful clothes for the Establishment, rising above the hipsters who couldn't afford them anyway.

Opera bouffe(ant)

Hair styles were "big." Teased, blow-dried bouffants or beehives contrasted with straight, center-parted manes of nearly down-to-the-waist lengths. Flips, left over from the '50s, were frequently paired with a half-bouffant, as were the straight, center-parted long styles. Giant rollers aided in producing the "big" look. The bouffant could be modified into a number of variations: the classic beehive; the classic combined with the addition of flip; the French twist; the half-do; the big updo; or the band/front bow.

Where the Boys Were

For men we had: the mop top (popularized by the Beatles); the "crew" or "buzz" cut (shaved close to the head); the pompadour (think *Grease* or Elvis); and the afro for

African Americans (also known as the "natural"). The long flowing manes were worn by either males or females and have evolved into the "man-buns" of today, which are often combined with a modified buzz cut (shade—think Kim Jong Un). Facial hair was ubiquitous: mustaches; sideburns; full beards, sometimes combined with sideburns; and mustaches with Van Dykes. Unless they were corporate suits, men, in general, looked as though there was a full moon every night.

The Nehru jacket for men came into fashion in the early '70s. Patterned on that worn by the Indian Prime Minister, they were fun and could be dressed up or down depending on the choice of accessories and/or fabric. In China, under the suppression of the Cultural Revolution, grey Mao suits (Zhongshan) were the mandatory height of fashion. Amusingly, they were transformed into earth-toned safari-style jackets for European men. More various influences could also be seen: films featuring James Bond; the hint of exotic adventurous travel (Great White Hunter); possible socialist leanings—pretense of a classless society; or more of that rebellion against traditional ideas of proper attire.

In the Upper Crust

At the other end of the spectrum, we have Jackie Kennedy, the style icon of icons. One of the most examined women of history, her style shadow was cast across the world. In her little pillbox hats with Oleg Cassini or Chanel suits, she epitomized the 1960s upper-class aristocracy.

Born Jacqueline Lee Bouvier in 1929, she and her sister Caroline Lee were the children of Wall Street stockbroker John Vernou Bouvier, III, nicknamed "Black Jack." Raised a Catholic, her upbringing was somewhat schizophrenic. On the one hand, she was used to only the very best of everything society could give her, on the other, her father was an alcoholic and philanderer. This caused her parents to separate in 1936, when Jackie was only seven, and divorce in 1940. This event seems to have affected her deeply and turned her inward. Their mother quickly married the heir to Standard Oil, Hugh Dudley Auchincloss, Jr. As a Catholic, Jackie is reported to have felt ill at ease with the Protestant Auchincloss family, so she sought her own company more and more.

After tragedy struck, her face grew sadder through time and her eyes lost their smile, but her look never fell below impeccable and never lost its influence. Nonetheless, even after her marriage to Aristotle Onassis, her face never regained the brilliance which had characterized her during her First Lady years. In an interesting development, both fashion-wise and psychologically, whereas simplicity had always been her signature, in the 1980s/90s she added more in the way of ruffles to her evening wear. Glamorous in a completely unstudied way, and the dramatic opposite to the kaleidoscope of fashion swirling around her, she maintained her considerable influence—greater than any movie star—until her death in 1994.

A similar icon of fashion, Grace Kelly, moved into even higher circles of prestige. Not just a First Lady, she became a princess—the purported dream of every little girl—with her marriage to Prince Rainier of Monaco in 1956. Although she retired from acting after her marriage, she continued to be an arbiter of aristocratic style until her death in a 1982 car accident.

A princess, as well, was Jackie Kennedy's younger sister, Lee Radziwill (Caroline Lee Bouvier). On her marriage to the Polish Prince Stanislaw Albrecht Radziwill, she became Her Serene Highness Princess Caroline. Possessed of the same sense of style as her sister, she attempted at first to make it as an actress, which was an abject failure. Her next attempt at an individual persona was as an interior decorator which made her a minor success among wealthy clientele. In 1972, she tried to make a documentary film about the Bouvier family which never materialized. Nonetheless, the footage concerning "Big Edie" (Edith Ewing Bouvier Beale) and "Little Edie" (Edith Bouvier Beale) which had already been shot by Albert and David Maysies was preserved. This footage later became the documentary *Grey Gardens* (1976) and then the basis for the 2006 Broadway musical of the same name. The story was also made into a television movie in 2009. In spite of her efforts, sadly, Lee's biggest hit was as a fashionista. In 1996 she was named to the *Vanity Fair* International Best Dressed Hall of Fame. The Bouvier sisters' story is actually quite a tragic one—an ironic example of "money can't buy happiness."

In service of these diverse role models, fashion see-sawed through the '60s and '70s from strange to even stranger. Who can forget Barbra Streisand at the 1969 Oscars in a sheer, bell-bottomed pantsuit covered with sequins and a Peter Pan collar complete with floppy bow tie? While opaque patches in front kept the ensemble from prompting a vice raid, the rear view was a different story. Or Cher's increasingly bizarre moments through the '70s? Or Angelica Huston? Or ... just about anybody?

"Dress of the Year" 1969. I am at a loss for descriptors. Ruffled? Girlish? Schlumpy? Anyone over 14 should know better? Take your pick (Mabalu, Creative Commons).

Looking at pictures of those rather fraught decades, it seems strange to realize that the response to extraordinary worldwide social upheaval was really what one might consider utter silliness. May I present the "Dress of the Year" for 1969?

But, on further consideration, what should the response to the madness of war be? Most particularly one that caused as much societal divisiveness as the Vietnam War. We will look further into other sources for answers.

Thirteen

Anti-Posters

Vietnam War Posters

> "We are the unwilling, led by the unqualified, doing the unnecessary, for the ungrateful."
>
> —Matthew Quick, *The Reason You're Alive*[1]

Shocking and virulent? Emotional and truthful? The United States propaganda posters of the Vietnam War are a jarring departure from those of World Wars I and II. Almost universally against the war, mainly displaying little sympathy for those fighting, they branded Richard Nixon and Lyndon Johnson as murderers and suggested that the men who resisted the draft got the girls—"Girls Say Yes to Boys Who Say No." Interestingly, these anti-posters are nearly all presented in red, black and white.

One Lyndon Baines Johnson image is particularly gruesome. A spider-legged insect with scorpion tail and human hands which hold bones and a skull, also bears a skull for a head and is surrounded by more skulls. In bleak black and white, without even the red, there is nothing subtle, objective, or reflective here. "Nixon's Peace" portrays Nixon waving a small flag, riding at the head of a fleet of bombers, over a map of Vietnam pinpointing the spots that have been heavily bombed, all in the ubiquitous red, black, and white. The title, just in case anyone should miss the message, is given in three languages, Spanish, French, and English.

A Nixon detractor says, "You Don't Have to be Vietnamese to Smell a Rat. Come Crown King Dick!"—not so subtle, there, either. A caricature of Nixon's face is welded on the body of a rat swallowing the body of a defenseless victim, whose blood flows copiously. A product of the Youth International Party, it's also red, black, and white.

Another anti-Nixon poster—he was probably the most popular target—depicts Nixon in a blood-red color on an off-white background, wearing an Uncle Sam hat, holding a gun and a bag of money. The caption states "Uncle Sam Bleeds You." Published by RITA (Resisters Inside the Army), it boldly proclaims the date and location of a protest in Berlin, in support of Cambodia, the week of May 16–23. We, the general public, are included in the massacre of innocents suggested by the poster's statement.

"Know Your Enemy" depicted a single black-and-white enlargement of a round-faced child, covered in what we assume is blood from a head wound. Since at least a million South Vietnamese died at the hands of both the Communists and United States, this tugs at the heartstrings, as it was intended.

A few leaned in a slightly sympathetic direction for the Unites States troops: one example reminded parents of the cost with the bald question "Your Son Next?" in stark black and khaki; another entitled "Bring the Troops Home" depicts a young soldier with helmet carelessly tossed aside, bare head cradled in his right hand, with red for the soldier's image, black for the lettering, all on a completely bare white background. There's also an example in the black-and-khaki color scheme which proclaims, "The War is Over," then goes on to say that it's "For 55,000 G.I.s and a Million Vietnamese [the numbers killed]), It's All Over." The poster exhorts us to "Vote YES for PEACE on April 6."

One of the few booster-ish examples I found, supposedly aimed at recruiting African Americans, was a poster for the naval services saying, "Your Son Can Be Black, and Navy too." It pictures a slender young man, wearing an afro and a tie-dye style shirt, looking puzzled, and, frankly, I am as well. Is the poster saying, "You don't have to be a 'hippie'?" "You don't have to be skinny?" "You don't have to wear that awful shirt?" "Get a job?" This cringe-worthy poster can scarcely be called an encouragement for the Black community.

A preferable one, which might have resulted in some enlistees for the Navy, shows an African American officer on the bridge and two regular seamen. The caption says, "You can study black history and you can go out and make it." Less insulting to the target audience.

Unsurprisingly, posters from both North and South Vietnam do a total one-eighty from those of the United States. The Communists portray heroic villagers fighting for their "freedom" as in one uncaptioned example. Or (and I love this one) "Uncle Ho: 'The Bringer of Light.'"[2] Depicting a smiling Uncle Ho right beside the hammer and sickle, it's executed in those colors seemingly favored for Vietnam posters—red, black, and white. Happy warriors precede him while trampling on an arrow marked USA. Several Communist-produced posters celebrate the downing of 4,000 American bombers. One of these depicts a smiling girl soldier looming over a dejected and possibly bound American airman. A second depicts an American bomber skewered on the end of a bayonet held by a Red soldier. There are an unusual number of front-line women soldiers portrayed: a profiled woman with a bayonet stands in front of a lotus flower—a frequent motif in Communist Vietnamese art; two women with guns creep through a field

A recruiting poster for the U.S. Navy, which must have resulted in very few takers. The young man looks as baffled as I am (courtesy Online Library).

Black officer on the bridge and one black, one white ordinary seamen. This at least acknowledges the abilities of African Americans (Online Library).

of lotuses, captioned "The Southern Guerillas are Truly Gutsy" in Vietnamese; and in a third, a woman soldier raising a sickle stands behind a man with a hammer. Both carry bayoneted rifles. In Vietnamese., the caption vows, "Under the glorious flag of the Vietnamese Communist Party, the people of Nghe An will crush their American enemies." Below the red background with its sickle and hammer emblem, an olive-green group of soldiers, farmers, mothers, etc., mill randomly.

Of course, a notable majority proclaim the happiness of North Vietnamese people, most often with "Uncle Ho" smiling above. One colorful example of this genre depicts a soldier, a mechanic, and a young woman holding a tablet—possibly a student, possibly a clerk or simply representative of women as a whole. They smile, Uncle Ho smiles, planes fly, ships navigate—everyone is happy, happy, happy.

The glacial dearth of poster support for our own troops, originating from United States sources, is really inexcusable. Where was the government which was sending men to fight? Why were they not combating the bad publicity with an opposite view? The answer, I'm afraid, is that they were afraid to manifest support. We have seen this sort of schizophrenic political attitude many times. There were a few examples. "Back Our Boys in Vietnam" was issued by the American Legion in patriotic red, white, and blue, but was far outweighed by those that were anti-war. One in particular struck me—very negatively, I must say, with its take-off of Uncle Sam's image, saying "I Want You for the US Army." It portrays a grinning, pointing skeleton bursting through Uncle Sam

A male and female carrying bayonetted rifles raise a hammer and sickle in their left hands. Not dressed as soldiers, they undoubtedly represent the people of North Vietnam as a whole. The caption states that *the people* will crush their American enemies (courtesy Saigoneer).

and replacing him with Death. It's not the only one to use the skeletal depiction—a second pictures a skull boasting an American flag top hat. "Mobilize Against the War," it exhorts, and in smaller print "March" giving time and date. One of the marches was to be held by the Vietnam Peace Parade Committee, on Fifth Avenue. The "Committee" was led by Norma Becker, an outspoken opponent to the war and a member of the War Resisters League. The committee used posters such as one taken from a famous news photo of a young girl with her clothes burned off as a result of bombing to drum up sympathy for their cause. The caption for that one reads "Aid the Victims of U.S. Bombing." Unconscionable, to my mind, not for being anti-war, but for mocking those who felt duty-bound to serve—unwillingly or not.

In the end, say what you will, whether it was a "just" war or not, it was *just* war: the dead were *just* as dead and the families *just* as devasted, as they had been in every war despite the lack of either clarity or unity.

Fourteen

Hosed But Not Supported

The unresolved aftermath of the war produced a spate of movies presenting opinions criticizing the war, but only one supporting it. Naturally enough, the "you bet we should fight" side was again represented by John Wayne, the indefatigable leader of heroes through 30 years of war. One of his best-known films, *The Green Berets* (1968), was heavily propagandistic in favor of the conflict. It also starred another tough guy, Aldo Ray, along with George Takei (of Mr. Sulu fame), Patrick Wayne, Jack Soo, and David Janssen. Based on a 1965 novel by Robin Moore, the scenario was radically altered for the movie, most probably at Wayne's request. Wayne was obsessively anti-Communist and strongly in favor of South Vietnam's position, so he requested full cooperation and source material from President Lyndon Johnson and the United States Department of Defense. Obtaining both was no problem since Johnson knew favorable publicity from a popular star, for an unpopular war, was invaluable.

Wayne, as Colonel Mike Kirby, handpicks two teams of his best Special Forces personnel. They are to be sent to Vietnam on two separate missions: one to replace troops at a base camp, where they would be working with South Vietnamese and Montagnard (hill-dwelling Vietnamese) soldiers; and the other to form a counterguerrilla force. Once there, they meet a skeptical journalist, George Beckworth (David Janssen), who is unconvinced of the need to be in Vietnam. Kirby demonstrates all the good they are doing for the population—irrigation ditches, candy for the little ones, clean bandages—all benefits of the Special Forces mission. Much of the rest is Wayne being Wayne. After much fighting, running, blowing up bridges, etc., most members of both teams have been killed with the exception of Wayne. In the final scene, he comforts a child they have saved in answer to the child's desperate question, "What will happen to me now?" "You let me worry about that, Green Beret [Wayne has placed a dead team member's beret on the child's head]. You're what this thing's all about." The two walk together along a beach at sunset while the "Ballad of the Green Berets" is heard. A financial success, the movie failed to win the hearts and minds of the critics. Nevertheless, in spite of popular sentiment regarding the war, viewers flocked to see it, inspired more probably out of curiosity—that, and the indomitable John Wayne.

Wayne himself, was (and continues to be posthumously) a controversial figure. A staunch Republican, a flag-waving patriot, and an icon of masculinity, Wayne was also given to racist, homophobic, and jingoistic statements which were uncensored by good taste. He is quoted in a 1971 *Playboy* interview as saying, "I believe in white supremacy until the blacks are educated to a point of responsibility," as well as "I don't feel we did wrong in taking this great country away from the Indians...." It gets worse but that makes the point.[1] On the other hand, all of his three wives were of Spanish or Hispanic descent. Unlike several other prominent actors, such as Jimmy Stewart and Clark Gable, Wayne did not serve in World War II (he was exempted due to age), which was purportedly a sore point with him. According to his last wife, he became the over-the-top patriot of his later years out of guilt at his failure to serve. Strangely, in my humble opinion, in 1980 he was posthumously awarded the Presidential Medal of Freedom by President Jimmy Carter.[2]

Speaking from the Past

As with World War I, more films about the Vietnam War appeared after the cessation of hostilities than during. In view of this fact, one can see the fashions of the 1960s/70s did not "come from Hollywood," but were an anti-establishment statement from the beginning. Two of the best-known and best remembered were *Platoon* (1986) and *Apocalypse Now* (1979).

Based in a loose way on Joseph Conrad's novel *Heart of Darkness, Apocalypse Now* starred a parade of big names: Marlon Brando; Robert Duvall; Martin Sheen; Laurence Fishburne, who was only fourteen at the time of shooting; Harrison Ford; and Dennis Hopper to name a few. Written by Francis Ford Coppola along with John Milius, and directed by Coppola, the story switched the jungles of the Congo to the jungles of southeast Asia. Marlon Brando, who plays Colonel Kurtz (based on Conrad's Mr. Kurtz) has been deemed insane and accused of murder. Martin Sheen, as Captain Benjamin Willard (based on a character named Marlow in *Heart*), has been chosen for a secret mission to assassinate Kurtz. The story follows Willard's action-filled river journey from South Vietnam to Cambodia. When he arrives at Kurtz's outpost, Willard is imprisoned by Kurtz. There he is tortured but released and allowed to walk freely in the compound. This partial freedom allows him to sneak into Kurtz's room and attack him with a machete. Kurtz is fatally wounded but manages a few last words: "The horror ... the horror..." which naturally, became a catchphrase.[3]

Platoon (1986) looks back nearly two decades in the memory of a genuine Vietnam veteran, Oliver Stone. Seven years after *Apocalypse Now* we have Charlie Sheen instead of his father Martin as a United States Army volunteer to Vietnam, Private Chris Taylor. Tom Berenger is the cynical Sgt. Bob Barnes, who is ultimately killed by Taylor. Willem Dafoe is Sgt. Elias, a more idealistic leader (who is presumably killed by Barnes). The script is a semi-autobiographical expansion of a film entitled *Break*, written by Stone but never produced. The violence is unremitting, and there is little in the way of ameliorating "morality." Sadly, and horrifically, this is the reality of war and most particularly, that war. The veterans of World Wars I and II returned just as disillusioned as those of Vietnam, but they at least had the slight comfort of feeling they had fought for a just cause. The veterans of Vietnam had nothing but ridicule, criticism, and disdain to return to. Perhaps that fact is why the psychological wounds from the war seemed so much worse than in previous conflicts. Veterans of World War II, for example, appeared to be able to go back to work, buy homes through the G.I. Bill, and generally maintain a semblance of stability. Of course, this was only a surface façade, but they, again, could feel they had been fighting for that same just cause and could return with pride. Vietnam veterans not only had to cope with their memories but be reviled for them.

In order to create the verisimilitude of their discouragement, Stone had the *Platoon* actors undergo an intensive 30-day "training" course in which they were subjected to restricted rations, lack of sleep, forced marches, and other forms of "abuse" until Stone felt they had the right attitude of exhausted, "don't give a damn," G.I.s. Like General Sherman, and as a veteran, Stone knew whereof he spoke. The morality of war is one of the central issues in *Platoon;* the movie seems to stress that none can be found.

Possibly due to the meager amount of war movies, or to the unpopularity of the war itself, fashions for the '70s leaned as far away from military style as possible with one or two specialized exceptions. A sketch by the Spanish designer Elio Berhanyer pictures a uniform-style fitted coat with large double-breasted buttons, accessorized with over-the-knee boots and a billed military cap with one of the large buttons centered over the bill. The sketch was probably a suggested design for Iberia Airline. The prize-winning Berhanyer not only designed commercially, but also for the stars Ava Gardner and Cyd Charisse, as well as Queen Sofia of Spain and the Infanta (Princess) Pilar.

For men's fashions, the disco era was in swing. Ties got wider, and toward the 1980s, shoulders began to widen as well. Polyester was still king, and in the late '70s into the early '80s, "glam" fashion reared it's not so attractive head and persisted for several years. A great deal of this influence can be laid at the feet of the iconic David Bowie. On him (and some runway models), it looked terrific. On the man in the street—not so much—not everybody can be Ziggy Stardust. Really not our finest hours.

Unlike the years just after talkies arrived in the late '20s, continuing through the Depression and into World War II, lighthearted musicals were not much a part of the Vietnam era. *Thoroughly Modern Millie* (1967) and *The Boyfriend* (1971), starring the supermodel Twiggy, stand out for their attitudes of sheer fun. Both were set in the Roaring Twenties—which might indicate a nostalgia for the past rather than the uncertain present of the 1960s/70s.

Millie starred Julie Andrews in the title role, along with a charming Mary Tyler Moore as the naïve orphan Miss Dorothy Brown. The plot brings Millie to the big city with the hopes of getting a job as a stenographer and marrying a rich gentleman. She rents a room at a boarding house where the owner, Mrs. Meers (Beatrice Lillie, a former musical comedy star herself), is selling lone girls into white slavery. The resulting action is screwball comedy of the old school. The film received mixed reviews for its abrupt changes of tone, veering from loving satire of the Flapper Age to Mack Sennett Keystone Cop slapstick, to utterly improbable. In other words, very much like a genuine silent film.

The not very inspired, and way off style-wise for the declared year of the film ("This is 1922!"), costumes were by Jean Louis.[4] Moreover, the dancers who wore them had trouble (a lot) with coordination. The Charleston, which was repeated several times, seemed to be beyond them. On top of that, the choreography was generally mediocre. Still, all of the mess added up to a really enjoyable evening.

The *Boyfriend* project had considerable difficulty getting off the ground. It had been a long-running stage production, premiering in 1954 with Julie Andrews in the lead. With Debbie Reynolds in the Julie Andrews role, it was announced as a coming attraction in 1958, but the idea was shelved. Reynolds later claimed it was one of three projects she really wanted to do but again nothing came of it. Finally, in 1971, the project came to fruition, with the leading role falling to Twiggy. It turned out to be a break-out performance for her, because she was neither a singer nor a dancer. Nevertheless, it gave her the start of an unexpected musical career.

Again, there were mixed reviews: Roger Ebert referred to the "joyless camera" of Ken Russell; Fred Astaire felt it mocked the old movies; Sandy Wilson, who wrote the '20s-style music, later claimed he hated it, and even the director repudiated it in a later interview. But it had Tommy Tune, one of the best hoofers around, Christopher Gable of the Royal Ballet, and a really charming Twiggy. Although she does not become a great singer, she does a workmanlike job with the dancing. Ken Russell's wife, Shirley, designed the costumes, however the movie does not appear on her filmography. The costumes are great and so are Tony Walton's sets. The choreography is a big improvement on *Thoroughly Modern Millie,* as is the dancing. The movie is a must-see just for Tommy Tune's performance alone. Yes, it's not a masterpiece, but it's a musical, so it doesn't have to be. These two were exceptions to the generally turgid product churned out by the studios through the '70s and '80s.

While movies have regained some sense of fun or adventure, the Janus-headed ambience of the Vietnam era lives with us still, in our attitudes, in our activities, in the very divided nature of our society, and in our wardrobes. Like Humpty Dumpty, we can't seem to put ourselves back together again.

FIFTEEN

Is There an After(war)d?

The 1970s, according to Tom Wolfe, ushered in the "Me" generation. These were deemed to be the Baby Boomers (born between 1946 and 1964) who were supposedly unwarrantedly self-involved. Since the '80s have also been described as the "Me" Decade, and the same term applied to the Millennials born after 1980, it would seem that every generation since Vietnam has been on a merry-go-round of self-indulgence.[1]

As I have suggested, the '70s was not the greatest of fashion eras. Even First Lady Betty Ford's formal wear was less than appealing. Flared pants were still in, but micro-minis were out. The "Hot Pants Patrol" was still functioning along with other less attractive trends. You wouldn't believe photos of Nigel Lythgoe ("So You Think You Can Dance)" and his dance group. Yves St. Laurent, however, was an outstanding exception to some pretty bad wardrobe designs from some eminent designers. One lovely example was a black evening gown pairing a velvet bodice with fuchsia satin sleeves and teal satin belt over a full black taffeta skirt. Furs were lush, no PETA then.

Formal wear for men was equally—I can't think of another word but "funny": Extra wide lapels, enormous bow ties and lots of piping trim in contrasting colors for evening, three-piece suits with those wide lapels for work, and flares, flares, flares—or conversely, jeans, jeans, jeans, which had straight, but not tight, legs.

In the 1980s, continuing the diversity of the '60s and '70s, fashion was still of a "come as you are" preference, but reverting to more formality when "dressing up."

An outstanding exception to informality is a photograph of First Lady Nancy Reagan in 1981, featuring her in the company of King Juan Carlos of Spain and his spouse, Queen Sophia. Mrs. Reagan, well-known for her sense of style, is gowned in a stunning creation. Mainly devoted to a geometric, black-and-gold, satin print, the gown has a square-necked, solid black bodice, with full, three-quarter sleeves of the print, above a belted, semi-full gathered skirt also in the print. Queen Sophia wears a gown which is better left undescribed.

One of the most eye-catching examples of '80s dressing is an ensemble by the designer John Galliano, whose "Dress of the Year" (1987) was a gray and black large-size plaid jacket and skirt with a solid black collarless bodice. This description does not begin to do justice to the design.

The jacket was long sleeved, full-length, and with a relaxed and unstructured fit. The skirt was high-waisted (virtually Empire), draped harem style, with the drape proceeding from two large side pockets, and midi-length, about three inches above the ankle. The whole ensemble was paired with a turban-like head-covering that culminated in a flirtatious little hat perched over one eye and low-heeled, x-strapped shoes. Fabulous!

The ’80s also saw the establishment of the Goths. Various use of the adjective “Gothic” had already been applied to rock music as far back as the ’60s, nevertheless a true subculture emerged in the early years after 1980. The influences shaping the Goth movement were many. Literary heroes included the “usual suspects”—Edgar Allan Poe, Bram Stoker, the author Sheridan Le Fanu (*The House by the Churchyard,* 1863), and H.P. Lovecraft. Others, more contemporary, were Storm Constantine, Gothic/horror author Poppy Z. Brite (Billy Martin) and Ian McEwan. The more literary Goths also harked all the way back to Ann Radcliffe, the author of *The Mysteries of Udolpho* (1794) and *The Italian* (1797), following in the footsteps of Horace Walpole (*The Castle of Otranto,* 1764). Very popular with young women, Radcliffe was one of the pioneers in the field of Gothic fiction. Unlike Walpole, who gave the name to the genre, her books included elements of the supernatural which generally turned out to have rational explanations. Mythology was also an inspiration for the Goth rationale, such as Celtic myth, Christian “theology,” Egyptian mythology, and pagan tradition, and they drew influence from such disparate sources as the pre–Raphaelites, Nietzsche, and Sartre.

Similar in many ways to steampunk fashion, Gothic clothing consisted mainly of black, accessorized with black, and contrasted with black. Laced, corset-like bodices, with figure-clinging long gowns, or full-skirted semi-ball attire; heavy boots, some with platforms; often with thigh-high hose and garters; derrière-revealing shorts and corsets; dark, heavy makeup; in other words, a mélange of Victorian-inspired anti-fashion in black. Fun. Steampunk concentrates on the Victorian era and is also fun. Straight punk, characterized by more chains and more rips, can be considered an offshoot. Not so much fun.

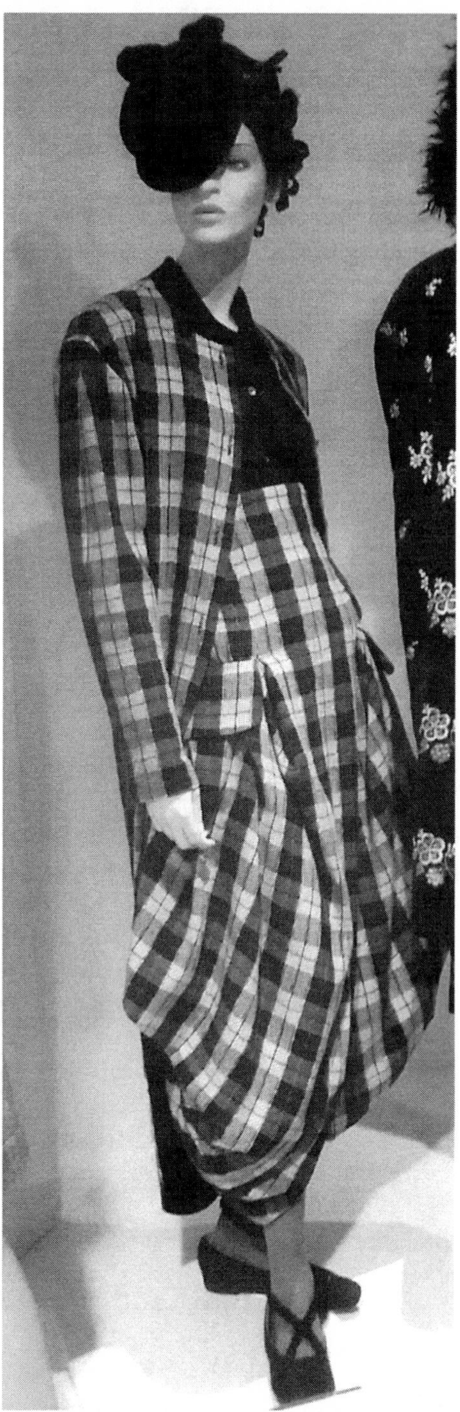

John Galliano “Dress of the Year” for 1987. Large-size black-and-white plaid with solid black bodice, draped skirt contrasts with high waist. Fabulous! (Mabalu, Wikimedia Commons.)

Goth has been one of the most enduring fashions of the after-Vietnam decades and has been brought up to date. We can now boast both the post-punk and Goth/Wave movement.[2]

A Return to Formality?

One interesting development, which can be seen featured more and more in publications such as the *WSJ* magazine (part of the weekend *Wall Street Journal*), is the revival of extravagant formal wear for evening. Nevertheless, extravagant does not always translate as flattering or tasteful, as photos of fairly recent red-carpet walkers would demonstrate. At the 2019 Oscars, one hopelessly misguided participant combined what appeared to be a shapeless, sleeveless, turtleneck tee shirt stretched into a full-length gown, with an embroidered, sheer, off-the-shoulder overdress, ending in a long train. The wearer shall remain nameless. At the other end of the spectrum there was, however, a glorious Elie Saab–designed gown of what resembled a cascade of Monet-inspired hand-painted flowers on a plunging-necklined bodice, just slightly off-the-shoulder above a gathered bouffant skirt ending in a short train. A bold George Chakra design in a pale orchid sheer was also an eye-catcher—almost indescribable. A one-shouldered peek-a-boo bodice that covered and revealed at the same time, and slit to the waist with the same peek-a-boo effect, underneath it displayed what looked like a totally sheer dotted romper. Just enough tease to be enticing and demure together.

Looking back at the Oscars throughout the years reminds us that there have always been more misses than hits, especially in those hit-or-miss years of the '60s and '70s.

Still there is hope. The 2019 Met Gala, naturally, takes extravagant to the very *n*th of the word, with the young singer and dancer Zendaya offering a take on Cinderella that was a bit more than Cindy ever had in mind. The popular and pop-singing star Lady Gaga (Stefani Germanotta) was magnificent, posing at the 2019 Golden Globes in the same shade of blue as Zendaya but with an elegant and simple flare-skirted gown accessorized with a puff-sleeved coat ending in a cathedral-length train of the same material as the gown. Wonderful! However, she appeared at the Met Gala in pink, then in black, then in pink again, and then in her black undies, panty hose, and umpteen-inch platforms. What's wrong with being short?

Sandra Oh was outstanding at the Golden Globes in a white, draped bodice, mermaid-style with an asymmetrical neckline, a flared ruffle on the right shoulder, and just the hint of train in the back. To the 2019 BAFTAs Kate Middleton (yes, that one) wore a white chiffon Alexander McQueen that looked like a mirror twin to Sandra Oh's. Although Kate's was more flared at the skirt, it featured an asymmetrical neckline to the left and ruffled left shoulder. Even the reporters were elegant and indistinguishable from the celebrities. Zanna Roberts Rassi, for example, covering the 2019 Golden Globe Awards, is a case in point. Wearing a lavender, form-fitting chiffon gown with a slight train which featured a cascade of posies in white and a darker shade of blue-purple, she resembled a mermaid rising from the foam.

There were others less successful at each of these events: the emerging from the shell, the tower of red ruffles, the sagging to the waist bare-chested drape, but overall, they were a sign of taste for the future. While the kaleidoscope of today's fashion

Zanna Roberts Rassi, reporter for *E! News* covering the Golden Globe Awards for 2019. Even the reporters are elegant (Amzrr, Wikimedia Commons).

democratizes everyone, it also takes a lot of the fun out of dressing for the occasion. The above examples prove that it's definitely a good thing to do. If one is going to pay up to $2,500 (and even upwards) for a ticket to a Broadway play, one really ought to dress like a Vanderbilt to match.[3]

On the other, more contemporary, hand, Ari Seth Cohen's exuberant, whimsical, and amusing book, *Advanced Style: Older and Wiser,* is a paean to eccentricity made top-of-the-line fashion. Two hundred sixty-eight pages of photographs, featuring women of a "certain age" dressing as they %$@* well feel like, offers a boost to the soul in its sheer joy. These ladies are fearless, eye-popping, and downright irresistible. They mix and match with abandon, pile on the jewelry with no restraint, and look wonderful (even the guys occasionally get into the act—think Elton John). I should mention that most of them have the money to carry it off without looking like bag ladies. Nevertheless, the final product is inspiring for the less affluent and could only happen in the post–Vietnam afterglow. An added plus, *they are* the occasion they are dressing for.

Perhaps the anything-goes mash-up of styles is a positive, rather than a negative, continuing trend. In the light of today's many gasp-worthy events, it remains to be seen.

Epilogue

Following the trajectories of the three major world wars focused on in this discussion—Vietnam could certainly be considered as global a conflict as either of the world wars—the arguments presented attempted to demonstrate that those great battles have led to profound shifts in fashion. What we have worn, both during and after each of these conflicts, has been directly affected by psychological considerations operating in those eras. Wardrobe choices have thus mirrored the societal *Zeitgeist* in interesting and very often controversial way's. Each era has left some enduring mark on the future: trousers for women from World War I; no-nonsense practicality from World War II, as well as tailored, take-charge suits and dresses (not to mention bikinis) and, in the most thought-provoking, and so far, enduring fashion upheaval of all, *anything goes* since Vietnam.

Still, was there a commonality? I asked, at the beginning, if a pattern would emerge from the seeming crazy-quilt of fashion. I would argue that, though there was ostensibly little similarity among the three wars, that the common fashion thread which ran through all was rebellion. Men were included, but it was mainly a woman's war being fought *sub rosa* in each instance. With each war, women gained a little more ground toward equality under the law and in the marketplace and their wardrobes reflected those gains. Not just for the everyday housewife, but those who aspired to career recognition: doctors, filmmakers, lawyers, scientists, and those plain "ordinary" workers who make up the bulk of wage earners. This commonality went hand in hand with an interesting "masculinization" of women's clothing culminating in the unisex attire featured since Vietnam.

When discussing the Vietnam conflict, I also asked the question: Has the Vietnam War ever ended? The answer, I suggested, was possibly a resounding No![1] It might be said with some authority that the fashion mélange of today lends considerable support to that assertion. In spite of the nearly half century since the cessation of outright hostilities, society has not settled into anything resembling the aftermaths of the previous two wars. There are, however, other considerations which, mingled with the clinging aftermath of Vietnam, add spice to the recipe.

A large part of this upheaval might be laid at the feet of the rising social media phenomenon, which provides open access to a multitude of diverse opinions. This diversity, in its turn, contributes to a wider psychological unease afflicting the entire global village. Ever growing population, global warming with its concomitant severe weather crises, and the lack of adequate food and water in areas which will be permanently drought-ridden, all these are contributors to that unease. In plain truth, we *see* too much. While this makes us more aware of global problems, it can result in paralyzing helplessness for many. Although it may appear to be a frivolous and fanciful statement, these drastic and random occurrences are mirrored by the helter-skelter nature of present-day fashion design. While we are not still dealing with an open war against a declared enemy, we are still fighting a societal war for increasingly scarce resources, increasingly scarce land, and an increasingly angry and divided population. What will we be wearing?[2]

Appendix A

The Women Warriors

Let's Be Civil

A surprising number of women actually served as soldiers in the Civil War. Ascertaining just how many is difficult since their names are lost, owing to the need the women had to disguise themselves as men. Nonetheless, it is thought that the count was between 400 and 750. Women also served on the Union hospital ship *Red Rover* and nursed Union and Confederate troops at field hospitals.

Mary Edwards Walker

One woman who stood out for her service—and the only woman who ever received the Medal of Honor—was the Union Army doctor, Mary Edwards Walker. Walker was born in 1832 into a strongly abolitionist family. Her father, a country doctor, participated in many reform movements and believed in equal education for both sexes. True to his word, he followed his beliefs by educating his five daughters in the same manner as he did his only son, Alvah. Of particular interest was his support of dress reform for women, feeling they were hampered from active pursuits by their cumbersome and tightly corseted garments. That enlightened outlook certainly found favor with his daughter.

Owing to her father's enlightened views regarding women, Mary Walker decided to pursue a career in the medical field and gained a place at Syracuse Medical College, achieving a Doctor of Medicine degree in 1955. After graduating she set up a private practice in Columbus, Ohio, where she met and married a physician colleague, Albert Miller. At the onset of the Civil War, she volunteered as a nurse at the Patent Office Hospital in Washington, D.C. During that time, she earned a degree from New York Hygeio-Therapeutic College in New York City which was the first to enroll women and men in equal standing. The institution, organized in 1853 by Russell Thacher Trall, focused on hydropathy. This was a type of water cure which professed to cure all disease through the use of copious amounts of water, internally and externally, and hygienic therapy which focused on sanitation. After obtaining this second degree, Walker returned to service in the war effort.

This was not as easy as it sounded. Walker had first applied for a commission as an Army surgeon in 1861 but was refused on gender grounds. Working in tent hospitals in both Warrenton and Fredericksburg, Virginia, and then in Tennessee, after the battle of Chickamauga, she once again applied for a commission. However, an Army medical board declared her "utterly unqualified for the position of medical officer." Nevertheless,

Dr. Mary Edwards Walker, winner of the Medal of Honor for service in the American Civil War. The first woman to win this honor, she sports it proudly on her left lapel (Library of Congress).

Major General George H. Thomas appointed her an assistant surgeon in the 52nd Ohio Infantry (also known as the Army of the Cumberland).

The suggestion has been made that she was also a Union spy. This truth of this rumor may be bolstered by the fact that she was captured and held by the Confederate

Army in the spring of 1864. Walker was imprisoned between four and six months before she was traded for a Confederate soldier and released in the fall. She retired from government service in 1865 and later that same year was awarded the Medal of Honor for Meritorious Service, the first woman to hold the honor. In 1917, the honor was unfairly withdrawn by the government, claiming she did not meet the requirements. However, she continued to wear it for the next two years before her death in 1919. In 1977, President Jimmy Carter posthumously restored the honor to this more than deserving woman. Photographs of Walker in her later years picture her dressed in her favorite ensemble, a man's coat and trousers, with wing-collared shirt, watch chains, and a top hat—certainly a reflection of her father's enlightened views. Also, I am positive, a thumbing of her nose at the established male hierarchy. Prominent on her left lapel is her Medal of Honor.[1]

Frances Clayton

Another name known from the annals of the Civil War was Frances Clayton, who served for months in Missouri artillery and cavalry units.[2] Also known as Frances Clalin and under her purported alias of Jack Williams, she disguised herself as a man and joined the Union forces as an ordinary soldier. Born in the 1830s, she was married with three children when she decided to adopt the name Jack Williams, disguise her sex, and enlist in the Army along with her husband. Accounts of her activities differ, nevertheless most sources agree that she fought in at least 17 battles and that she was wounded more than once. At the Battle of Stones River, her husband was killed by her side, but Frances continued to fight on.

Again, accounts differ as to the manner in which she was discovered to be a woman (even Frances' own accounts). Nonetheless, she was finally found out and discharged. In the course of attempting to collect money owed to her and her husband, she was robbed by renegade Confederates, who took her papers and all her money, leaving her at a loss. Friends and former soldiers who had known Frances (as Jack) got together a fund to help assist her in her application for redress, but the end of her story is lost to time. Photographs of Frances dressed as both a woman and a man reveal a tall, high-cheek-boned, masculine appearing woman who passes very well for the opposite sex.

World War I—1914–1918

A Tragic Heroine of World War I: Dorothy Lawrence

The story of Dorothy Lawrence, an Englishwoman who disguised herself as a man and served in the British Army during World War I, reads like a Greek tragedy. Born in 1896, stories of her birth differ widely. Some accounts claim she was abandoned by her mother early; others that she never knew either parent; some sources claim she was the second daughter of Thomas Hartshorn Lawrence and Mary Jane Beddall and knew at least one parent; and still others that her mother died when she was a teen. Her birthplace has been variously given as Hendon Middlesex, Polesworth, Warwickshire, and London. However, all agree that at some point she was adopted by a member of the Church of England. The relationship was not a happy one.

Wanting very much to be a journalist, she moved to Paris, and when the war broke sought to become a war correspondent. Rejected, owing to the reluctance of editors to send a woman to the Front, she befriended two homesick British soldiers, whom she persuaded to procure her a uniform. They passed her separate pieces of the uniform until she had a complete set, whereby she forged papers naming her as Private Denis Smith. After an arduous journey, she befriended another soldier, who hid her for a time until he felt it was safe, then took her to the front line. "Private Smith" served for 10 days until her health took a bad turn and the truth came out.

Embarrassed by their lack of perception, the authorities detained her in a French convent and interrogated her as a spy until she swore to keep her adventure a complete secret. However, in 1919, she published a memoir entitled *Sapper Dorothy Lawrence: The Only English Soldier*. Unfortunately, it was heavily censored by the War Office and never became a commercial success. Dorothy herself disclosed in 1925 that her guardian was sexually abusive, but she was not taken seriously. In fact, the result of this disclosure was that she was taken into care and deemed insane. Committed first to a mental hospital, she was later institutionalized in the Colney Hatch Lunatic Asylum (later Friern Hospital) in North London. She died there, after living in deplorable conditions, in 1964. Penniless, she was buried in a pauper's grave, the site of which is no longer known.

Flora Sandes

Flora Sandes has the distinction of being the "only British woman to *officially* serve as a soldier in the trenches during World War I."[3] An unabashed tomboy from her earliest childhood, she left her middle-class Suffolk background behind and set out for a life of adventure. Trained as a stenographer, she found work in Cairo, Canada, and the United States, before returning to England. There she drove fast cars, joined a shooting club, and trained as a nurse.

When war broke out, Flora was 38 and still eager for adventure. Thinking the war might provide what she sought, she volunteered for the St. John Ambulance Service and was sent to Serbia. There she became fluent in the language and transferred to the Serbian Red Cross. She worked first as a nurse with a Serbian infantry troop, and then enlisted into the Serbian Army which allowed women to fight. She rose to the rank of sergeant-major, during which time she published a book entitled *An English Woman-Sergeant in the Serbian Army* with the hopes of raising money for the Serbian cause. Severely wounded, she received the King George Star from the Serbian government for her bravery under fire and was later promoted to captain.

After the war, dissatisfied with the tame life of England, she returned to Serbia, married the White Russian General Yuri Yudenitch (12 years younger), and moved to what was now Belgrade, Yugoslavia. When that country was invaded by the Nazis in 1941, she re-enlisted at age 65. The Gestapo arrested her, in April of that year when Yugoslavia fell, but she was soon released. Her husband died in September of the same year, leaving her penniless and alone. However, Flora was not held back by either misfortune. Although living again in Suffolk, she continued to travel, sometimes with her nephew. In 1956, Flora died there at the age of 80 (she had just renewed her passport in the prospect of more travel), and her ashes were scattered in the Garden of Remembrance at Ipswich Crematorium.[4]

The Peril of Being Humanitarian: Edith Cavell

Edith Louisa Cavell was born December 4, 1865, in Norfolk, England. After high school, she went to several boarding schools where she gained a fluency in French. In 1887, she began working in Europe as a governess for various European families; however, the illness of her father brought her back to England. Caring for him inspired her to seek a nursing career. Although not joining the nursing profession until 1895 at nearly 30, her aptitude and diligence saw her appointed the first matron of the Berkendael Institute in Brussels, Belgium, in 1907, a position she still held when the country was occupied by the Germans. Cavell then became involved in an underground group trying to help Allied soldiers to reach the Netherlands, a neutral country. They were aided in this process by a native Belgian, Philippe Baucq, who provided money and guides.

Not a combatant, but a dedicated nurse, Cavell was to discover that a white apron and a red cross were no guarantee of either protection or mercy. Accused of "conducting soldiers to the enemy," i.e., helping stranded Allied soldiers to escape from occupied Belgium, she was arrested by the Germans and subject to the death penalty under German law. During her imprisonment she behaved with unswerving dignity and an outward semblance of calm. Cavell must have frustrated her captors, passing the time with letter-writing to friends and family, little domestic duties such as her laundry, and embroidery work.

When her court-martial trial approached, she stated that she preferred to be tried in civilian clothing in order to avoid the appearance of the nursing profession being on trial. She was allowed to send home for garments and chose a blue suit and white blouse which she wore during the entire proceedings. As did Emmeline Pankhurst, she knew that clothing played an important role in projecting one's character.

The verdict was, of course, death. When friends begged her to appeal, she refused. "They want my life," she is reported to have said. She was executed by firing squad at dawn on October 12, 1915, wearing the same blue suit and white blouse. Philippe Baucq was executed on the same day.[5]

The outrage aroused at her death was genuine; nonetheless, it did not hold the British government back from making political capital from her demise. It made invaluable recruitment propaganda and was used unabashedly for that purpose.

World War II—1939–1945

Due to the increased emphasis on physicals in World War II, it was virtually impossible for women to disguise themselves as men and wangle a way into the fighting. Women, however, did serve honorably and courageously, although until recently their service has been undervalued.

"Indomitable" Florence Finch

The exploits of Florence Finch (Loring May Ebersole Smith Finch) read like a spy thriller by John le Carré. The daughter of a veteran of the Spanish-American War who served in the Philippines, she was raised there after the war was over, when her father decided to reside there permanently with his Filipino wife. Not fully belonging to either country, Florence grew up facing the burdens of a mixed-race child.

Beginning her activist career early, she started working for General Douglas MacArthur's Army Intelligence Manila Department (G-2) immediately after graduating from high school. She married an American naval officer, a PT boat operator; however, he was killed when the Japanese invaded the Philippines in 1942. Heroically, he died while trying to resupply Allied troops trapped on Corregidor and the Bataan Peninsula.

After the Japanese occupation of Manila, Finch traded on her Filipino heritage and avoided internment in a Japanese camp, instead being given a job at the Philippine Liquid Fuel Distribution Union with the responsibility of writing vouchers for the distribution of the fuel. In close connection with the Philippine resistance, she diverted fuel supplies to them and took part in arranging acts of sabotage against the Japanese. On hearing of how badly the prisoners of war were being treated in the internment camps, she also joined with a resistance group smuggling food and medicine to the internees.

She was discovered and arrested in October 1944 and sentenced to three years at hard labor. During this time, she was beaten and otherwise tortured, but she refused to reveal any information that would lead to the discovery of the underground resistance group or its members. When Manila was liberated in 1945, so was Finch, who, in short order hopped on a Coast Guard troop transport vessel and headed for the United States. Once there, she took up residence in Buffalo, New York, the birthplace of her father, and joined the Coast Guard. After the war she married an Army veteran, Robert Finch, and moved to Ithaca, New York, for the rest of her life.

Finch was the only member of the Coast Guard Reserve (SPARS) to be honored with the American Medal of Freedom in 1947. She was also the first female recipient of the Asiatic-Pacific Campaign Ribbon. On her death—at the age of 101—she was awarded a complete military funeral with full honors.[6]

Jane Kendeigh

At the age of 22, Jane Kendeigh, a Navy flight nurse, landed on Iwo Jima on March 6, 1945, as reportedly the first United States Navy flight nurse to land on a Pacific battlefield and the first to fly evacuation missions to an active battlefield. The real-life counterparts of Joan Blondell and Ann Southern (*Cry Havoc*), she and her fellow flight nurses would go on to evacuate more than 2,300 Marine and Navy personnel from Iwo Jima, along with an estimated 1,176,048 hospital patients, of whom only 48 were said to have died en route.

Nancy Wake

Born in New Zealand but raised in Australia, Nancy Wake was working as a journalist in New York when she married a wealthy Frenchman and went to live with him in France. She was living in Marseilles when the Germans invaded and occupied France. After the German invasion, Wake went to work for the French Resistance, smuggling men out of occupied France, ferrying supplies and falsifying documents. Captured for a time by the Germans and interrogated, she gave nothing of her activities away. In 1943, she managed to escape to Britain, where she joined the Special

Operations Executive (SOE). After training, she was airdropped back into France as an official spy and was also an out-and-out warrior known as "The White Mouse." Not in the least fazed by blowing things up, shooting foes, etc., she is reported to have killed a SS sentry with her bare hands. For her courageous actions she received the George Medal from Britain, as well as the Medaille de la Résistance and three Croix de Guerre medals from France.[7]

Susan Ahn Cuddy

Cuddy, the daughter of a Korean father who was killed in Seoul in 1937 for raising his voice against the Japanese occupation of Korea, joined the United States military, along with her two brothers, shortly after the Japanese attack on Pearl Harbor. Wishing to join the WAVES, she was at first rejected—most probably due to her Asian-American heritage. Undaunted, she applied again, this time with success, and became the first Asian-American woman in the United States Navy.

First as a link trainer, then as the first female gunnery officer in the Navy, she instructed male recruits in air combat tactics and how to fire a .50-caliber machine gun in the air. She retired from service at the rank of lieutenant and then followed up with a career in the United States Navy Intelligence, a stint with the Library of Congress and the National Security Agency (NSA). Susan Ahn Cuddy was 100 years old when she passed away in 2015.[8]

Colonel Ruby Bradley

One of the most decorated women of World War II, Ruby Bradley spent most of the war interned in a Japanese concentration camp. Colonel Bradley was taken prisoner by the Japanese only three weeks after the Pearl Harbor attack and transferred to the Santo Tomas Internment Camp in Manila, Philippines. For the entire 37 months of her captivity, she provided medical attention to other prisoners, smuggled food to those in need, often giving up her own rations to feed others, delivered babies, and assisted on surgeries. By the time she was liberated, she weighed only 84 pounds, having given away most of her sustenance.

Undaunted by her ordeal, she continued in the Army, serving again in Korea and achieving the rank of colonel. She retired in 1963, the owner of 34 decorations, medals and awards, which included the Bronze Star.

Vietnam—1964–1975

The Vietnam War presented the need for a different kind of bravery in the face of such widespread hostility to the conflict.

Most of the women who served in Vietnam were American nurses, both Army and Navy, starting as far back as 1956, when the first members of the Army Nurse Corps arrived. By 1973, at least somewhere between 5,000 and 7,500 American women were serving or had served in the country (estimates differ). By some miracle, only a few died while in service, two receiving posthumous awards for bravery. Both had previously served on the battlefields in prior wars: Lieutenant Colonel Annie Ruth Graham in both

World War II and Korea and First Lieutenant Sharon Lane in Korea. For her service in Vietnam, First Lieutenant Lane was awarded the Vietnamese Gallantry Cross with Palm and the Vietnamese Bronze Star for Heroism, as well. Lieutenant Colonel Graham died of a stroke while still on duty in the country; it was her third active participation in an American war.

Also serving were the United States Naval and Air Force Flight Nurses. The first group to arrive in Saigon in 1963, all received Purple Hearts for injuries incurred during a bombing raid on Saigon on Christmas Eve. Eight of the Women's Airforce Nurses (WAF) were killed in performance of their duties.

Of all the women who served, only two performed a role as anything but a nurse: Lieutenant Elizabeth Wylie, who was Commander of Naval Forces in the Vietnam Command Information Center; and Commander Elizabeth Barret, considered "the first female naval line officer to hold command in an official combat zone."

Beside the American and some Vietnamese women, there were a few Australian nurses, and a fairly large number of non-medically trained volunteers from the Red Cross and other humanitarian organizations.

A few names of those heroic women stand out.

Claire Brisebois Starnes

Claire Brisebois Starnes enlisted in the United States Army Signal Corps at 17 in 1963. Rail thin, she was ordered to eat bananas to put on some weight. At 23, she volunteered for a tour of duty in Vietnam. Once there, she worked as a photojournalist and oversaw publications at Military Assistance Command Vietnam Office of Information (MACV *Observer*). She learned to detach herself from the sights she photographed, carefully never letting herself feel anything at the time. Only later did this become a problem. Starnes served five tours in Vietnam before returning to the United States, where the same contempt and dismissal awaited her that it did for the men. Nevertheless, the Allied Armies recognized her for her outstanding service, and she received the Vietnam Service Medal with Silver Star, the Republic of Vietnam Campaign Medal and the Republic of Vietnam Gallantry Cross. After returning to civilian life, she tried to put the past behind with work, career, and children; nevertheless, the horror of her memories lingered until she felt she needed to seek help in group therapy. To her dismay, she was the only woman in the group and received the same treatment from the male veterans as from the public at large. As a result, the verbal abuse caused her to leave treatment and never seek help again. Instead, for the past 17 years, she has searched for women who served in non-nursing roles to put their stories forth before the public. A book has now been written about those forgotten heroines: *Women Vietnam Veterans: Our Untold Stories*. By Donna Lowery, it finally honors them as they should be honored.[9]

Women Who Died Were Just as Dead

For some reason, it seems that women who died at the front lines, in any war, were somehow seen as not worthy of acknowledgment. Here is a list of just a few who are known to have died in the Vietnam conflict:

Second Lieutenants Carol Drazba and Elizabeth Jones, February 1966 (helicopter crash near Saigon)

Captain Eleanor Alexander and First Lieutenant Hedwig Orlowski, November 1967 (plane crash)
First Lieutenant Sharon Lane, June 1969 (shrapnel wounds)
Second Lieutenant Pamela Donovan, July 1968 (illness contracted on duty)
Lieutenant Colonel Annie Graham, August 1968 (mentioned above, from a stroke; she was only 52)
Captain Mary Therese Klinker, April 1975 (plane crash while attempting to evacuate Vietnamese orphans out of the country)

Along with these servicewomen, 59 female civilians died, including Georgette "Dickey" Chapelle, working as a writer for the *National Observer,* who was killed by a mine while on patrol with the United States Marines in November 1965, and Phillipa Schuyler, killed in a firefight at Da Nang, May 1966. Also killed was Virginia E. Kirsch, who was murdered by a member of the United States Army (August 16, 1970).[10]

All the above were volunteers in the United States armed services or volunteer civilians. Heaven only knows how many Vietnamese women, on both sides, died in active service to the cause they believed in.

These women listed above, not just in the three wars which are our focus, but others mentioned in the text, are but a few of those whose names are known. They stand as exemplars of all those unknowns who served with courage the equal of any man. What differentiates the brave women of World War II and Vietnam from the women of the earlier conflicts was the fact that they served openly as women. No adoption of men's uniforms or trying to pass themselves off as the opposite sex. Heroism was a wardrobe of its own.

Appendix B

"The Light of Europe"

This, to our minds, very peculiar article appeared in the May 1916, issue of *Photoplay.* The tone strikes us as odd—lacking in any awareness of either the realities of war in general or the realities of those under the German heel. Kitchen seems to save what little compassion he possesses for the people of Berlin—who admittedly were suffering privations, nevertheless, were not suffering the abuses of foreign invaders.

Concerning the Continental Photoplay, War's Opiate from Budapest to Brussels

Karl K. Kitchen

There is but one topic of conversation in Berlin—the war. There is but one place where the Berliner can forget it and its concomitant horrors and sorrows—the *Lichtspiele*—"the movies"; and then only for an hour or so because war scenes are a part of every film program. And though the common grief of the nation cannot be wholly forgotten even in the common recreation, the "movies" go far toward making life bearable.

In Vienna and Budapest, capitals of the dual kingdom, where everyday life has not been so poignantly tainted by the nearness of the blood demon, they laugh aloud at the antics of the film comedians. In Berlin, they only smile, for in *Kultur's* center, they take even their pleasures seriously. Even in Brussels, the humbled Belgian enjoys the tragedies and comedies of the *cinema* and forgets, for a time, the grief that came with the gray-clad hordes from the East.

Well, it might be worse, soliloquizes the philosophic Belgian. The tyranny of the ancient or medieval conqueror was tempered by the *cinema.*

At the hour when New Yorkers are sitting down to dinner, the first number on the program in half a hundred *Lichtspiele* in Berlin is being flashed on the screen. Half past seven is the very latest for a moving picture show to begin in the German capital, and 7 o'clock is the usual time. Then Berlin goes in on an empty stomach—or rather, without having dined. For dinner is a midday repast in Germany and supper's a movable feast taken any time between 9 and midnight.

Seven o'clock, my first night in Berlin, found me in a loge of the *Linden Lichtspiele,* a moving picture theatre in Unter den Linden, near the Friedrichtstrasse. Being invited to a 9 o'clock "supper" with a Berlin family, I adopted the usual method of killing time in a strange city.

The *Linden Lichtspiele,* despite its imposing entrance and its uniformed commissionaries, is a comparatively small theatre built after the fashion of our early motion picture theatre—in shape an oblong with a steep pitch to the floor. Along both sidewalls are loges and for the sum of "two mark fifty"—about sixty cents—I was given the privilege of sharing a loge with three monocled and much iron-crossed Prussian officers. Every seat on the floor was taken, but the officers who had reached the loge before me realized the generosity of making room for me, which they did with exact bows and *stereotyped* (emphasis mine) expressions.

A moment after I adjusted myself to my surrounding [sic] the orchestra, composed of a pianist, not more than two violinists and drummer, struck up the opening bars of a typical German air and the lights were dimmed.

"Sein Schwierigster Fall" (His Hardest Case) was flashed on the screen amid murmurs of anticipatory excitement from the audience. As in many films the principals were revealed one at a time and greeted with applause according to their popularity. A rather attractive girl name Mia May was greeted enthusiastically when her face was shown and when Max Landas' [sic, the name is Landa] impressive features were disclosed there was stamping of feet, applause and a buzz of conversation.

It will not be necessary to describe the film, which was given in five parts, although a synopsis of the story was given in the programs which were sold for 10 pfennigs each. Suffice to say it was a fairly good detective film of German manufacture.

For the present time Germany has to depend almost entirely on films made within her borders or in Sweden and Denmark. In fact, during a dozen visits to moving picture theatres in Berlin and other German cities, I did not see a single film that was made outside of Germany or Sweden. The importation of French and English films was, of course, forbidden after the outbreak of war and while Germany is not officially at war with Italy, no Italian films have been imported for nearly a year. There are surprisingly few American films being shown in Germany at the present time. Following the detective film at the Linden Lichtspiele there was an American film—a railroad thriller in which the sweetheart of a sleepy telegraph operator prevents a wreck by riding a horse at full speed and signaling the fast freight with her petticoat—you know the kind—but it was the only American film I saw during all my visits to picture houses in Germany and Austria-Hungary.

A series of war pictures followed this American film, but I did not remain to see them, for there is not a motion picture house in Germany that does not show at least one reel of war pictures at every performance. In fact, the war films are the most important feature of the motion picture industry in Germany today. In several Berlin theatres war pictures are being shown exclusively. At the Urania Theatre at the Taubenstrasse, for instance, I saw a war picture called "Die Kriegeschauplatze auf dem Balkan"—a very interesting film showing the topography of the Balkans as well as some of the recent fighting there. At the Marmorhaus, another moving picture playhouse, I saw part of a film called "Von die Karpathen vis Brest Litowak," which disclosed some of the fighting in the Carpathians and the fall of the above-named fortress. At both playhouses every seat was taken and there many soldiers present whose comments vouched for the accuracy of the pictures.

The U.T. Lichtspiele in the Friedrichstrasse has a good orchestra and while the auditorium is smaller than the leading picture houses in the larger American cities its appointment compare very favorably with them. The best seats are two marks (normally 48 cents), programs are 10 pfennigs (2½ cents), and 10 pfennigs is charged for checking your coat. Like all the other moving picture houses in Berlin it is conducted on a different principle from picture houses in America. Three performances are given at 5, 7 and 9 p.m. Continuous performances are unknown in Berlin and vaudeville and films are rarely combined. Generally speaking, "movie going" is more expensive in Germany than in America. There are no theatres with one price of admission for the reason that class lines are more sharply drawn than they are here. Two marks is the usual price for the best seats, loge seats an extra mark, while the cheapest seats are rarely less than 50 pfennigs (12 cents). Occasionally in the poorer sections of the city we will see announcements that school children are admitted at matinees for 25 pfennigs but 12 cents is the minimum for grownups. And the average admission at the majority of theatres must be over a mark.

But to get back to the bill at Friedrichstrasse Lichtspiele. Here I had my first glimpse of Germany's funny film man, Max Pallenberg, the Teutonic Charley Chaplin, who can assimilate a custard pie with the same éclat portrayed by his Anglo-Saxon brother. Chaplin is unknown in Germany, although in England and France he is a tremendous favorite. I saw Max first in "Der Rasende Roland," a succession of slapstick stunts—a film in which Chaplin would have been perfectly at home.

Loud laughter, the first I had heard in a Berlin movie, greeted Max's antics, which were undeniably funny, but from the conversation I overheard the serious Swedish photoplay which followed was much more appreciated.

This was entitled "A Ghetto Tragedy" made in and about Stockholm. It had a truly tragic theme, which is the entertainment that appeals most to Berliners at the present time. When it was concluded there was prolonged applause and the program ended with a reel of very good war pictures showing the Kaiser reviewing his troops on the East front.

During my stay in Berlin I visited the Lichtspiele "Mozart Saal" in the Nolendorfplatz and the Kammer Lichtspiele on the Potsdamerplatz—two of the largest and highest class moving picture theatres in the German capital—and at both of them I was impressed with the fact that the serious films interested the audience far more than the comedies. At the Kammer Lichtspiele a three-act comedy by Arthur Landberger called "Pension," Lampel disclosed several German film favorites—Hanni Weise, Senta Stoneland, Albert Paulig, Herman Picha and Ferry Sikla. From what I could gather during my brief excursions into the movies in Germany, Albert Paulig is one of the most popular film stars of the hour. Max Mack seems to be the D.W. Griffith of the German movies although it must be admitted that there are no German films that compare with "The Birth of a Nation." Fern Andra is the nearest approach to a Mary Pickford that I saw.

The moving pictures are daily becoming a more important part of the life of the people in the larger cities of Germany and in Berlin especially. The number of travel and educational films he encounters is a revelation to an American movie fan. There is almost a total absence of the cheap "thrillers" that abound in the less important picture houses in America. Films in Germany are under strict supervision of the police, to whom the mishaps of a film counterfeit bring no particular joy. While many of the photoplays are more daring than the films approved by our own variegated censors, good taste is rarely violated.

There is no doubt that the war has stimulated movie going, due chiefly to the great interest in war pictures and the nervous state of mind of a very large proportion of the population. I talked with many Berliners and nearly all of them told me that a visit to a *lichtspiele* took them away from the bitter realities of life more quickly and completely than a visit to a legitimate playhouse. To be sure the playhouses in Berlin that are offering serious plays are crowded nightly, but it is also true that the moving picture houses have never attracted such crowds.

Strangely enough, moving pictures do not play such an important part in the lives of the inhabitants of Vienna and Budapest. Although Vienna is nearly as large as Berlin it is doubtful if it has one-third as many picture houses.

As in Berlin, the moving picture theatres in Vienna give performances at 5, 7 and 9 o'clock. Their scale of prices is somewhat lower for the reason that the unit in Austria—the crown—is worth a trifle less than 20 cents in normal times. A crown buys an orchestra seat at most of the *kinos* in the Austrian capital, although the front seats and the places in the loges are usually two crowns. When I was in Vienna in December the crown had depreciated to 13 cents in American money—consequently my movie going was not expensive.

Generally speaking the *kinos* in Vienna are conducted along the same lines as the *lichtspiele* in Berlin. The films are of German or Swedish origin, with war pictures occupying the most important part of every bill.

At the Opernkino, which is the smartest of the *kinos* for the reason that it is located near the Opernring, or boulevard adjacent to the Great Opera House, I saw very interesting bills on two occasions. Officers in uniform were very much in evidence. I did not see any soldiers for the reason that they are always given places in the balconies. However, I heard them for they were most vigorous in their applause when pictures of their comrades were flashed on the screen.

The program at the Opernkino which are [sic] sold for 10 heiler (normally 3 cents) contain the synopses of the comedy films which are shown there. And I noticed that nearly everyone bought a program. In fact, it is characteristic of movies audiences abroad to understand what they are shown as well as be amused or instructed by it.

The travel films—mountain climbing scenes in Switzerland on one occasion and Bulgarian village scenes on the occasion of my second visit—will long linger in my memory They were in color and of remarkable beauty.

Following them were war pictures of the Austrian General Staff reviewing troops in Galicia and the fighting on the Italian front. When the picture of the aged Austrian emperor was flashed on the screen there was genuine enthusiasm and even the pictures of the German Kaiser and his great generals, von Hindenburg and Mackensen, were also applauded to the echo.

I was very much surprised to see pictures of King George of England reviewing his troops with Earl Kitchener. Not only were they received in respectful silence but when Gen. Joffre was revealed with his staff officers you could have heard a pin drop. Only when the French commander began to kiss the various officers on whom he was pinning decorations was the silence broken. There was a black officer in the line—evidently a Sengalese [sic]—and everyone in the audience wondered if Gen. Joffre would kiss him. I heard tittering in a dozen different parts of the theatre and when Joffres planted two kisses on the cheeks of "der Schwartzer," the entire audience burst into roars of laughter.

The Viennese are a lighter hearted people than the Berliners. And they are not nearly as serious about the war. In Berlin, Shakespeare's tragedies and other serious plays are playing to crowded houses, while lighter forms of theatrical diversion are neglected. In Vienna, just the reverse is true. The light, amusing musical plays are more popular than ever. Add in the movies, aside from the war pictures, the comedies seem more popular than the serious films.

In Budapest I visited just two moving picture playhouses. At one of them, the Mozgo Septthon, a typical picture house of the better class, I saw "Der Tunnel," a film version of Bernard Kellerman's story "The Tunnel."

This film is one of the most popular as well as one of the most pretentious German films of the day. At the six o'clock performance—four performances, at 3:30, 6, 8 and 10 P. M., are given daily—the theatre was crowded. Of all the capitals in warring Europe Budapest has been least affected by the war. The gay night life has continued without interruption and the "movies," have prospered.

As in Berlin and Vienna the capital of Hungary has to depend upon German, Danish and Swedish films. War pictures are everywhere in evidence and, of course, are first in popularity. Evidently there is a shortage of new films for I saw a screen version of Hauptmann's "Atlantis," a picture nearly three years old. It was evidently familiar to many in the audience, but it held their interest, nevertheless. It must be admitted that moving pictures have not entirely come into their own in Budapest but there are unmistakable signs that they are becoming more popular every year.

Of all the war capitals Brussels seems to be the real home of movie fans. The city is dotted with *cinemas,* as they are called there, and they are filled morning, noon and night.

There are several reasons for this surprising condition. Brussels, of course is under German rule and the native population is in mourning for the sad plight of their little country. They have no heart for theatre going—that is, attending regular dramatic performances. The Germans are trying to bring "Kultur" to the Belgians and there are two theatres devoted to German plays, which of course are avoided by the Brusselois [sic]. As the opera is closed and travelling French dramatic and musical companies are unable to reach Brussels, moving pictures have become the popular amusement for all classes. They have the advantage of being inexpensive—a very important consideration in war striken [sic] Belgium.

Of course, all the films shown in Brussels are censured by the German military authorities. But the most surprising liberality is shown in this censorship. The war films which I saw in a *cinema* on the Boulevard du Nord near the metropole Hotel gave glimpses of the French, English and Russian armies as well as the victorious Teutons.

In addition to the German, Swedish and Danish films, numerous American films are to be seen in Brussels at the present time. Cowboy films are particularly popular. Because of the work of the Belgian Relief Commission Americans are extremely popular in Belgium and American film actors are applauded to the echo.

> The *cinemas* of the Belgian capital are more like our American moving picture houses than the *lichtspieles* and *kinos* of Berlin and Vienna. The prices are extremely low, the best seats selling for one franc, less than 20 cents. The majority of movie goers in Brussels pay less than half that sum for their entertainment. The performances in many of the play houses are continuous but end promptly at 11 p.m. when the lid is clamped down by regulations in the former Belgian capital (article entirely as written).

Kitchen's apparent disregard of the fact that he was dealing with enemies of the American people—the United States having declared war, although without sending troops as yet—demonstrates just how unaware the populace at large was, as well as just how unconcerned. Just at the movies, Kitchen dressed as though going to an appearance at court, overlooking the resplendent militarism of his companions, who attend with a similar appearance but with a more chilling purpose. Both these fashion choices bespeak their underlying characters—the unaware American, the well-aware conquerors.

Appendix C

The New York World's Fair

1939–1940

The 1939 World's Fair was built on 1,202 acres of what had been a marshy-grounded ash dump in Queens, after four years of planning, building, organizing, and scouring for funds by the World's Fair Corporation. "Unusual" was probably the best thing that could be said about the choice. The site was out of the way, unattractive, and became the "largest land reclamation project in the Eastern United States."[1] This was paid for by the corporation, which consisted of Police Chief Grover Whalen, who had been elected president of the corporation by the NYWFC (New York World's Fair Committee), Mayor Fiorello La Guardia, Winthrop Aldrich (chairman of the board of Chase Manhattan Bank), Percy S. Straus (president of Macy's), and a host of other important business leaders. They worked closely with Robert Moses, the City Parks Commissioner. In the end, the costs were astronomical for 1939. Around $26.7 million for the land reclamation and a permanent fair building for the corporation. Over and above that, New York State spent about $6 million for its own temporary building and a permanent theater where the *Aquacade* was held. The corporation laid out another $42 million for construction, and other investors contributed around $32 million—all in all, about $160 million. However, foreign nations paid between $30 and $35 million for their chance to be represented and defrayed some of the expense, with attendees expected to make up the rest. This was along with a hoped-for profit from the ticket prices of 75 cents per adult, and 25 cents for children up to age 14. Some interior exhibits were ticketed as well, adding to the rather high price for the time. Just as a comparison, children under 11 could go all day to the movies for 14 cents—watching the cartoons and serials in the morning, and the featured presentations in the afternoon.[2]

Where the ground was hardest to fill, a lake, known first as Fountains then in 1940 changed to Liberty Lake, was created and became the location for Billy Rose's *Aquacade*. Rose (William Samuel Rosenberg) was virtually the entire gamut of entertainment in one person. Not just an impresario, he produced musical theatre and was a lyricist ["Me and My Shadow" (1927), "Without a Song" (1929), "It Happened in Monterrey" (1930), and "It's Only a Paper Moon" (1933), among many others]. He produced not only the *Aquacade,* even before the fair, but also *Carmen Jones,* a Broadway musical (1943), which was remade as a movie (1954). He was married for nine years to Fanny Brice, who would later be played by Barbra Streisand in *Funny Girl,* with James Caan cast as Rose. The couple divorced in 1938, and in 1939 he married Eleanor Holm, the star of his *Aquacade.* He married three more times before his death in 1966.

Entrance to the New York World's Fair, 1939. Summer dresses, but hats and heels. One of the last moments of hope for a long time. By the end of the fair season, the world was at war (Library of Congress).

Exhibits

Divided into seven "zones," each with a separate theme, the fair stretched like a gigantic millwheel centered on the *Trylon* and *Perisphere*.

The various foreign countries represented were housed in the *Government Zone*. The others were *The Community Interest Zone, The Food Zone, The Communications and Business Zone, The Production and Distribution Zone, The Transportation Zone*, and *The Amusement Zone*.

The *Government Zone*, very popular in spite of its sober, less than inviting name, offered visitors a taste (both literally and figuratively) of all the nations represented.

The *Italian Pavilion* was a rising almost ziggurat-styled structure, dominated by a waterfall which poured from below an armored female representation of *Italia*. The waterfall dropped three separate elevations down to a monument celebrating Guglielmo Marconi, topped by a nude female sculpture holding a small box in her right hand.

The pavilion from the USSR was surprisingly attractive—even though still in the block-like Communist style. It employed a good bit of red lighting at night—only to be expected. The striding worker—*The New Soviet Citizen*—with arm held high bearing a star, was entirely engulfed in flame-like red light. Rising an impressive height above the ground, it towered over the pavilion itself which consisted of a classically inspired central gallery that joins two identical, forward-stretching wings. The pamphlet which visitors received was unabashed propaganda as well as untruths, stating that 170,000,000 … were "united in a voluntary equal federation of eleven Socialist Republics." The pavilion was razed in 1940 after those "voluntary Republics" aligned themselves with Nazi Germany. One wonders how Stalin managed to get it so wrong. The spot which the pavilion had occupied was changed into the American Common in celebration of Free Speech.[3]

The *French Pavilion*, on the other hand, was undoubtedly where one wanted to have lunch or dinner—if your wallet was in good shape. Noted for its *haute cuisine,* the prices matched the quality of the food (*haute prix*). The light-filled terrace restaurant, with its glass-enclosed façade, overlooked the Lagoon of Nations so that the evening patrons could see the nightly display of fireworks. Angled wings swept backward from there, giving the appearance of an onrushing luxury liner.

The Town of Tomorrow was the showcase feature of the *Community of Interests Zone*. There one could visit fifteen complete homes, each designed around a different theme, with explanations of the range of materials that went into the building of that particular home.

The *Temple of Religion*, located not far from the *Avenue of Patriots* within the *Community of Interests Zone*, was Spartan, non-denominational, and really more cold than comforting. A vast white space, with endless rows of uncomfortable looking folding chairs, it was presumably aimed at Christians, but the cut-out window designs, resembling large doilies but which were actually meant to suggest stained glass, could just as well have fit a mosque or synagogue.

In the *Amusement Zone,* there was a space devoted entirely to children—*Children's World*. Here, the kiddies could take a trip around the world, or "...take the usual side trips, sailing in small boats on the waterways of Holland and the Italian lakes, or travel by burro to the crater of an active Hawaiian volcano and through an Indian village on a Mexican mesa."[4] The world trip also included a seven act, one ring circus, and a museum of toys. There were babysitters, as well, available to entertain the children when the parents were off to more adult pursuits.

The zone also included the Parachute Jump and other rides, Old New York, watched over by the comedian George Jessel, a "ghetto" restaurant (meaning a Jewish delicatessen), the Arctic Girl's Tomb of Ice, which featured a number of bathing beauties (not renewed in 1940), numerous restaurants, and a recreation of P.T. Barnum's museum.

One of the most interesting, as well as dismaying, exhibits to look back on, although overwhelmingly a huge hit at the fair, was the *Futurama Ride* sponsored by General Motors. Located in the *Transportation Zone*, aerial photographs of the fair show long lines stretching back for blocks from the swooping hook shape of the building entrance. Consisting of 600 chairs which whirled the seated audience around a 36,000-square-foot scale model city, which provided a glimpse into the *World of Tomorrow* circa 1960. Seven-lane highways—yes—one hundred mile an hour speed limits—thankfully no. Abundant energy, perfect climate, plenty of parks, no slums—not even close.

With the final closure of the fair in September 1940, the World of Tomorrow became the World of Today, as only a year later the United States joined the countries swirling in the maelstrom of all-out war.

Back to the Future

In 1964, another group of businessmen along with the still active Robert Moses as president, who remembered their childhoods with nostalgia, hosted a second World's Fair in the same spot. With undiminished enthusiasm, they recreated the *Futurama*, again under the auspices of General Motors. A purported 26,000,000 people viewed the 3D model which gave them a glimpse of the "near future." A little closer to the actuality of the present because it includes images of a machine felling rain forest after rain forest and leaving a divided multilane superhighway behind it.

A pale imitation of the 1939 fair, both in execution and imagination, the 1964 version provides a presage of the tumultuous '60s with its confusion and division. What strikes us as rather eerie about the photos and movies of the 1964 World's Fair is that with the exception of the '60s "big hair," the women look almost exactly the same. Heels, dresses, hats, hardly a single pair of slacks to be seen. It's symbolic of the stasis we experienced in those intervening years. In short order this image would be swept away as we plunged headlong into one more catastrophic conflict. The tumultuous years of the remaining '60s were lurking just outside the fair gates and linger with us yet. Only the triumph of the 1969 moon landing provided a taste of that elusive "world of tomorrow." We still wait for that "Peace with Understanding."

Appendix D

What They Were in the War

Women Behind the Camera in World War I

From the inception of the moving picture, women had been availing themselves of the opportunity to move from stage acting to the "big screen." The lure of the newly designated "Hollywood" attracted a horde of young women from all over the United States, most hoping for their big break in front of the cameras; however, there were those who hoped to also make those pictures themselves.

A lucky few, such as Alice Guy-Blaché in France, Lois Weber, Francis Marion and the actress, Mabel Normand, had been actively engaged in the process prior to the conflict, however many more women were able to move into positions emptied of men even before the United States had officially joined the fray. Here is just a sampling of their brief success stories.

Gene Gautier

A less recognizable name than some of the others, Gene Gautier (née Genevieve Gautier Liggett in 1885) was one of the first female pioneers in motion pictures. Starting as a stage actress, she began her screen career in 1906 in a daredevil stunt, as a helpless maiden thrown into a river. In 1907, now working for the Kalem Company, she immersed herself thoroughly in acting, writing, directing, editing, and every other facet of the creative process. After leaving Kalem in late 1912, Gautier formed the Gene Gautier Feature Players Company, along with Sidney Olcott and husband Jack Clark. The partnership with her husband lasted only a short time; they were divorced in 1918. In 1920, after an incredibly prolific career, she left the film business entirely, stating she was "worn out." Afterwards, she worked as a film and drama critic for the *Kansas City Post,* then left for Europe to be near her sister. She was in Cuernavaca, Mexico when she died in 1966.[1]

Helen Gardner

A serious Renaissance woman, and considered to be the first of either sex to solely own her production company, was Helen Gardner (Helen Gardner Picture Players). Not content with just that achievement, she was a writer, producer, costume designer—she designed her own costumes for her own movies—and actress. The last may be a bit of an overstatement. Ms. Gardner came from the stage tradition and played to the balconies at all times. Without a hint of irony, one of the prologue text insertions for her 1912 adaptation of *Cleopatra*, and the first film released from her company, states:

> Certain stage traditions originally founded in ignorance and preserved after they became traditions, *have not been considered* (emphasis mine): The object of the Director has been to insure naturalness in an atmosphere of romance. The object of the Author to intimate the nobilities and grandeur of the woman who was devotedly loved by Julius Caesar. Perfect freedom has been exercised in the adaptation.

Since Ms. Gardner was also the "atmosphere of romance" object of the director Charles Gaskill (or vice versa), "perfect freedom" was also exercised in Ms. Gardner's "naturalness." She managed to achieve the look of a one-woman ballet company. Wearing a black wig of enormous proportions (which tended to increase or decrease depending on the scene) and her own admittedly effective costumes, she is by turn, regal, sexy, petulant, haughty, and pleading, all the while conveying the story by semaphore. In spite of this, the movie is really watchable and worth the experience.

She only operated the production company for two years before closing the studio in 1914, just on the eve of the war; however, the company produced 11 feature films in that two-year interval. After the closure, she returned to working for Vitagraph and others, but by 1924 her film career was over.[2]

Lois Weber

The article (mentioned in Chapter Three) written by Elizabeth Peltret, which appeared in the October 1917 issue of *Photoplay,* "On the Lot with Lois Weber," pays bounteous tribute to Lois Weber—"the greatest of all woman directors." It is unstinting in its praise of Ms. Weber, ending with "...she *seems* so ordinary. She has the tactful simplicity that is inseparable from the great director, the director who achieves big things." The article stresses the fact that Ms. Weber is emphatic that she is *not* going to do any more propaganda films. This is most interesting, since that is the very thing she was known for and what made her "the greatest." With films like *Where Are My Children,* a strong statement in support of family planning—although anti-abortion—she joined Margaret Sanger in her unwavering support of a woman's right to contraception and limitation of births. Her background as a street-corner evangelist is obvious from her choices of topics along with birth control: alcoholism, drug addiction, prostitution, and abortion.

Working for Universal Film Manufacturing (Universal Studios), by 1916 she had successfully established herself with them as their top director. Considered the first American woman to be acknowledged as a director in the same way as the men, in 1917 she opened her own production company, Lois Weber Productions, directing, writing and producing those propaganda films she disavows in the article. All in all, Weber directed over 100 films, but ultimately, her production company went into bankruptcy in the '20s. She only made one talking picture, however that was the fairly successful melodrama, *White Heat* (1934).

Her rationale for the perplexing change of heart she espouses in the article seems to have been the need to uplift the audiences' spirits rather than to preach causes at a time when there was only one paramount cause.

As World War I drew to a close, a new atmosphere of idealism took hold of the country. Even the government stepped in semi-officially to suggest that movies should be uplifting and raise people's spirits—this may be the impetus behind Weber's change of directorial direction.

Frances Marion

Born Marion Benson Owens in 1888, Frances Marion was one of the most successful screenwriters of the 20th century, male or female, writing several hundred scripts (estimates differ according to source—from 325 scripts to 187) and winning two Oscars. She also directed at least three films and produced two. Well compensated for her efforts, in 1917 her salary was rumored to be in the neighborhood of $50,000 a year, a time when the average household income was less than $3,000. By 1926, Marion's salary was $3,000 a *week*.

Already possessed of a varied career as a commercial artist, model, journalist, and actress before entering the film world, she was hired in 1914 as a general assistant and actress for Lois Weber's production company. Finding she liked working behind the camera rather than in front, she learned screenwriting under Weber's tutelage. During World War I, Marion worked as a war correspondent at the Front, always emphasizing women's contribution to the war effort and was the first woman to cross the Rhine after the armistice. As a dedicated feminist, she was an active participant in marches for women's suffrage. Making the transition to sound films easily, she won both her Academy Awards for talkies: *The Big House* (1930) and *The Champ* (1931). In the Silent era she worked as Mary Pickford's official writer; from her pen came some of Pickford's best and most memorable films, including *The Poor Little Rich Girl* (1917).

She left Hollywood in the '40s and concentrated on writing plays and novels with continued success.

Anita Loos

Most famous for the creation of the character Lorelei Lee in *Gentlemen Prefer Blondes* (1925 novel, 1928 and 1953 films), Loos wrote more than 150 scripts over a three-decade career in Hollywood. Noted as well for her intertitles, she was lauded by a 1917 issue of *Photoplay* as having elevated the intertitle "first to sanity then to dignity and brilliance combined." Many others added their voices, claiming that she raised intertitles to an art. From 1915 to 1918 she collaborated with director John Emerson to market Douglas Fairbanks, Sr., whose screen persona was partially defined by Loos' scripts. Fairbanks left then to begin the swashbuckling roles he became so well-known for. Loos finally married Emerson in 1920. The marriage was not made in heaven because Emerson was a philanderer, a hypochondriac, and ultimately had to be hospitalized for schizophrenia. He also ran through her money, evidently on his other women. She continued to support and care for him without divorce, until his death freed her.

Gentlemen Prefer Blondes was, of course, her biggest hit. Very funny in the '20s, she was taken to task by feminists after the 1953 release of the film starring Marilyn Monroe for perpetuating the stereotype of the dumb blonde. Late scholarship has revised that opinion to show the work was originally intended as a satirical reproach to H.L. Mencken. Loos had adored Mencken, but after watching him try to beguile a young blonde on a train, while completely ignoring her, she became disillusioned.

Lorelei Lee, a caricature, not a portrait, would have made Loos' point more obviously in the Jazz Age than in the strait-laced, humorless '50s.[3] In actuality, Lorelei Lee wasn't a dumb blonde—a gold digger, it's true—but knew her way around and had ambition if nothing else. Shrewd, and not afraid to parlay sex appeal into material returns, Lee began life in a series of short sketches, rather like diary entries, for *Harper's Bazaar.* Their success prompted the book which sold out overnight and went through three more printings through year's end (1925). The book has gone through 85 more editions and has been translated into 14 languages, including Chinese.

It's a shame that the success of *Gentlemen Prefer Blondes* has kept film scholars from paying more attention to Loos' filmography. Most of her later movies are still extant although a great many of the early ones have been lost. What remains is still a treasure trove for film buffs. If nothing else, just her scenario for *The Women* (1939) could be considered a screen triumph. The earlier *Red Headed Woman* (a pre–Code 1932) is another well worth watching. Billed as a rom-com, it's actually a barely concealed melodrama incorporating comedic elements, starring Jean Harlow in one of her best-known films. Wearing a red wig and a succession of stunning outfits, Harlow played an amoral gold digger who carries on several affairs at once.

These examples represent about 1 percent of her remarkable output from a career which ran for over half a century.

Alice Guy-Blaché

A French prodigy, Alice Guy-Blaché (Alice Ida Antoinette Guy) was one of, and possibly *the* first female pioneer in moving pictures on any continent. Seeing opportunities in film in the late 19th century, she broke into the business in 1896. An avid experimenter, she tried out Gaumont's Chronophone synch-sound system, color-tinting and special effects. Casting an even broader innovative net, she cast her films interracially, as well. From 1896 to 1906, she held the position of only female filmmaker anywhere in the world.

She began her career simply as a secretary for a camera manufacturing and photographic supply company. When the company changed hands and was renamed Gaumont et Cie, she made an effort to familiarize herself with many aspects of the business. As a result of close observation, she became convinced she could make an interesting film incorporating fictional elements into the straight reportage—which, surprisingly, had never been done up until then. Guy sought permission from Gaumont to make her own short film and was given the go-ahead. Thus, was born *La Fée aux Choux,* considered the world's first narrative film. It's an endearing and charming little *bijou* (running time 60 seconds) of children born under the cabbages, although the fairy's treatment of the infants is a bit alarming. *Les infants* think so as well, which is only too apparent from their flailing limbs and wide-open mouths.

When she married Herbert Blaché in 1907, the two established the Solax Company in Flushing, Queens, New York, partnering with George A. Magie. At the time, it was the largest pre-Hollywood studio in the United States. With their divorce several years later (1922), their partnership in moving pictures also dissolved. Sadly, even though she had started her own studio—an offshoot of Solax—after having directed her last film in 1919, she was forced to auction the studio and declare bankruptcy in 1921. She returned to France in 1922 and never made another film.

Nearly forgotten, in spite of her own efforts to retain her position in filmmaking, she has finally been rediscovered. In 2018, Kino Lorber released a six-disc collection—*Pioneers: First Women Filmmakers*—which devotes the first disc of the compilation to Guy-Blaché. A documentary of her career, *Be Natural: The Untold Story of Alice Guy-Blaché,* narrated by Jodie Foster, was simultaneously released in 2018. Her many film firsts—before either male or female film pioneers—should never be forgotten.

Dorothy Arzner

The last leaf on the tree of women directors was Dorothy Arzner, who began her career in the Silent era and managed to continue through the "Golden Age" of Hollywood. Born in San Francisco anywhere from 1897 to 1900 (as always, sources differ), she was the daughter of restaurant owners. The café run by her parents was frequented by such silent film celebrities as Charlie Chaplin and William S. Hart, as well as the director Erich von Stroheim, an exposure which was undoubtedly influential in her choice of career.

Beginning in film as a script typist for Famous Players-Lasky Corporation, in only six months Arzner was hired as a cutter and editor at Realart Studio, a division of Paramount. She had cut and edited 52 films for them when Paramount called her back to edit *Blood and Sand* (1925) with Rudolph Valentino. This was her first major picture release and her breakout opportunity.

After working with the director James Cruze at Paramount, she branched out on her own as a scriptwriter for several independent companies. In short order, however, she returned to Paramount where she wrote the shooting script for *Old Ironsides* (1926). Columbia then dangled an offer to write and direct a film, but Paramount responded by offering the opportunity to direct an "A" film which had more cachet. Arzner directed four more silent films for Paramount, and then got the prestigious position of directing the studio's first sound film, *The Wild Party* (1928), starring Clara Bow.

Following a decade of directing for Paramount, she decided to leave in 1932 to be independent again as a freelance director for RKO, United Artists, MGM, and her earlier employer, Columbia. In 1943, she left Hollywood to make training films for the Women's Army Corps (WACS) and commercials for Pepsi at the request of Joan Crawford, produce a radio program, and teach filmmaking at the Pasadena Playhouse in California.

Arzner has been touted as the most "prolific woman studio director in the history of American cinema." With a career in Hollywood from 1919 to 1943, six credits as a writer, eight as an editor and 21 as a director, not to mention her commercial and instructional work for a number of years afterward, she can certainly be deemed the most durable.

Other women who were not strictly directors but continued their film work into the era of talkies included Wanda Tuchock, who was a co-director on the movie *Finishing School* (1934). The primary directorial credit went to George Nichols, Jr. Tuchock was also a continuity writer on the 1923 film *Show People,* which starred Marion Davies.

Again, the primary credit went to Agnes Christine Johnston who wrote the treatment. However, Tuchock was credited with the scenario for the all-Black movie classic, *Hallelujah* (1929), directed by King Vidor, who wrote the original story. *Hallelujah,* like other films produced "on the cusp," was released in both silent and sound versions.

All together Tuchock received credit for writing over 30 films, as well as racking up credits for copywriting and producing. She is but one of several other women who began in the Silent era and hung on to their careers after the transition to sound by wearing more than one hat. However, once the boys were back from "over there" the whittling down began, and the lucky few were few indeed.

Glossary

Aktiengesellschaft Essentially, corporation or stock company. *Aktien* translates as share, as in stock. (See UFA, below).

Bliaut A close-fitting, long sleeved women's overgarment which defined the figure to below the waist, then widened into a full, flowing skirt. Generally belted low on the hips and sometimes laced up the front. There was a somewhat differently styled garment for men, also called a *bliaut*. Generally, most popular in the 12th century.

Brucellosis Also called Malta fever. A bacterial infection causing intermittent fever and malaise, more common in the Mediterranean area.

"Castle Walk" A derivation of the one-step, combined with the trot. The dancers strut, holding their bodies firm, with sharply executed pivots on the supporting foot. The steps are taken toe first, then heel.

Chronophone An early attempt to synchronize a sound disc with a moving picture by the use of an air compressor. Gaumont showed *Phonscènes*—something like music videos—and *Filmpariants*—more or less "talking" films—nearly every week for at least six years, from 1911 to 1917, in their cinema. A *Chronophone* theatre was opened in Los Angeles, California, in 1908, operating for an unknown length of time.

Crimean War October 1853–February 1856. Ostensibly over the rights of Christian minorities in the Holy Land, the war pitted Russia against a declining Ottoman Empire allied with the United Kingdom, Sardinia, and France. One might think this an unlikely alliance, but the real reason was to prevent Russia from gaining more territory and more power. At great cost to all, Russia was defeated in her bid to expand her territories.

Drill Cloth A fairly light-weight cotton material with an obvious diagonal weave. Used in service uniforms and standardized in the khaki color in the mid–1880s. The fabric soon became popular for casual civilian dress.

Fortuny Pleating A method developed by the Spanish designer Mariano Fortuny c. 1906. Done entirely by hand, the method consisted of incredibly narrow tucks of fabric—in silk, by Fortuny. Reinvented in the 1980s by designer Mary McFadden using polyester.

Gaiters Similar to spats, gaiters were made of cloth (canvas, primarily) or leather and worn over a shoe ostensibly for protection. Laced up the sides, they became a fashion must-have in the teens of the 20th century. Still being shown in the *Sears Catalog* in the early '20s, they had mostly disappeared by 1925.

Gangrene Serious bacterial infection causing the death of tissue, most often seen in the extremities. Treated best by excision of the infected tissue or, if necessary, amputation of the affected limb.

***Jupe-culotte*, also *Jupe-sultane*, or *Jupe-pantalon* (trouser-skirt)** Introduced circa 1910/1911 by Paul Poiret, it consisted of wide-legged pants, frequently conflated with his "harem" pants which were blousy but tied in at the ankle. The wide-legged trouser style was also presented by couturier Jeanne Margaine-Lacroix in 1910.

Kinos Movie theatres—*cinemas.*

Korean "Police Action" Taking place from 1950 to 1953, the so-called police action concerned the attempted Communist takeover of the entirety of Korea. The cost to the United States was nearly 34,000 of our troops, and approximately $30 billion dollars. Approximately 138,000 military deaths were reported from South Korea. The country remains divided to this day.

Lichtspieles Literally, light-speak. Loosely referring to movie theatres.

Lisle High/hard-twisted cotton thread, two or more ply, very popular for hosiery, but also used for gloves and other knitted wear.

Marabou A variety of feather plumes taken from the marabou stork.

Morganatic marriage between persons of unequal rank, generally a royal with a commoner. The children of this union are legitimate; however, they may not succeed to the royal position.

Moyen-Age French for the Middle Ages.

Panniers Blousy poufs sitting below the waist of a frock on the outside of either hip—popular for either day or evening. From the French word for basket.

Pipits Tawny pipits are medium-sized migrant birds with a widespread breeding range extending from northwest Africa to Portugal, but also including Central Siberia and Inner Mongolia. Their appearance in the discussed film celebrates what would be an exceedingly rare occurrence in England.

Puttees Wraps for the lower leg from the ankle to the knee—rather like Ace bandages. Worn by soldiers in the First World War, below their knee-length uniform trousers. They could also be a complete legging which was secured by a strap.

Redingote A fitted, generally belted garment, either dress or lightweight coat, with a flared skirt, sometimes with a contrasting gore in the front.

***Rondel* (also *Rondelle*)** Refers to any circular object, whether a brooch, paintings presented within a circular shape, or an architectural feature. Also refers to a fixed type of 14-line poetry.

Schwartzer German word for African Americans (meaning black).

Trotteur Suit Literally, walker suit, more often reserved for afternoon wear.

Universum-Film-Aktiengesellschaft (UFA) German film company which made excellent films during the First World War. The name translates as Universal Film Corporation (*aktien* is share, as in stocks).

Notes

Preface

1. *Delineator Magazine*. September 1917.

Chapter One

1. Sherman's hardline, "scorched earth" approach did not set well even with his supporters. His March to the Sea, "hard war" according to Sherman, resulted in the capture of Savannah, but caused (according to Sherman himself) more than $100 million in property damage and has become a catchphrase for all-out destruction. However, the cost in lives appears to have been minimal. Supposedly, speaking to a crowd in Columbus, Ohio, he said, "There is many a boy here today who looks on war as all glory, but, boys, it is all hell."

2. "Civil war casualties." *American Battlefield Trust*. www.battlefields.org/learn/articles/civil-war-casualties. *American Civil War Story*. www.americancivilwarstory.com/civil-war-casualties.html.

3. "William Alexander Hammond." *AMEDD Center of History and Heritage*. It was rumored that the original verdict of the court-martial was acquittal; however, it was disapproved and a second verdict of guilty was rendered. He was later restored to the Army as a brigadier general (retired) but without pay or allowances. achh.army.mil/history/surgeongenerals-w-hammond. "William A. Hammond." *National Park Service*. www.nps.gov/people/william-a-hammond.htm. William A. Hammond. *A Statement of the Causes Which Led to the Dismissal of Surgeon General William A. Hammond from the Army with a Review of the Evidence Adduced Before the Court*. (Reprint paperback) Forgotten Books, February 7, 2018.

4. A district in Istanbul, Turkey, on the shores of the Bosphorus. This area is now known as *üsküdar*.

5. The conditions were so unspeakable that Nightingale wrote: "I have been well acquainted with the dwellings of the worst parts of most of the great cities of Europe, but have never been in any atmosphere which I could compare with that of the Barrack Hospital at night." Rappaport. *No Place for Ladies*.

6. Brucellosis is a highly contagious bacterial disease generally caused by the ingestion of contaminated milk or meat. It can, however, spread from animals to humans with contact.

7. A very good, informative, extensive, and well-researched article from Wikipedia. en.wikipedia.org/wiki/Crimean_War.

8. The word "woman" would never have been used; females were "girls" until they became "ladies." "Women" walked the streets.

9. "Dorothea Lynde Dix." *History*. www.history.com/topics/womens-history/dorothea-lynde-dix. "Dorothea Dix." *National Women's History Museum*. www.womenshistory.org/education-resources/biographies/dorothea-dix. "Women Nurses in the Civil War." ahec.armywarcollege.edu/exhibits/CivilWarImagery/Civil_War_Nurses.cfm. The impetus to put women in something like a uniform was also felt by Nightingale in Britain.

10. "Clara Barton." *History*. www.history.com/topics/womens-history/clara-barton. "Women Nurses in the Civil War." ahec.armywarcollege.edu/exhibits/CivilWarImagery/Civil_War_Nurses.cfm.

11. This included the applications of leeches to "bleed" him. The treatment that had killed George Washington.

12. And many images which make the claim of being from the Civil War are seriously misdated, as the dress styles are obviously not from that era. However, a lovely drawing appeared in *Harper's Weekly* for September 6, 1862, depicting "The Influence of Women." The image showed women knitting, sewing, nursing, writing letters, and generally offering comfort.

13. John Banks. "Five Minutes with Chris Foard, collector of nursing artifacts." john-banks.blogspot.com/2016/01/five-minutes-with-chris-foard-collector.html.

Chapter Two

1. Quoted in Robert Gerwath. *The Vanquished: Why the First World War Failed to End, 1917-1923*. New York: Farrar, Straus and Giroux. 2016.

2. For those interested, I recommend either Christopher Clark's *The Sleepwalkers* or Margaret MacMillan's *The War That Ended Peace;* both are comprehensive and exhaustively researched.

3. Morganatic marriage—generally to a commoner—is one where the children of that union do not inherit the titles of royalty and have no claim to the throne.

4. Amelia Bloomer had already set the stage for the "jupe-culotte" with her voluminous contribution to "pantelettes" for the ladies. Not really her invention (she borrowed the idea from the Middle East), she was a tireless advocate. However, Poiret has to be credited as the first fashion designer to promote the idea seriously.

5. "Paul Poiret: French Fashion Designer." *Britannica.* www.britannica.com/biography/Paul-Poiret.

6. "The Hobble Skirt." *Wikipedia.*

7. Quoted by Kanupriya Goenka. "Why did the Hobble skirt become popular?" I hate to be a traitor to my sex, but women seem bound (pun intended) to follow every silly fashion they possibly can.

8. It should be noted that these ideas—and the "new vocabulary"—only appeared in high fashion magazines or catalogs. They were much slower to trickle down to the Sears or Wards catalogs intended for the average housewife.

9. Nina Edwards. *Dressed for War: Uniform, Civilian Clothing and Trappings, 1914 to 1918.* London: I.B. Tauris and C., Ltd., 2015. 58.

10. Photo and quote courtesy of the National Archives/Wikimedia Commons collection.

11. A 14th century Italian census showed that nearly 25 percent of women declared themselves "head of household." This means, of course, that they were the primary breadwinners.

12. "Women's Work in World War I: 1914-1918." *Striking Women.* University of Leeds. www.striking-women.org. Robert Wilde. "Women and Work in World War I."

13. Barton Hacker. "Women in Uniform, World War I Edition." Blog. September 8, 2011.

14. The museum is still adding to the collection and still photographing them so the website changes continually. Women still wore foundation garments but eschewed the binding effect of stays—most often by simply removing them from their ordinary corsets for greater mobility.

15. Edwards. 62.

16. americanhistory.si.edu/collections/object-groups/women-in-wwi/women-s-uniforms.

17. "The Women's Auxiliary Army Corps." *History Learning Site.* www.historylearningsite.co.uk/the-role-of-british-women-in-the-twentieth-century/the-womens-army-auxiliary-corps/.

18. John Simkin. "Woman's Auxiliary Army Corps." *Spartacus Educational.*
spartacus-educational.com/FWWwomen.htm.

19. Kate Lindsay. "The She-Soldiers of World War One." *World War I Centenary.* University of Oxford. w1centenary.oucs.ox.ac.uk/unconventionalsoldiers/the-she-soldiers-of-world-war-one. The issue of women's service in combat is still a dilemma. Should women wholeheartedly embrace war? On the other hand, should they sit by and tacitly signal approval? Again, if need arises to protect and defend, shouldn't both men and women rise to the occasion? The answer is not at all straightforward.

20. Interview with Gladys Brockwell. *Photoplay,* November 1917. 21. I think Ms. Brockwell was unaware of the fact that her argument simply bolstered the unfortunate reality that women not only have to do what women do, but also have to shoulder men's work on top of it.

21. Baroness Williams of Crosby. "World War One: The Many Battles Faced by WW1's Nurses." *BBC News Magazine,* April 2, 2014. www.bbc.com/news/magazine-26838077.

22. Vera Brittain. *"Lament of the Demobilised."* 1918.

23. Colonel Elizabeth A. P. Vane. "Contributions of the U. S. Army Nurse Corps in World War I." *Army Nurse Corps Association.*

24. "Women's Royal Air Force (WRAF) 1918-1920." *Royal Air Force Museum.* John Simkin. "Women's Royal Air Force." *Spartacus Educational.* "Women in World War I." *The National WWI Museum and Memorial.* I was also unable to discover if they actually drove the motorcycles or were just passengers. The photograph of the dispatch girl is ambiguous.

25. Paula Becker. "Kitting for Victory—World War I." *HistoryLink.org.*

26. *Wikipedia.* The complete song can be heard on YouTube. I recommend listening if you need a lift in spirits.

27. Elizabeth June Christie. "Now *Every* Woman Can Make Her Own Clothes." *Photoplay.* December 1917. 121.

28. French. *Photoplay.* July 1916. Pink and silver were most definitely "in" for 1916.

29. French. *Photoplay.* August 1916. 75-77.

30. Actually Romain de Tirtoff. He called himself by his initials in French—Air-Tay.

31. Stella Blum (Selections and Introduction). *Fashion Drawings and Illustrations from Harper's Bazar.* 17.

32. Erté's designs were not always executed just as drawn. The final product was sometimes more restrained for wearability.

Chapter Three

1. Ormi Hawley (née Ormetta Grace Hawley and known during her stardom as "Opulent Ormi") had but a short career in films (1911-1919), but made over 300 films—most of them shorts—in the course of that few years. Also an artist, she painted portraits and wrote stories for children after her retirement to a farm in Camden, New Jersey. She died at only 53, in Rome.

2. Karl K. Kitchen. "The Light of Europe." *Photoplay.* May 1916. 58-64.

3. Landa's (1873-1933) story was ultimately tragic. Starting as a stage actor, he was discovered in Berlin by the star, Asta Nielsen, with whom he

made several movies. Very popular as Joe Deebs, the fictional detective intended to rival Sherlock Holmes, the Jewish Landa was forced to flee Germany in 1933 when the Nazis seized power. Despondent, he committed suicide in Yugoslavia shortly thereafter.

4. Kitchen. 62ff.

5. Tim Luckhurst. "War Correspondents." *International Encyclopedia of the First World War.* encyclopedia.1914-1918-online.net/article/war_correspondents.

6. Luckhurst. 4.

7. This was not as outlandish as it sounds. Cuba had been ostensibly neutral up until then, but there was suspicion that U-boats could have been operating from those waters, and there was an active Bund in the country. However, Cuba declared war on Germany on April 7, 1917, the day after the United States entered the war.

8. Jami L. Bryan. "Fighting for Respect: African-American soldiers in WWI." *National Museum. United States Army.* www.military.com/history/fighting-for-respect. Heather Michon. "The Role of Black Americans in World War I." www.thoughtco.com/african-americans-in-wwi-4158185.

9. "Blackface - Origins of Jump Jim Crow." www.black-face.com/jim-crow.htm. "The History of Minstrelsy: "Jump Jim Crow." USF Library.

10. Ross. *Working Class Hollywood.*

11. Steven J. Ross. *Working Class Hollywood.* Princeton University Press, 1998. 124ff.

12. Brownlow. *Behind the Mask of Innocence.* 61. Susan L. Speaker. "Fit to Fight." October 18, 2018.

13. Elizabeth Peltret. "On the Lot with Lois Weber." *Photoplay,* October 1917. 89ff.

14. *Shadowland Magazine.* September, October 1919.

15. An interesting partnership, all things considered.

16. Lyn Macdonald. *1914-1918, Voices and Images of the Great War.* Quoted in Peter Craddick-Adams. "The Home Front in World War One." *History Trails: Wars and Conflict.*" www.bbc.co.uk/history/trail/wars_conflict/home_front/the_home_front_04.shtml.

17. Quoted in Stuart Klawans. "Film: How the First World War Changed Movies Forever." *The New York Times.* November 19, 2000.

18. World War I German Newsreels. "On the Firing Line with the Germans." *You Tube.* www.youtube.com/watch?v=riK0pPfpsL4.

19. Belinda Davis. "Food and Nutrition (Germany)."1914-1918 Online. *International Encyclopedia of the First World War.* encyclopedia.1914-1918-online.net/article/food_and_nutrition_german.

20. Paul Cornish. "Rationing and Food Shortages During the First World War." www.iwm.org.uk/history/rationing-and-food-shortages-during-the-first-world-war.

21. Wolfgang Mühl-Benninghaus. "Film/Cinema (Germany)." *International Encyclopedia of the First World War: 1914–1918 Online.* encyclopedia.1914-1918-online.net/article/filmcinema_germany.

Chapter Four

1. Lillian Howard. "Back to Babylon for New Fashions." *Photoplay.* April 1917. 39-40.

2. Yes, guilty as charged. This is a highly prejudiced personal opinion.

3. *Photoplay.* April 1917. 157.

4. John Ten Eyck. "Mollie of Manhattan." *Photoplay,* October 1917. 36ff.

5. Illustrated in the *St. Louis Dispatch,* April 1918.

6. "The Trenchcoat." *Burberry.* us.burberry.com/the-trench-coat/. The Burberry trench is now available in five "silhouettes": the Kensington; the Westminster; the Chelsea; the Waterloo; and the Pimlico, all named after London locations. Jay Hemmings. www.warhistoryonline.com/instant-articles/history-of-the-trench-coat.html.

7. Although, as Nina Edwards remarks in *Dressed for War,* at the beginning of World War II, even the British were retaining some of the old-fashioned flashy features. The Russians, who wished to look as suave as the English, still wanted a "Russian" flair. 23.

8. *Moving Picture Weekly.* September 25, 1918. 270-277.

9. *Photoplay.* April 1918.

10. John Dolber. "These Are Russians." *Photoplay.* May 1918.

11. *Moving Picture World.* April 6, 1918. 6-9.

12. *Moving Picture World.* April 13, 1918. 182.

13. *Moving Picture World.* February 2, 1918.

14. "How War Affects Pictures." *Moving Picture World.* February 2, 1918. 648.

15. "The Motion Picture and the War." *Moving Picture World.* February 2, 1918. 678.

16. *Moving Picture World.* February 17, 1918.

17. Illustrated songs were performances usually preceding silent films and consisted of a (usually) singer and pianist who accompanied magic lantern slides. A number of film stars owed their careers to this form of entertainment.

18. Vernon and Irene executing the Castle Walk is available on YouTube. A trifle blurry, but nonetheless spectacular for speed, innovation, and athleticism. Not to mention, it's really fun, as well.

19. Sylvia, Emmaline's youngest daughter, who wrote the definitive story of the Suffragette struggle, was later estranged from her mother, who disapproved of Sylvia's methods, her other espoused causes, and her illegitimate son.

20. Sylvia Pankhurst. *The Suffragette.* 454-455.

21. Adlington. *Great War Fashion.* 25.

22. "Lillian Forrester." *Wikipedia Republished.* Marina Nenadic. "Six Sites of Suffragette Sabotage." *Heritage Calling.* heritagecalling.com/2018/06/08/6-sites-of-suffragette-sabotage/.

23. Victoria Bernal. "The Suffrage Stories Connected Through the Archives." 2. This short, but excellent, article briefly delineates the story of several women who were active, and activist, clubwomen. One such was Charlotta Bass, considered to be the first African American woman to own and run a newspaper. In 1952, Ms. Bass was the first African American woman to be nominated for Vice President as a candidate of the Progressive Party.

24. In spite of their efforts, the Triangle factory continued their oppressive ways, culminating in the Triangle Shirtwaist Factory fire in 1911.

Chapter Five

1. Poster. The United War Work Campaign, American YWCA. The YWCA was the first organization to send women overseas for the purpose of ministering to soldiers serving at the Front. This, second to empowering women, had been their mission from their Civil War founding.

2. Martin Hardie and Arthur K. Sabin, Eds. *War Posters: The Historical Role of Wartime Poster Art 1914-1918*. (1920). Mineola, New York: Dover Publications reissue, 2016.

3. *The Face in the Pool* is a (very) old-fashioned fairy tale in the Han Christian Andersen/L. Frank Baum tradition. It can be read, or downloaded for your kids, on the National Archives website. It's kind of fun. archive.org/details/faceinpoolfaerie00stjo.

4. "J. Allen St. John: American, 1972-1957." *The Korshak Collection: Illustrations of Imaginative Literature*. www.korshakcollection.com/j-allen-st-john.

5. Hardie and Sabin, 31.

6. The Church Army was established in 1882 by Wilson Carlile [sic] with the intent of reaching out to those most in need. Recognized in 1883 by the Church of England, in the same year the Army opened a training college for men at Oxford, followed by one for women in 1889. In addition to providing recreation huts during World War I, the army also operated ambulances, mobile canteens and kitchen cars. "Our History." *The Church Army*. www.churcharmy.org.uk/Group/Group.aspx?ID=290554.

Chapter Six

1. Such as the perfectly deplorable *Merry Widow*, directed by Erich von Stroheim and starring John Gilbert and Mae Murray. Murray chews the scenery unrestrained, and Gilbert looks as though he wishes he were back in *The Big Parade* (or he wishes Murray was, preferably under a collapsed roof).

2. Susan King. *Los Angeles Times*. January 7, 2020.

3. "The Big Parade." *AMC Filmsite*.

4. *Creating the Illusion*. 16-17.

5. There are actually several writing credits besides Remarque and Anderson. George Abbott is credited with the screenplay, Del Andrews with yet another "adaptation," C. Gardner Sullivan as the supervising story chief, Walter Anthony (uncredited) for the titles, and an uncredited Lewis Milestone, for heaven knows what, since he was the director.

6. The wreckage of the battleship *Scharnhorst* was discovered in 2019. In a fit of hubris, the Reich built the *Schornhurst* and the *Gneisenau* anew with similar results, although the *Scharnhorst* inflicted much damage on Allied ships before her final demise.

7. Geoffrey Bennett. *The Battles of Coronel and the Falklands, 1914*. "Battle of Coronel - British Battles." www.britishbattles.com/first-world-war/battle-of-coronel/. *Wikipedia*.

8. Ross. *Working Class Hollywood*. 117.

9. Ross. 129. "World War I Agencies." *U S History.com*. u-s-history.com/pages/h4302.html. The Fuel Administration was discontinued in June 1919, but revived in October through December of that year during the bituminous coal strike of 1919. "Records of the U.S. Fuel Administration (USFA)." *National Archives*. www.archives.gov/research/guide-fed-records/groups/067.html.

10. *Film Daily*. March 4, 1917. 1-2. Quoted in Crafton. *The Talkies*. 109.

11. Crafton. 169.

12. *Film Daily*. July 15, 1928.

13. Crafton. 166.

14. *Variety Magazine*. October 2, 1929. 16-17.

15. "Tinting and Toning." Brian Pritchard. www.brianpritchard.com/Tinting.htm. "Colourful [sic] stories no. 12—Tinting and toning." *The Bioscope*. thebioscope.net/2008/07/05/colourful-stories-no-12-tinting-and-toning. "Film Tinting." *Wikipedia*.

16. *The Sea Hawk* is my personal favorite, but *Snow White* is surreally beautiful. The costumes and sets are gorgeous for this one. It's too early for costume credits but they are exquisite. *Snow White* uses just about every tint available. The evil queen is always lavender. I highly recommend both films which can be seen online.

17. Yes, that's a double pun. Forgive me.

18. Emma Baxter-Wright. *Vintage Fashion*. 46.

19. *Photoplay*. June 1932. 16.

20. The official Fair pamphlet stated: "The eyes of the Fair are on the future—not in the sense of peering toward the unknown nor attempting to foretell the events of tomorrow and the shape of things to come, but in the sense of presenting a new and clearer view of today in preparation for tomorrow; a view of the forces and ideas that prevail as well as the machines. To its visitors the Fair will say: Here are the materials, ideas, and forces at work in our world. These are the tools with which the World of Tomorrow must be made. They are all interesting and much effort has been expended to lay them before you in an interesting way. Familiarity with today is the best preparation for the

future." Six months into the celebration, Hitler rolled over Poland.

Chapter Seven

1. Tristan Bass. Quoted in "Costume Designer Orry-Kelly: The Frock Flicks Guide." www.frockflicks.com/costume-designer-orry-kelly-the-frock-flicks-guide/.

2. Evidently suffering silently from depression, she jumped from a bathroom window at the Knickerbocker Hotel in November 1962.

3. *Creating the Illusion*. 73.

Chapter Eight

1. There is an exhibit hosted by the National World War II Museum entitled "So Ready for Laughter: The Legacy of Bob Hope" which pays tribute to his unceasing devotion to bringing entertainment to those far from home. At the time of this writing the exhibit is still in the future.

2. It was praised by the *New York Times,* which called it "utterly beguiling" and suggested "it would be a grave error not to see it."

3. Susan Peters was a young dramatic actress with a promising career when she was accidently shot through the abdomen while on a hunting trip. The shotgun pellets pierced her spine, resulting in permanent paralysis from the waist down. She suffered from serious depression after this and her health began to decline due to complications from her paralysis, ending in her death at 31.

4. The contemporary reviews were anything but complementary. *The New York Times* reviewer call it "strangely empty." *Variety* stated that the protagonists were charming, but that Colman looked too old for the role. James Agee, the playwright and critic, recommended the film to those who "can with pleasure eat a bowl of Yardley's shaving soap..." More recently, it has earned considerable praise. Call me sappy, but I love it.

5. Quoted in Boland. "Hitler's Use of Film."

6. A purge which removed as many as 500 (some sources say 700 to 1,000) of Hitler's opponents. At the very least, 85 died, many members of the Sturmabteilung, the Nazi's paramilitary organization.

7. In my opinion, a must-see, for many reasons: just the atmosphere alone is a strong recommendation; the acting, while sometimes overwrought is compelling; the feel of the medieval influenced sets; and the militaristic feel of the costumes.

Chapter Nine

1. Not that it matters, but my money is on Mary Doyle Keefe. The resemblance is strong, and the fact that there was another woman whose married name was Doyle makes me think there was some confusion of one Doyle with another.

2. Mae Krier, age 93 in 2019, designates herself *an original* Rosie the Riveter, but doesn't say *the* Rosie.

3. I am using this term a little loosely—it really refers to a continuing musical theme rather than a graphic image, but it does become the instant theme of the war in the Pacific.

4. *World Digital Library*. Library of Congress. There were four slightly different images used, including one with civilians raising a giant number 7.

5. We are all painfully aware of the internment of Japanese-American citizens until the end of the war. Some had been here for at least two, and sometimes three, generations.

6. I say seemingly, however, it was actually the assumption that men, in spite of all evidence to the contrary, could/should do what women were unable to do. Within that definition, the sexism was quite conscious. If I may be forgiven a personal anecdote, I will hark back to my senior year in high school, when I had signed up for physics. I was called into the Girl's Dean's office where I was told that girls were not allowed to do this. When I inquired "Why not?" I was told that they "knew" that girls could not keep up with the boys. I should add that the Dean was talking to a fifteen-year-old—I was two years ahead of my grade and it was the boys who needed to keep up with me.

7. Sara Collini. "Women Airforce Service Pilots (WASPs) of WWII." *National Women's History Museum*. April 23, 1919. Michael Ray. "Women Airforce Service Pilots." *Britannica*. www.britannica.com/topic/Women-Airforce-Service-Pilots.

8. Her drab coverall becomes a fashion statement by 1942, at least in the U.S., as the *Sears Catalog* for that year features them with "matching work caps, in "sturdy, sanforized, cotton work cloth."

9. My husband's grandmother lost her arm to a drop-hammer during World War II, owing to careless safety procedures.

10. "Anti-Black Imagery." Jim Crow Museum of Racist Memorabilia. Ferris State University. Big Rapids, Michigan. At the time of this writing, Aunt Jemima, Uncle Ben, and Mrs. Butterworth have at last been removed from the grocer's shelves.

11. Above their heads appear the words "Hazánkért, Jövönkert," which seems to allude to being home soon. I am unable to give the precise meaning, but Jövön refers to the future, and Hazán can be loosely translated as homeland.

Chapter Ten

1. "Utility clothing." *Wikipedia*. Ian Baylay. "An Introduction to Utility Clothing." *1940s Society*.

2. "An Introduction to Utility Clothing."

3. "Paris in World War II." *Wikipedia*. This is one of *Wikipedia's* better articles, lengthy, detailed, and well-cited. "Paris." *The Holocaust Encyclopedia*. encyclopedia.ushmm.org/content/en/article/paris. Jonathan Yardley. "A

History of Paris during Nazi Occupation." *Washington Post.* August 29, 2014. Yardley quotes Ronald Rosbottom's book, *When Paris Went Dark,* regarding the role of the French police as "active collaborators of the Germans." www.washingtonpost.com/opinions/a-history-of-paris-during-nazi-occupation/2014/08/29/fce9e112-222c-11e4-958c-268a320a60ce_story.html. "The *Velodrome d'Hiver* (Vel d'Hiv), Roundup." encyclopedia.ushmm.org/content/en/article/the-velodrome-dhiver-vel-dhiv-roundup.

4. My one-time French teacher told of partying every night for weeks after the Liberation. One early morning after an all-nighter he dropped on the side of his bed and bent over to remove his shoes. He awoke, hours later, still bent over his shoes and nearly paralyzed.

5. Catherine Hokin. "An Appearance of Serenity. www.historiamag.com/french-fashion-industry-ww2/.

6. "This Day in History, June 14." *History.* www.history.com/this-day-in-history/germans-enter-paris. "Paris in World War II." en.wikipedia.org/wiki/Paris_in_World_War_II. "Paris falls to the Germans." *The Guardian.* www.theguardian.com/world/1940/jun/15/secondworldwar.france.

7. Sarah Goethe-Jones. "Hats Against Hitler." February 2019.

8. *The New York Times.* January 22, 1942. In all fairness, the *Times* may have just been considering the ages of the participants.

9. Becker. "Knitting for Victory." As a matter of interest, the National World War II Museum in New Orleans has an organization inspired by the knitters of World War II called "Knit Your Bit." This organization, which was founded in 2006, has provided over 50,000 scarves for veterans' centers, hospitals and service organizations.

Chapter Eleven

1. Ceil Chapman was Marilyn Monroe's favorite designer. Her specialty was glamorous cocktail attire and elegant streetwear.

2. "The "New Look" Revolution." *La Maison Dior.* www.dior.com/couture/nl_nl/a-maison-dior/the-story-of-dior/the-new-look-revolution.

3. This was not necessarily an across-the-board thing. Harvard, for example, allowed women to major in astronomy, and the first woman was allowed into the medical school in 1945, followed by the law school in 1950. Colleen Walsh. "Hard-earned gains for women at Harvard." *The Harvard Gazette.* April 26, 2012. "Allowance" did not mean they were welcomed, however.

Chapter Twelve

1. Although it had first been proposed by Harry Truman in the 1940s as a justification for sending military aid to Greece and Turkey. "Who's Been Counting My Fish? The Quotable Quotes of Dwight D. Eisenhower." *Eisenhower National Historic Site.* ParkNet. National Park Service. www.nps.gov/features/eise/jrranger/quotes2.htm

2. "The Domino Theory: Cold War Explained." *HRF (Health Research Funding).* healthresearchfunding.org/the-domino-theory-cold-war-explained/ "Drawn History: The Domino Theory." *History Channel.* "The Domino Theory." *Wikipedia.*

3. "Vietnam War Timeline." *Encyclopedia Britannica.* www.britannica.com/list/vietnam-war-timeline. Alan Rohn. "Vietnam War Timeline." thevietnamwar.info/vietnam-war-timeline/.

4. "Vietnam War." *History.* www.history.com/topics/vietnam-war/vietnam-war. *Britannica.* www.britannica.com/event/Vietnam-War. *Wikipedia.* en.wikipedia.org/wiki/Vietnam_War. *National Archives.* www.archives.gov/research/vietnam-war.

5. Mary Quant. *Quant by Quant.* London: Cassell, 1966. "Mary Quant." IMDb. www.imdb.com/name/nm0702877/bio?ref_=nm_ov_bio_sm. "Mary Quant—Fashion Designer—Biography." www.biography.com/fashion-designer/mary-quant.

6. Gaile Robinson. "The Signs of an American Renaissance." *Los Angeles Times.* December 21, 1990.

7. I realize I throw the word "ironic" around a great deal, but for the '60s, there is simply nothing else I find appropriate. Carangi's demise being a particular example. Her story was dramatized in 1998 with Angelina Jolie as the lead.

Chapter Thirteen

1. Matthew Quick. Novel regarding a veteran of Vietnam searching for his enemy.

2. It's more than possible he might have been, if the United States had come to his aid when he asked for it.

Chapter Fourteen

1. Quoted in Ronald L. Davis. *Duke: The Life and Image of John Wayne.* 289.

2. *IMDb. Wikipedia.*

3. I'm afraid this describes my opinion of the movie. As melodramatic and overwrought as *East Lynne,* it was nevertheless critically acclaimed. Conrad's novella struck me the same way.

4. Jean Louis (née Jean Louis Berthault), the French designer, who was known for his fabulous designs and designed for virtually every big star in Hollywood, was a surprising flop in *Millie* (this is strictly a personal opinion). He was nominated 14 times for an Academy Award (including *Millie*), so mine is a minority vote.

Chapter Fifteen

1. As of the time of this writing, recent events would seem to bear this out.

2. Angel Melendez. "The Rise of 21st Century Goth/Post Punk Revival." *Obscura Undead.*

3. As of this writing, the world is undergoing a pandemic, the likes of which has not been seen in a century. Many establishments are closed, movie houses and theatres stand empty, and both work and school are conducted from home in one's pajamas. The extent or length of the pandemic is unknown and many businesses will remain shuttered while many white-collar workers will continue to telecommute. What will the future hold for fashion in a world so different from even one year previous to the onset of Covid?

Epilogue

1. To clarify, this condition probably affects the United States more than other countries; nevertheless, in our now global village, what affects one affects all.

2. Owing to the worst pandemic since 1918, at this moment, the answer to the question "What will we be wearing?" is either masks or breathing tubes.

Appendix A

1. "Mary Walker: 1832-1919." *Biography.* www.biography.com/activist/mary-walker. *Karpeles Museum.* Mary Walker Biography. "Hygiene Therapy." *ND Health Facts. Naturopathic Medicine Profession.*

2. DeAnne Blanton. "Women Soldiers of the Civil War." *National Archives. Prologue Magazine.* Spring 1993, Volume 25, No, 1.

3. J.R. Thorpe. "10 Heroic Women Who Helped Win WWI, Because The Great War Wasn't Only Fought by Men." *Bustle.* www.bustle.com/articles/48404-10-heroic-women-who-helped-win-wwi-because-the-great-war-wasnt-only-fought-by-men.

4. Julie Wheelwright. "The Life of Captain Flora Sandes." *History Today.* June 2013. www.historytoday.com/reviews/life-captain-flora-sandes. "Flora Sandes - Historic UK." www.historic-uk.com/HistoryUK/HistoryofBritain/Flora-Sandes.

5. www.britannica.com/biography/Edith-Cavell. edithcavell.org.uk. www.iwm.org.uk/history/who-was-edith-cavell.

6. Theisen. "The Long Blue Line: Florence Finch." *History.* May 14, 2020. "Florence Finch." *Wikipedia.* Stuart McClung. "A heroine gets her due." Book Review. *Los Angeles Times.* Sunday, August 6, 2020.

7. "Meet Nancy Wake: Socialite, Spy, and the Most Decorated Heroine of WWII." crimereads.com/meet-nancy-wake-socialite-spy-and-the-most-decorated-heroine-of-wwii. "Nancy Wake, Proud Spy and Nazi foe, Dies at 98." *New York Times.* August 13, 2011. Russell Braddon. *Nancy Wake: The Story of a very Brave Woman.* 1956. "Nancy Wake." *Wikipedia.*

8. "Susan Ahn Cuddy—Tales of Awesomeness." www.talesofawesomeness.com/susan-ahn-cuddy. "Susan Ahn Cuddy - Women's Activism NYC." womensactivism.nyc/stories/7361.

9. Lee Karen Ctow. "The Women Who Served in Vietnam." July 5, 2016.

10. "Women in the Vietnam War." *History.* August 2, 2011 (updated March 5, 2020). Stow. "Women Who Served." Barbara Will. "American Women Died in Vietnam, Too." *The Conversation.* October 1, 2017. "American Civilian and Military Women Who Died in the Vietnam War." *The Virtual Wall.*

Appendix C

1. Stanley Appelbaum. *The New York World's Fair.* Introduction, ix.

2. Applebaum. ix.

3. Andrew Wood. *New York's 1939-1940 World's Fair.* 36-37.

4. Wood. 108.

Appendix D

1. Gretchen Bisplinghoff. "Gene Gautier." *Women Film Pioneers Project.*

2. *IMDb, Wikipedia, Women Film Pioneers Project.* earlysilentfilm.blogspot.com/2013/04/the-mystery-of-helen-gardner.html.

3. "Anita Loos." JoAnne Ruvoli. *Women Film Pioneers Project. IMDb. Wikipedia.*

Bibliography

Adlington, Lucy. *Great War Fashion: Tales from the History Wardrobe.* Stroud, Gloucester, UK: The History Press, 2013.

"American Civil War Story." www.americancivilwarstory.com/civil-war-casualties.html.

"American Civilian and Military Women Who Died in the Vietnam War (1959–1975)." *The Virtual Wall, Vietnam Veterans Memorial.* November 29, 2012. www.virtualwall.org/women.htm.

"American Propaganda in World War II." www.warhistoryonline.com/world-war-ii/american.

Appelbaum, Stanley (text). *The New York World's Fair 1939/1940: In 155 Photographs by Richard Wurts and Others.* Mineola, NY: Dover Publications, Inc., 1977.

Backus, Paige Gibbons. "Angels of the Battlefield: Female Nurses During the Civil War." *American Battlefield Trust.* www.battlefields.org/learn/articles/female-nurses-during-civil-war.

Balio, Tino. *Grand Design: Hollywood as a Modern Business Enterprise, 1930–1939.* New York: Charles Scribner's Sons, 1993.

Banks, John. "Five Minutes with Chris Foard, collector of nursing artifacts." *John Banks Civil War Blog.* john-banks.blogspot.com/2016/01/five-minutes-with-chris-foard-collector.html.

Bass, Tristan. Quoted in "Costume Designer Orry-Kelly: The Frock Flicks Guide." www.frockflicks.com/costume-designer-orry-kelly-the-frock-flicks-guide/.

Baxter-Wright, Emma. *Vintage Fashion: Collecting and Wearing Designer Classics, 1900–1990.* New York: HarperCollins, 2007.

Baylay, Ian. "An Introduction to Utility Clothing." *1940s Society.* www.1940.co.uk/acatalog/an-introduction-to-utility-clothing.html.

Becker, Paula. "Kitting for Victory—World War I." *HistoryLink.org.*

Bennett, Geoffrey. *The Battles of Coronel and the Falklands, 1914.* Barnsley, South Yorkshire: Pen and Sword Books, 2014.

Bernal, Victoria (Women in the Archives Social Media Manager). "The Suffrage Stories Connected Through the Archives." *The Autry Museum.* August 17, 2020.

Bisplinghoff, Gretchen. "Gene Gautier." *Women Film Pioneers Project.* Columbia University Library. 2013.

Blanton, DeAnne. "Women Soldiers of the Civil War." *National Archives. Prologue Magazine.*

Blue Sky Metropolis Episodes 1–5.

Blum, Stella. (Selections and Introduction) *Fashion Drawings and Illustrations from "Harper's Bazar."* Mineola, NY: Dover Publications, Inc. 1976. Spring 1993, Volume 25, No. 1.

Boland, William K. "Hitler's Use of Film in Germany, Leading up to and During World War II." *Inquiries Journal.* www.inquiriesjournal.com/articles/206/hitlers-use-of-film-in-germany-leading-up-to-and-during-world-war-ii.

Brownlow, Kevin. *Behind the Mask of Innocence: Sex, Violence, Prejudice, Crime: Films of Social Conscience in the Silent Era.* New York: Alfred A. Knopf, Inc., 1990.

Bryan, Jami L. "Fighting for Respect: African-American Soldiers in WWI." *National Museum. United States Army.* www.military.com/history/fighting-for-respect.

Burns, Stanley B., MD. "Nursing in the Civil War." *Behind the Lens: A History in Pictures.* PBS SOCAL. www.pbs.org/mercy-street/uncover-history/behind-lens/nursing-civil-war.

Card, James. *Seductive Cinema: The Art of Silent Film.* New York: Alfred A. Knopf, Inc., 1994.

Chapman, James, Mark Glancy, Sue Harper, Eds. *The New Film History: Sources, Methods, Approaches.* New York: Palgrave Macmillan, 2007.

Christie, Elizabeth June. "Now *Every* Woman Can Make Her Own Clothes." *Photoplay.* December 1917.

"Civil War Casualties—American Battlefield Trust." www.battlefields.org/learn/articles/civil-war-casualties.

"Clara Barton—HISTORY." *History.* www.history.com/topics/womens-history/clara-barton.

Clark, Christopher. *The Sleepwalkers: How Europe Went to War in 1914.* London: Allen Lane, 2012.

Clouting, Laura. "Fashion on the Ration: The Story of Clothing on the Home Front during World War Two." *Museum Crush.* museumcrush.org/fashion-on-the-ration-the-story-of-clothing-on-the-home-front.

Cohen, Ari Seth. *Advanced Style: Older and Wiser.* New York: PressHouse Books, 2016.

Cornish, Paul. "Rationing and Food Shortages

During the First World War." www.iwm.org.uk/history/rationing-and-food-shortages-during-the-first-world-war.

Craddick-Adams, Peter. "The Home Front in World War One." *History Trails: Wars and Conflict.* www.bbc.co.uk/history/trail/wars_conflict/home_front/the_home_front_04.shtml.

Crafton, Donald. *The Talkies: American Cinema's Transition to Sound, 1926–1931.* Berkeley: University of California Press, 1999.

Davis, Belinda. "Food and Nutrition (Germany)." *1914-1918-online. International Encyclopedia of the First World War.* encyclopedia.1914-1918-online.net/article/food_and_nutrition_germany.

Delineator Magazine. September 1917. *Internet Archive.*

Deroeux, Iris. "Anne Morgan, an American Heart." *France-Amérique: The Best of French Culture.* July 13, 2017 (translated from the French by Alexander Uff).

DeSimone, Danielle. "These 5 Heroic Women of World War II Should Be Household Names." USO Organization/Stories. September 2019 (updated 2020).

Dirks, Tim. "The Big Parade: Filmsite Movie Review." *AMC Filmsite.* www.filmsite.org/bigp.html.

Dolber, John. "These Are Russians." *Photoplay.* May 1918.

"Dorothea Dix." ahec.armywarcollege.edu/exhibits/CivilWarImagery/Civil_War_Nurses.cfm.

______. *National Women's History Museum.* www.womenshistory.org/education-resources/biographies/dorothea-dix.

"Dorothea Lynde Dix—HISTORY." www.history.com/topics/womens-history/dorothea-lynde-dix.

Dunn, Terry. "Funnies in Uniform: The Role of Comic Strips during WWII." *Tested.* October 26, 2017.

Edwards, Nina. *Dressed for War: Uniform, Civilian Clothing and Trappings, 1914 to 1918.* London: I.B. Tauris and C., Ltd., 2015.

Erté: Twenty-four Picture Cards. Mineola. New York: Dover Publications, Inc., 1984.

"Facts About Vietnam: Women Veterans You May Not Know." National Veterans Foundation. *Lifeline for Vets.* February 8, 2016.

"Fashion in World War I: December 1918." *Fashion History and Quilt History.* clarerosehistory.com.

Fashion, Society, and the First World War. London: Bloomsbury, 2021.

"Flora Sandes—Historic UK." www.historic-uk.com/HistoryUK/HistoryofBritain/Flora-Sandes.

"Frances Clalin [sic] Clayton—Women of the Civil War." womenofthecIvIlwar.weebly.com/frances-clalin-clayton.html.

"Frances Clayton—Civil War Filing Cabinet—Liberty Letters." libertyletters.com/resources/civil-war/frances-clayton.php.

French, Lucille. "Outing Fashions—All Our Own." *Photoplay.* August 1916.

______. "Wartime Fashions—Always the Same." *Photoplay.* July 1916.

Gerwath, Robert. *The Vanquished: Why the First World War Failed to End, 1917–1923.* New York: Farrar, Straus and Giroux, 2016.

Goenka, Kanupriya. "Why Did the Hobble Skirt Become Popular?" medium.com/@kanupriya.goenka/why-did-the-hobble-skirt-become-popular-e86dbdd06880.

Goethe-Jones, Sarah. "Hats Against Hitler: How Headwear Became Part of the Resistance." *Dismantle Magazine.* February 2010. dismantlemag.com/2019/02/10/hats-hitler-turbans-resistance/.

Guo Pei: Couture Beyond. Exhibition Catalog. Anaheim, CA: Bowers Museum, 2019.

Hacker, Barton. "Women in Uniform, World War I Edition." Blog, September 8, 2011. *National Museum of American History.* americanhistory.si.edu/collections/object-groups/women-in-wwi/women-s-uniforms.

Hallett, Hilary. *Go West, Young Woman!: The Rise of Early Hollywood.* Berkeley: University of California Press, 2013.

Hammond, William A. *A Statement of the Causes Which Led to the Dismissal of Surgeon General William A. Hammond from the Army with a Review of the Evidence Adduced Before the Court.* London: Forgotten Books. February 7, 2018 (Reprint).

Hancock, Joseph H. II, Toni Johnson-Woods, Vicki Karaminas, Eds. *Fashion in Popular Culture: Literature, Media and Contemporary Studies.* Chicago: Intellect, 2013.

Hardie, Martin, and Arthur K. Sabin, Eds. *War Posters: The Historical Role of Wartime Poster Art 1914–1919.* Mineola, NY: Dover Publications, Inc., 2016 (Reissue, 1920).

Hemmings, Jay. "A History of the Trench Coat—A Military Garment with Origins Far Older Than WWI." *War History Online.* us.burberry.com/the-trench-coat/.

Hess, John P. "Early Experiments in Sound During the Silent Era." *The History of Sound at the Movies.* filmmakeriq.com/lessons/setting-silent-stage/.

Hokin, Catherine. "An Appearance of Serenity: The French Fashion Industry in WWII." *Historia: Magazine of the Historical Writer's Association.* April 2019. www.historiamag.com/french-fashion-industry-ww2/.

Howard, Lillian. "Back to Babylon for New Fashions." *Photoplay.* April 1917.

Howell, Geraldine. *Wartime Fashion: From Haute Couture to Homemade, 1939–1945.* London: Berg Publishers, 2013.

"Hydrotherapy." www.ndhealthfacts.org/wiki/Hydrotherapy. www.britannica.com/science/hydrotherapy.

"Hygiene Therapy." www.ndhealthfacts.org/wiki/Hygiene_Therapy.

Kendall, Elizabeth. *The Runaway Bride: Hollywood Romantic Comedy of the 1930s.* New York: Doubleday, 1990.

King, Susan. "The Movies Soar into World War I." *Los Angeles Times.* January 7, 2020.

Kitchen, Karl K. "The Light of Europe." *Photoplay.* May 1916.

Klawans, Stuart. "Film: How the First World War Changed Movies Forever." *The New York Times.* November 19, 2000.

Korda, Holly. *The Knitting Brigades of World War I: Volunteers for Victory in America and Abroad.* Wilmington, DE: New Enterprise Publishing, Inc., 2019.

Koszarski, Richard. *An Evening's Entertainment: The Age of the Silent Feature Picture, 1915–1928.* Berkeley: University of California Press, 1994.

Kracauer. Siegfried. *From Caligari to Hitler: A Psychological History of the German Film.* Princeton, NJ: Princeton University Press, 2004 (Reprint).

Krist, Gary. *The Mirage Factory: Illusion, Imagination, and the Invention of Los Angeles.* New York: Broadway Books, 2018.

"Lillian Forrester." *Wikipedia Republished.*

Lindsay, Kate. "The She-Soldiers of World War One." *World War I Centenary.* University of Oxford. wlcentenary.oucs.ox.ac.uk/unconventionalsoldiers/the-she-soldiers-of-world-war-one.

Literature Catalog. New Haven, CT: William Reese Co., 2019.

Luckhurst, Tim. "War Correspondents." *1914-1918-online. International Encyclopedia of the First World War.* encyclopedia.1914-1918-online.net/article/war_correspondents.

Macdonald, Lyn. *1914–1918, Voices and Images of the Great War.* Quoted in Peter Craddick-Adams. "The Home Front in World War One." *History Trails: Wars and Conflict.* www.bbc.co.uk/history/trail/wars_conflict/home_front/the_home_front_04.shtml.

MacMillan, Margaret. *The War that Ended Peace: The Road to 1914.* New York: Random House, 2014.

Mahar, Karen Ward. *Women Filmmakers in Early Hollywood.* Baltimore, MD: Johns Hopkins University Press, 2006.

"Mary Walker: 1832–1919." *Biography.* www.biography.com/activist/mary-walker.

"Mary Walker: Physician and Women's Rights Advocate Remains the Only Woman Recipient of the Medal of Honor." *WWII Times—Remembering our Nation's Veterans.* April 2000.

McClung, Stuart. "A Heroine Gets Her Due." Book review. *Los Angeles Times.* August 6, 2020.

Melendez, Angel. "The Rise of 21st Century Goth/Post Punk Revival." *Obscura Undead.*

Michon, Heather. "The Role of Africans in World War I." www.thoughtco.com/african-americans-in-wwi-4158185.

Monaghan, Peter. "Detecting the History of Sound on Film." *Moving Image Archive News.* August 24, 2010 (added clarification, February 17, 1916).

Moving Picture World. Issues: February 2, 1918; February 17, 1918; April 6, 1918; April 13, 1918.

"*Mrs. Miniver.*" *IMDb.* www.imdb.com/title/tt0035093.

______. *Rotten Tomatoes.* www.rottentomatoes.com/m/mrs_miniver.

______. *Wikipedia.* en.wikipedia.org/wiki/Mrs._Miniver.

Mühl-Benninghaus, Wolfgang. "Film/Cinema (Germany)." *1914-1918-online. International Encyclopedia of the First World War.* encyclopedia.1914-1918-online.net/article/filmcinema_germany.

Nenadic, Marina. "Six Sites of Suffragette Sabotage." *Heritage Calling.* heritagecalling.com/2018/06/08/6-sites-of-suffragette-sabotage/.

The New York Times. January 22, 1942.

Olds, Lauren. "World War II and Fashion: The Birth of the New Look." Ohio: Wesleyan University, 2001.

Olian, JoAnne, Ed. *Everyday Fashions 1909–1920 as Pictured in the Sears Catalogs.* Mineola, NY: Dover Publications, Inc., 1995 (Reprint).

"Our History." *The Church Army.* www.churcharmy.org.uk/Group/Group.aspx?ID=290554.

Pankhurst, Sylvia. (Preface, Emmeline Pankhurst). *The Suffragette: The History of the Women's Militant Suffrage Movement.* Mineola, New York: Dover Publications, Inc., 2015 (Reprint).

"Paris Falls to the Germans." *The Guardian.* www.theguardian.com/world/1940/jun/15/secondworldwar.france.

"Paris in World War II." en.wikipedia.org/wiki/Paris_in_World_War_II.

Peltret, Elizabeth. "On the Lot with Lois Weber." *Photoplay.* October 1917.

Photoplay Magazine. Issues: April 1917; April 1918; May 1918.

Pitogo, Heziel. "How the Great War Changed Fashion for Women." *War History Online.* www.warhistoryonline.com/war-articles/great-war-changed-women-fashion.html.

Posters of World Wars I and II. Mineola, NY: Dover Publications, Inc., 2005.

"The Power of Propaganda in World War II." *SAGU.* www.sagu.edu/thoughthub/the-power-of-propaganda-in-world-war-ii.

Quant, Mary. *Quant by Quant.* London: Cassell, 1966.

Quick, Matthew. *The Reason You're Alive.* New York: HarperLuxe, 2017.

Rall, Denise N., Ed. *Fashion and War in Popular Culture.* Chicago: University of Chicago Press, 2014.

Rappaport, Helen. *No Place for Ladies: The Untold Story of Women in the Crimean War.* London: Aurum Press Ltd., 2008 (Kindle Edition).

Reddy, Karina. "1940–1949." *Fashion History Timeline.* August 2020. fashionhistory.fitnyc.edu/1940-1949/.

Robinson, Michael, and Rosalind Ormiston. *Art Deco: The Golden Age of Graphic Art and Illustration.* New York: Metro Books, 2008.

Ross, Steven J. *Working Class Hollywood: Silent Film and the Shaping of Class in America.* Princeton, NJ: Princeton University Press, 1998.

Ruvoli, JoAnne. "Anita Loos." *Women Film*

Pioneers Project. New York: Columbia University Libraries, 2014.

Ryan, Robert. WWI Mystery series featuring Dr. Watson (various titles). London: Simon & Schuster, 2012–2016.

St. Louis Dispatch. April 1918.

Schatz, Thomas. *Boom or Bust: American Cinema in the 1940s*. Berkeley: University of California Press, 1999.

Simkin, John. "Dorothy Lawrence." *Spartacus Educational*. September 1997 (updated January 2020). spartacus-educational.com/FWWlawrenceD.htm.

______. "Woman's Auxiliary Army Corps." *Spartacus Educational*. spartacus-educational.com/FWWwomen.htm.

Speaker, Susan L. "'Fit to Fight': Home Front Army Doctors and VD During WWI." *NIH National Library of Medicine: Circulating Now*. October 18, 2918.

Stow, Lee Karen. "The Women Who Served in Vietnam." *BBC, Vietnam War*.

Summers, Julie. *Fashion on the Ration*. London: Profile Books, 2016.

Sundell, Spencer. "The Pre-History of Sound Cinema, Part 1: Thomas Edison and W.K.L. Dickson." spencersundell.com/writing/pre-history_of_sound_cinema_part_1.html.

Ten Eyck, John. "Mollie of Manhattan." *Photoplay*, October.

Theisen, William H. "The Long Blue Line: Florence Finch." *History*. May 14, 2020.

"This Day in History, June 14." *History*. www.history.com/this-day-in-history/germans-enter-paris.

Thorpe J.R. "10 Female WWI Heroes You've Never Heard Of." *Bustle*. www.bustle.com/articles/48404-10-heroic-women-who-helped-win-wwi-because-the-great-war-wasnt-only-fought-by-men.

Todd, Charles (Mother and son writing team). WWI Mystery series featuring Inspector Ian Rutledge. London: William Morrow, 1996–2019.

Topor, Lauren. *War and Fashion: Political Views and How Military Styles Influence Fashion*. (Master of Science Thesis). Ypsilanti, MI: Eastern Michigan University, 2008. commons.emich.edu/cgi/viewcontent.cgi?article=1167&context=theses.

"Trall's New York Hydropathic and Physiological School." *Kook Science*. hatch.kookscience.com/wiki/New_York_Hygeio-Therapeutic_College.

Vane, Colonel Elizabeth A.P. "Contributions of the U.S. Army Nurse Corps in World War I." *Army Nurse Corps Association*. e-anca.org/History/Topics-in-ANC-History/Contributions-of-the-US-Army-Nurse-Corps-in-WWI.

"The Vera Brittain Collection." *Lament of the Demobilised* [sic]. *Digital Archive: The First World War Poetry*.

"Vietnam War." *Britannica*. www.britannica.com/event/Vietnam-War

______. *History*. www.history.com/topics/vietnam-war/vietnam-war.

______. *National Archives*. www.archives.gov/research/vietnam-war.

______. *Wikipedia*. en.wikipedia.org/wiki/Vietnam_War.

Walsh, Colleen. "Hard-Earned Gains for Women at Harvard." *The Harvard Gazette*. April 26, 2012.

Webb, Michael, Ed. *Hollywood: Legend and Reality*. Boston: Little Brown and Company, in association with the Smithsonian Institution. Exhibit Catalog. 1986–1988.

Western Americana Catalog. New Haven, CT: William Reese Co., 2019.

Wheelwright, Julie. "The Life of Captain Flora Sandes." *History Today*. June 2013. www.historytoday.com/reviews/life-captain-flora-sandes.

Wilde, Robert. "Women and Work in World War I." *ThoughtCo*. August 20, 1919.

Will, Barbara. "American Women Died in Vietnam, Too." *The Conversation: Academic Rigor; Journalistic Flair*.

"William A. Hammond." *National Park Service*. www.nps.gov/people/william-a-hammond.htm.

"William A. Hammond: Surgeons [sic] General." *U.S. Army Medical Department, Office of Medical History*. history.amedd.army.mil/surgeongenerals/W_Hammond.html.

Williams of Crosby, Baroness. "World War One: The Many Battles Faced by WW1's Nurses." *BBC News Magazine*. April 2, 2014. www.bbc.com/news/magazine-26838077.

"Women in the Vietnam war." *History*. www.history.com/topics/vietnam-war/women-in-the-vietnam-war.

"The Women's Army Auxiliary Corps." *History Learning Site*. www.historylearningsite.co.uk/the-role-of-british-women-in-the-twentieth-century/the-womens-army-auxiliary-corps/.

"Women's Royal Air Force (WRAF) 1918–1920." *Royal Air Force Museum*.

"Women's Work in World War I: 1914–1918." *Striking Women*. University of Leeds. www.striking-women.org.

Wood, Andrew. *New York's 1939–1940 World's Fair*. Chicago: Arcadia Publishing, 2004.

"WWII Propaganda." *Baylor University*. blogs.baylor.edu/propagandaovertime.

"YWCA History." *Temple University Libraries*. digital.library.temple.edu/cdm/ywcahistory.

Index